SLOW WALKS IN

Continuing the unique travel series es
PARIS, short-listed for the Thomas
Award, Michael Leitch now introduce
from its tragic past to find a new role

SLOW WALKS IN BERLIN offers twenty-two leisurely walks around the historic yet changing city. The visitor is invited to join in the local life of Berlin: to stroll past the jewellers, fashion shops and café terraces of Kurfürstendamm, jolt through Köpenick in an ancient tram or just laze around on a lake boat bound for Peacock Island. Other walks concentrate on particular themes such as the route of the infamous Wall – reflecting Berlin's political past.

Each walk is carefully planned and utterly enjoyable. Detailed route guides and specially drawn maps accompany each walk, while helpful information about the language, public transport, currency and places to eat take the worry out of travel and enhance the pleasures of exploration.

Travellers will be able to relax and enjoy themselves as they soak up Berlin's cultural life in the Kulturforum, amble down Unter den Linden – one of Europe's most famous avenues – wander in the pine and birch woods of Grunewald or explore the charming baroque town of Potsdam.

MICHAEL LEITCH spends a good deal of time travelling, both in Europe and the United States. He and his wife have two daughters and live in Oxfordshire.

SLOW WALKS IN

MICHAEL LEITCH

A VISITOR'S COMPANION

HODDER AND STOUGHTON
London   Sydney   Auckland

ACKNOWLEDGMENTS

I am grateful to many people in Berlin for their generous help with this book. First of these has been my principal hostess in Berlin, Fr. Ursula-Marie Roy, who has given me countless words of advice and amusing asides about life in the city. My thanks also to the following people: Fr. Editha Gelbin, Fr. Gertrude Hempel (and her famous bicycle), Fr. Eva Wulff, the Wensky family – Manfred, Jutta and Norman – and Herr Horst Ulrich of the Presse und Informationsamt. Many others have helped me in various ways, from answering my questions to just behaving as Berliners do, spontaneously and with the refreshing directness that singles out the people of this city.

I shall also be forever grateful to my wife, Gwydwr, for tolerating my long exile in Berlin and remaining cheerfully at the centre of our family intelligence network for so many months.

The excerpt from *Goodbye to Berlin* by Christopher Isherwood is reproduced with the kind permission of the author's Estate and his publishers, Chatto & Windus.

British Library Cataloguing in Publication Data
Leitch, Michael
  Slow Walks in Berlin
  I. Title
  914.315504

ISBN 0-340-57209-4

Route maps and illustrations by Alec Spark

Copyright © Michael Leitch 1993

First published in Great Britain 1993

Published by Hodder and Stoughton,
a division of Hodder and Stoughton Ltd,
Mill Road, Dunton Green, Sevenoaks, Kent TN13 2YA
Editorial Office: 47 Bedford Square, London WC1B 3DP

Photoset by SX Composing Ltd, Rayleigh, Essex

Printed in Great Britain by
Cox & Wyman Ltd, Reading, Berks.

CONTENTS

History notes; The German language – words and phrases; Where to stay; Transport – S-Bahn, U-Bahn, buses, taxis; Telephones; Money; Opening times; List of public holidays; Clothing sizes; Watering holes; Toilets; What's on/further information; Berlin by night; Quick Berlin.

WELCOME!

Welcome to *Slow Walks in Berlin*. While researching this book I have been living in Berlin for the best part of a year. It has been a remarkable experience. The months have flown by. At first, everything that happened served somehow to confirm previous impressions of the city. Then something else would happen to enlarge and change those earlier thoughts. As if through a curtain parting, the extraordinary future potential of Berlin was slowly revealed.

After the political upheavals of 1989-90 Berlin had begun, as expected, to reassume its old position as the capital of Germany. That prospect alone was enough to set the world's economists and power-brokers in a whirl of speculation, and to sound warning bells around the European Community and in other neighbour-states; in Poland most of all.

Then, as Eastern Europe collapsed westwards, it became clear that Berlin's new role was going to be greater than it had ever been in peacetime. Berlin was destined to become the magnet city of the next Middle Europe, and not inconceivably that of the whole Continent.

This new role will not be filled easily. So far, officially, it does not even exist, but it now seems inevitable that it will come into some form of being. In the meantime there is a huge amount to be done, and the city has settled down to what must be a long period of restoration and renewal.

This is not to say that Berlin has gone quiet. The tragic dramas of a city split in two halves by a monstrous wall – those have gone. Their place has been filled by more mundane problems of economic insecurity, of soaring property prices and a new openness which for many has produced an uncomfortable draught compared with the cosy days of 'when we were walled in (*eingemauert*)'. Without the danger and the ideological strife, bourgeois values have firmly taken over. Among the intellectual classes there is a constant moan that Berlin no longer gives them the sharp kick that used to be their source of inspiration.

On those levels there is a discernible lull. However, if quiet is to be measured on the ordinary register of noises made by builders and road-menders, Berlin has gone through the roof. So be it. This is no longer a place where EC-acceptable decibels have much relevance. The city is in a hurry, and you cannot have *Restauration, Rekonstruktion, Umbau* and all the rest that Berlin needs without frightening a few horses.

Now is an excellent time to come to the city. Not for much longer will the visitor be able to see the two sectors of Berlin so acutely divided: the comfortable, smooth-running, glamorous and sometimes flashy West and its evacuee twin, now restored to the family but still ravaged by the marks of its deprived and shell-shocked past.

Berlin is the most political city I have ever seen. As an indicator of this, out of the twenty-two walks in the book only one – through the forest paths of Grunewald – is untarnished by recent history. By that I mean the combined legacy of Nazi crimes and the bombs of the Second World War, followed by the harsh imprint of the Cold War which in the minds of many is not over yet.

In some of the walks I have concentrated on a particular theme thrown up by those past decades – the route of the Wall, for example, or the GDR showplaces and the Eastern enclaves that got left behind, or, more specific still, the concentration camp at Sachsenhausen. In others the pattern is much more general, taking life as it comes. Here the reader is invited to join in the life of the city: to stroll like some secret millionaire past the jewellers and café terraces of Kurfürstendamm, or jolt through Köpenick in an ancient tram, or just laze around on a lake boat bound for Peacock Island. (The greenery in and around Berlin – in the parklands of Tiergarten, Grunewald, Wannsee and Grosser Müggelsee – is one of the city's special delights.)

In every season of the year Berlin is a boundless source of things to see and do. Such is the choice, it can seem dazzling. My best advice is: don't try to see it all in one go. Relax, slow down and enjoy Berlin as you might a rich and filling dinner at the home of a generous host. One course at a time is the only way.

And good luck!

BERLIN from A to Z

This alphabet is meant as a light-hearted introduction to some of the customs and paradoxes that make up the character of Berlin life. The compound is a mixture of spice and formality, vigour and crudeness that no other German city can emulate.

A   **Altes Museum (Old Museum)**. The building which sets the mould of Berlin's architecture. Schinkel's glorious pavilion palace (1830), the city's first public museum, spans one end of the Lustgarten in an audacious parade of eighteen columns, a sublime piece of neo-classical design adapted for the flatlands of the Brandenburg Plain. Now chiefly reserved for big international art shows, offering the chance to mingle with Berlin's culture-hungry residents who invariably spend more time reading the explanatory cards on the wall than they ever do looking at the pictures.

B   **Bier** Delicious universal remedy, good for visitors acclimatising to diet of bread, cake, potato, off-cuts of pig, etc. Local versions include Berliner Kindl and Schultheiss. Tastiest in draught form (*vom Fass*) but takes ten minutes to pour with much froth-settling palaver. Seasoned residents fill the interval with a spirit chaser of *Korn*.

C   **Chaoten** Professional non-grownups who live in District 36 of East Kreuzberg, to embarrassment of Turkish population which settled there with diametrically opposite bourgeois intentions of making a living and *getting on*. *Chaoten* like to herd in large numbers and throw bricks at police – and get in a bit of shoplifting – but lack energy to do this often. In between, lurk muttering in unspeakable cafés, worship vegetarianism and encourage their mangy dogs to defecate on pavement. Many carry mark of some recent injury. Since 1989, numbers have migrated to Prenzlauer Berg (q.v.).

D   **Doppelt** Double. United Berlin's way of having two of everything, usually one in East, one in West. Museums are particularly prone to doubling-up, the result of a post-1945 carve-up when buried art treasures were reassembled in rival zones, yielding two Egyptian collections, two Islamic, two Far Eastern, etc., and clumps of European masters all over the place. For enthusiasts, involves much shuttling between Dahlem, Charlottenburg, Kulturforum (q.v.) and Museuminsel.

E   **Eck-kneipen** Corner bars, often dingy, TV mounted high on wall. The typical patron enters with his dog at about 11 a.m. and swills beer until thrown out much later. Good for arguments, but sometimes these get out of order. The ensuing commotion is called *Keilerei*; patrons make a lot of *Krach* and *klopfen* each other.

F   **Fernsehturm** TV Tower, near Alexanderplatz. Ingenious piece of plumbing 365m (1197ft) high with upper ballcock and painted spike. In bright weather, best all-round views of Berlin from inside ballcock, where revolving café turns through whole cityscape twice an hour. In GDR days, TV Tower served as a great sock-in-the-eye to West Berlin which had nothing to match it. Western counter-joke was that sun glinting on ballcock, thereby forming a cross, was the Pope's Revenge on atheist Easterners.

G   **Gedenkstätte** Memorials. Hitler's ex-capital is now intent on expunging old horrors with dozens of refurbished sites where real and perceived enemies of Third Reich were tortured, hanged, shot. Exhibitions feature miles of earnest wallboard, grim photos, study centres, libraries and usual excess baggage of today's museum culture.

H   **Hundebadestelle** Dogs' bathing station. At eastern end of Grunewaldsee, a whole sandy beach set aside for Berlin's dogs to bathe and quietly perfect the paddle-stroke named after them. Across lake is *Nacktbadestelle*, where naked humans are similarly catered for.

I   **Imbiss** More a way of life than just a snack or snack bar. Reflects the Berliner's endearing need to lever food into his/her face at least ten times a day. Sweets, ices, cakes and sausage, *Bouletten* meatballs, smelly chips with mayonnaise or red sauce, *döner kebaps* – wherever you look, on the street or in the U-Bahn, someone will be snacking on the run.

J   **Jüdisch** Things Jewish. Biggest thorn in Germany's collective conscience. Although number of Jews resident in Berlin is not surprisingly low (about 7,000), vast homage is paid in books, films, newspaper articles and *Gedenkstätte* (q.v.) to victims of Nazi persecution. Latest conflict surrounds huge cost of building an adequate Jewish museum. With each delay critics ask, 'Will

Berlin really put its money where its mouth is?' Official reply: 'Yes, but Berlin is broke.'

K   Kulturforum Expanding tribe of cultural monsters, partly gold-plated, which in 1960s began settling near Potsdamer Platz. Have Romantic cousins in Charlottenburg, and dusky friends in Dahlem. Will consume anything but prefer paintings, porcelain and sheet music.

L   Luft Air. Howling winds that cut across the flat Brandenburg Plain and through city canyons, sending icy fingers down steps of U-Bahn stations. Berliners believe their *Luft* is healthy and bang on endlessly about it in song and tourist propaganda. As a popular delusion, compares with Paris and its obsession with being *gai*. Reality is more like cartoon of old woman on park bench, glaring at nearby mother and baby. 'That's not Berliner Luft,' she rasps. 'Your brat's just filled its nappies!'

M   Mauer Berlin Wall, erected 1961 by GDR authorities to keep citizens of East Germany in place and stop then rampant brain and worker drain. The cause of appalling hardships and private tragedies, affecting almost every Berlin family. Pulled down in 1989. Some stretches preserved, e.g. at East Side Gallery and next to Topographie des Terrors Museum. Fragments of painted stone on sale at Brandenburg Gate and Checkpoint Charlie should be made to carry 'guaranteed fake' labels.

N   Nikolai Viertel Another fake, but relaxing and pretty if you don't mind prefabricated concrete slabs masquerading as Old Berlin. Launched by GDR in 1980s around restored Nikolai Church, the quarter is a maze of cobbled streets with snazzy boutiques and transplanted favourites such as the Zum Nussbaum pub, formerly in Fischerinsel.

O   (O) Stands for *Ost* or East. The dreaded telephone prefix of former *Ossi*-land, signalling that this number will be unobtainable from West Berlin in business hours. German Telekom promise huge improvements very soon; few consumers share their confidence. The shortage of lines in the East remains desperate; ask any group of Easterners how many of them have a telephone.

P   Prenzlauer Berg Old battle site left largely untouched since Russian troops hacked through it in 1945. Blackened buildings pitted with shell and bullet holes remain as a tribute to GDR housing policy. Some newly restored blocks exist, e.g. in over-tarty Husemannstrasse, but for true picture explore side streets off Schönhauser Allee and around Zionskirche.

Q **Quasimodo** Berlin's best-known jazz venue, also presents R & B, Blues, R & R. Go early to secure a seat. Hot; even the eyes of dedicated smokers smart in the fug. Noisy; musicians rarely high-class, but clientele rate heavy beat and on-stage spectacle more highly than musical finesse.

R **Rekonstruiren** Ugly Anglo verb used to describe savage process of redesigning East Berlin to fit more neatly with Western or *Wessi* preconceptions. Berlin has always been a restless city, tearing down buildings as casually, so one writer put it, as you would throw out a pair of ageing trousers. This bout of reconstruction is likely to run until well after 2000, when the national government will at last be installed in the city – which God then preserve.

S **Schlagsahne** Whipped cream. The topping without which no cake, tart or ice cream is seen as fit to eat. Domestic version comes in a ready-to-spray canister. Shake well, remove cap, invert over target and press button. Hold close for pretty floral effect, or whack all over in lascivious mounds.

T **Toleranz** New street name for Otto-Grotewohl-Strasse, sited at heart of Hitler's state security network. Only a committee could come up with a name so dim. Let it also stand for the furious whirl of renaming which in 1992 ran to a list of more than eighty East Berlin streets, nine U-Bahn and six S-Bahn stations. Top names for the ideological chop were: Lenin (6), Marx-Engels (4) and Albert Norden (3) – this last one of many old GDR Communists whose names until recently adorned the lampposts of this city.

U **Umbau** Conversion. Sub-branch of *rekonstruiren* (q.v.). Usual reason given for temporary closure of shops and restaurants. In East Berlin, these are the ones that did not quite go out of business after the *Wende* ('The Turn' after 1989). However, they would have done so without a rapid facelift to match the needs of new times; these include customers who won't put up with a sloppy product.

V   **Volk** The People. According to one GDR encyclopedia, published in 1978, these wonderful souls are:
'*The masses*: 1. Category of historical materialism, comprises the working classes and social strata, and all progressive-minded classes and social strata by reason of their objective historical position and role. The people are the creators and chief forces of history.' RIP the *Volk* of East Germany.

W   **Wählerisch** Fastidious, picky. Watch a Berlin couple come into a café. They look around cautiously, choose a table, sit down, look around, then get up and move to another one. The ritual repeats, like birds choosing a place to nest, until both parties are settled and content. Then they have to get up again, take their coats off and hang them on the coatstand.

X   **Xenon** Cinema in Schöneberg. One of the few in Berlin to show foreign language films in original version (*OF*), thanks to maddening habit here of dubbing almost every foreign movie in sight, big-name Hollywood releases included. The Berlin Film Festival, in February, is by contrast a truly international feast, with films in all languages, and fully attended by the public. So who needs all this relentless dubbing?

Y   Pass.

Z   **Zitty** Fortnightly listings magazine which overlaps with **Tip**. Both are excellent sources of information on concerts, theatres, cinemas, special events, jazz and rock venues. *Zitty*'s editorial opinions can be quaint or plain silly (*Tip*'s are a little more sane) but its cartoons are lively and the info pages of both are necessary stuff.

THE GEOGRAPHY OF BERLIN

Berlin is very big and growing fast. Its population of three and a half million is set to rise to five million in the next decade, and its resources and services are already under strain. The traffic problem is acute and, as my local paper stated in triumph the other day, when reporting the results of the latest official survey: 'Proof at last – it's too loud, and it stinks to the heavens.' (To many Berlin readers this was *good* news, confirming that yet again their city led the way.)

How calm it must have been back in the twelfth century, when fishermen set up a village of huts on an island in the River Spree and another group settled on the far bank, together forming the communities of Cölln and Berlin from which all else followed. Then came a stone castle, and walls and a jagged moat, ringing what is now the Eastern centre. Then came Unter den Linden, a long avenue breaking out to the west. The Gold Rush was on, fuelled by Prussian monarchs, politicians and

speculators. They created Charlottenburg, laid out the Tiergarten and built ever westwards. After Germany was united under Prussian rule, the Avenue of the Electors (Kurfürstendamm) thrust away towards the forest of Grunewald and Berlin took on its present form.

From on high, the city has the amazingly inefficient shape of a dumbbell. Everything of consequence happens in one of the two spheres at each end of the bar, and the bar itself is a huge long park – the Tiergarten – which rightly cannot be tinkered with (except by underground tunnelling).

For the visitor, naturally intent on seeing as much of both centres as time allows, there is little for it but to commute to one sector and settle there for the day. As luck would have it, this is entirely in keeping with the spirit of *Slow Walks*. Far better, indeed, to camp in one quarter and get to know its highlights and byways and welcoming cafés, than to hurtle this way and that in an unplanned frenzy.

To profit best from commuting time, ride on the S-Bahn between Zoo Station and Friedrichstrasse (the old border station), continuing if necessary to Alexanderplatz. The raised view as the train leaves Lehrter Stadt Bahnhof and rumbles round the river bend (*Spree Bogen*) is marvellous. Sit on the right side of the train, facing forwards, and watch the Reichstag draw near across a wasteland of shattered watchtower and fragments of Wall; beyond, at the western end of Unter den Linden, is a glimpse of the Brandenburg Gate, key to the Eastern centre.

Two other rewarding ways to cross from West to East, or vice versa, are to take one of the following buses. Both offer an excellent parade of sights.

Bus 100   From Zoo Station to the other side of Alexanderplatz. Runs along Budapester Strasse and up through Tiergarten to the Victory Column (Siegessäule), Schloss Bellevue and the Kongresshalle. Passes through the Brandenburg Gate, along Unter den Linden to Karl-Liebknecht-Strasse, the Television Tower and Alexanderplatz. Terminates at Mollstrasse.

Bus 142   From Wittenbergplatz to Hauptbahnhof. Takes a more southerly route to Stauffenbergstrasse and the top of the Kulturforum. Passes through Potsdamer Platz and Leipziger Strasse to Spittelmarkt, the Nikolai Quarter and Alexanderplatz. Turns along Mollstrasse and winds through Friedrichshain to Hauptbahnhof.

A good round trip would be to take the 142 outward to Mollstrasse, walk back to the 100 terminus and return westward along Unter den Linden.

Maps Most of the walks in this book take place in the two centres or the area between them, or in one of the adjoining suburbs such as Schöneberg or Dahlem, former villages which were swept up and enclosed by the spreading city. In each chapter the Route map carries enough detail to guide the visitor through the district. For a broader overall view, buy one of the many maps on sale at newsstands and bookshops. The best is the *Stadtplan* published by Falk. Its patent folding system allows you to look at one section at a time without having to unfold the complete map.

Arriving in Berlin The principal airport is **Berlin-Tegel**. It lies on the north-western edge of the city. Transport to and from the city centre is simple and direct. From the terminal building, take Bus 109 through Charlottenburg to Kurfürstendamm and Zoo Station. To travel onward to East Berlin, take the S-Bahn either from Charlottenburg Station or the Zoo (two stops along). A single journey ticket (*Einzelfahrschein*) is valid for up to two hours on all parts of the transport network and passengers may change as often as they wish. Current cost is DM 3.20. For further details, see the section on 'Transport'.

Other flights arrive at **Berlin-Tempelhof**. Across the road is U-Bahnhof Platz der Luftbrücke (Line 6). Trains run up to Friedrichstrasse Station, a major junction, and on the way there are connections with other U-Bahn lines at Mehringdamm (Line 7, to Adenauerplatz and Spandau), Hallesches Tor (Line 1, to Kurfürstendamm and Kreuzberg) and Stadtmitte (Line 2, to Alexanderplatz, Prenzlauer Berg and Pankow).

Main-line trains from East and West run in beside the S-Bahn network and stop at one or more of a chain of central stations, variously Zoo, Friedrichstrasse, Hauptbahnhof and Lichtenberg. From each of these there are connections to all parts of the city.

BERLIN ON FILM

This section is a kind of 'Geography-plus'. I include it here because it offers an enjoyable way of seeing Berlin through the perceptive eyes of others who know it well. Although it is not true of every big city, it so happens that Berlin is the star (or figures strongly in the background) of a remarkable number of documentaries and feature films. These are regularly shown in Berlin cinemas but are rarely seen outside German-speaking countries. Look in the 'Film ABC' section of *Zitty* magazine for dates and venues; *Tip* has a similar section, called 'Filme von A-Z'. Below is a selection.

Berlin–Alexanderplatz, Germany, 1931. Dir. Piel Jutzi. Movie version of Alfred Döblin's frenetic Twenties novel. Franz Biberkopf, newly released from jail, adapts to the brutalities of life outside.

Berlin–Die Sinfonie der Gross-stadt (*Berlin – Symphony of the Big City*), Germany, 1927. Dir. Walter Ruttmann. Documentary. Twenty-four hours in the life of the city, seen through the camera's eye.

Berlin wie es war (*Berlin as it was*), Germany, 1943. Dir. Leo de Laforgue. Documentary. One day in Berlin, filmed mainly between 1938 and 1939, completed in 1943 before the city was destroyed, banned by the Nazis as 'too authentic' and first shown in 1950.

Bomben auf Berlin (*Bombs over Berlin*), West Germany, 1983. Dir. Irmgard von zur Mühlen. Everyday life in the bombing onslaught of 1943-45. Sharply contrasts what really happened with official Nazi accounts.

Deutschland im Jahre Null (*Germany in the Year Zero*), Germany/Italy, 1947. Dir. Roberto Rossellini. Story of a fifteen-year-old boy living in Berlin with his sick father in the 'difficult years' after the war. He grows up under the tutelage of a former teacher, an ex-Nazi turned black marketeer now busy exploiting the skills he learned under Hitler.

Emil und die Detektive (*Emil and the Detectives*), Germany, 1931. Dir. Gerhard Lamprecht. Charming adaptation of Erich Kästner's famous novel for children. Emil, robbed on a journey to Berlin, hunts the thief through the city with the help of a new, ever-increasing gang of friends.

Himmel über Berlin, Der (*Wings of Desire*), West Germany/France, 1987. Dir. Wim Wenders. Two unemployed guardian angels roam the streets of Berlin, unmoved by human feelings until one of them falls in love with a trapeze artist.

Jahrgang 45 (*Class of 45*), GDR, 1965. Dir. Jürgen Böttcher. Formerly banned, the love story of Al and Li, struggling to find a right way of life in a back courtyard in Prenzlauer Berg.

Legende von Paul und Paula, Die, GDR, 1973. Dir. Heiner Carow. As the old streets of Friedrichshain are torn down, Paul and Paula begin their touching and tragic affair. Adapted from Ulrich Plenzdorf's atmospheric novel, *Die Legende vom Glück ohne Ende* (*Legend of Fortune without End*).

Liebe auf den ersten Blick (*Love at First Sight*), Germany, 1991. Dir. Rudolf Thome. One year after reunification, a young archaeologist from former East Germany meets a Western futurologist from Berlin. An unlikely partnership, but in Berlin that year there was revolution in the air . . .

Here are some other films which closely reflect events in post-war Germany, in particular the gulf between Eastern and Western hopes and desires:

DDR – Ohne Titel (*GDR – No Title*), Germany, 1990. Dir. Harry Rag. Documentary. The director's journey through the GDR; views and interviews culled from every age-group.

Deutschland Deutschland, Germany, 1991. Dir. Peter Fleischmann. Documentary. Fleischmann taps the mood of a country grown suddenly bigger, half-populated by strangers.

Märkische Trilogie, GDR, 1988-90. Dir. Volker Koepp. Three-part study of East Germany's transformation in the years of 'The Turn'. For '*Märkische*' read border country, the part of Germany which was always the historic buttress between the Elbe and alien neighbour-states. The three parts are (1) *Märkische Ziegel*, (2) *Märkische Heide, Märkischer Sand*, (3) *Märkische Gesellschaft mbH*.

Winter ade (*Goodbye, Winter*), GDR, 1988. Dir. Helke Misselwitz. Documentary. An exploration of the day-to-day life of women in the GDR. A grey, predominantly sad portrait.

Wunderjahre (*Wonder Years*), Germany, 1991. Dir. Arend Agthe. It's 1957 and the economic boom in West Germany is under way. Hanna, an orphan, moves to a new home of her own in a small village, whose life mirrors that of the country at large.

BERLIN FROM A WALKER'S EYE VIEW

Berlin stands on the flat Brandenburg Plain and its weather is mixed – partly hot and continental, partly cold and windy (from the flatlands of Eastern Europe) and partly the wet stuff that comes in over Britain from the Atlantic.

In winter it can be as cold as −20°C, though such depths are increasingly rare. In the middle of the year, from May to the end of September, it is generally warm and dry (up to 30°C) with frequent spells of humid heat broken by thunderstorms.

Try to be warm, dry and comfortable at all times. Wear sturdy shoes and carry a folding umbrella if it is cloudy.

Security Berlin is a law-abiding place, though it is fair to say that theft and crime are on the increase. Be on the lookout for bagsnatchers in crowded areas, such as around Zoo Station and on buses and trains. The incidence of car thefts has spiralled since the opening of the Wall, so take every precaution if you leave a vehicle parked somewhere in the city.

Since 1989, too, the rising wave of hostility to foreigners (*Ausländerfeindlichkeit*) has become a worrying trend. It is a particularly nasty, racist phenomenon. Its victims are the poor of Eastern Europe and the Third World – the asylum-seekers (*Asylanten*) who have poured into Germany in search of work and a new life.

All visitors, of whatever race or colour, should be wary of groups of skinheads – the bully-boys of the Extreme Right factions. In general they keep to the more outlying Eastern estates where most of them live; Lichtenberg and Marzahn are the districts that come first to mind. However, they lurk too in the more cosmopolitan streets of Prenzlauer Berg and Kreuzberg, and are not readily distinguishable from the more harmless dropouts and *Chaoten* who have lived in these districts for a number of years. Wherever they plant their boots, skinheads are unpleasant animals. When drunk, they are a universal danger.

THE WALKS

Each Slow Walk opens with a Summary, then a Map and Route guide with street-by-street instructions, beginning at an S-Bahn or U-Bahn station. The essay which follows is suitable for reading either before setting off, as a trailer to the reader's personal experiences, or afterwards as a record.

The following symbols are used, mainly in the Route sections:

⊚   Special visit recommended

Ⓢ   S-Bahn station

Ⓤ   U-Bahn station

☂   Suitable for a rainy day.

The following abbreviations are used in the Route sections:

N, NE, E, etc., to indicate directions

14C   Fourteenth century.

All maps are drawn from north to south.

Many streets and stations in East Berlin and Potsdam were renamed in 1992. Old names appear in italics after the new name. Example: S-Bahnhof/Hackescher Markt (*Marx-Engels-Platz*).

Walk 1

Ku'damm

Kurfürstendamm – most famous promenade in Germany, vibrant with improbable glitter. Stroll beneath the plane trees and explore the attractive hinterland around Savignyplatz and Pariser Strasse. Visit the excellent Käthe-Kollwitz Museum, the Kaiser Wilhelm Memorial Church, the gaudy Europa-Center and KaDeWe ('Kaa-Day-Vay'), the Continent's biggest department store.

Allow 5-6 hours.

Best times Wednesday to Saturday, though KaDeWe closes Saturday at 13.00 (except on 'Long Saturday', the first in each month).

ROUTE

Begin at Ⓢ/Ⓤ Bahnhof Zoologischer Garten ('Zoo'); Buses 100, 109, 119, 129, 145, 146, 149, 219, 245, 249. Opposite main exit in Hardenbergplatz, buy Travel Pass (*Fahrausweis*) from **BVG Pavilion** on island in road, or from ticket window in station hall.

Cross Hardenbergstrasse and turn right under railway bridge. Continue to Steinplatz. At end of gardens turn left and next right at Goethestrasse. Post Office useful place to buy telephone card (*Telefonkarte*).

At next corner, turn left down Knesebeckstrasse to **Savignyplatz**. Explore cafés and restaurant menus, and leave square at far end, turning right beside railway arches. Take next left down Bleibtreustrasse, passing under Ⓢ Bahnhof Savignyplatz. Arrive in **Kurfürstendamm.**

Turn right and wander past luxury shops. At Leibnizstrasse, cross left to Olivaer Platz and bear left through square, along Lietzenburger Strasse. Turn right to **Pariser Strasse** and continue past cafés, galleries and boutiques to Ludwigkirchplatz.

Turn left up Pfalzburger Strasse. At Lietzenburger Strasse, cross road and to right of green-balconied block go in at entrance to **Ku'damm Karree**, where shopping/café arcade runs through to Ku'damm.

Here turn right past Theater am Kurfürstendamm and continue to Fasanenstrasse. Turn right and at No.24 visit **Käthe-Kollwitz Museum** ☞; open 11.00 to 18.00, closed Tuesday. *Admission.*

Return to Ku'damm. Turn right to Ku'damm Eck (opposite Café Kranzler) and walk on to **Kaiser Wilhelm Memorial Church (Kaiser-Wilhelm-Gedächtniskirche)** ☞; visit Memorial Hall at base of ruined tower, open 10.00 to 18.00, Sunday opens 11.00, closed Monday. Also see interior of new church, its walls filled with 11,000 panes of blue stained glass.

Continue across Breitscheidplatz (with its strange globular fountain) and look in at **Europa-Center** shopping-and-café complex. Take express lift to Viewing Platform (*Aussichtsplatform*) above 20th floor ☞; open 09.00 to 24.00, in winter opens 10.00. *Admission.*

At exit, turn left along Tauentzienstrasse and cross road to **Kaufhaus des Westens (KaDeWe)**, the Continent's biggest department store, widely admired for its glitzy food hall on 6th floor with brimming snack counters☞.

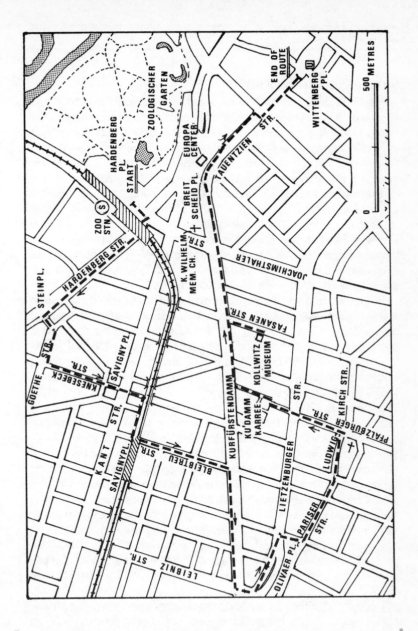

Walk ends here. Nearest Ⓤ Wittenbergplatz; Buses 119, 129, 142, 146, 185. Nearest refreshments in KaDaWe or cafés in Wittenbergplatz.

Stocking up at the Zoo

When West Berlin was a political island, Zoo Station's long arcade of steel and glass was the principal feeding-point for main-line trains to the West, and for the *S-Bahn* line running east to the border crossing-point at Friedrichstrasse. Today it remains as busy as ever. Below ground, Lines 1 and 9 of the *U-Bahn* pass through its needle's eye. The fore-court, on Hardenbergplatz, is the city's biggest bus station.

Three years after the Wall came down, transport arrangements are still not fully integrated in the city, and Zoo Station is the best place to go for up-to-date information. Public transport is run by the BVG ('Bay-Fow-Gay') and at their island pavilion in Hardenbergplatz visitors can buy a transport map (*Linienplan*) and ask about Travel Passes (One Day, One Week, Monthly, etc.) which are usually on sale there; if not, you may be directed to the station booking hall.

From Zoo Station, look southward to the impressively shattered tower of the Kaiser Wilhelm Memorial Church. It stands at the top end of Kurfürstendamm (the 'Avenue of the Electors'). From dusk, neon messages drench the surrounding sky, screaming the virtues of 'DUN-LOP – *REIFEN* – DUNLOP', of 'SONY' and 'HITACHI', and promise of financial heaven for investors in *'Die grossen drei* [The big three] LOTTO TOTO Spiel 77'.

At all hours it's a hard-nosed commercial quarter, smelly with onion fumes from the *Imbiss* (snack) stands, awash with grotesques lolling on street corners with their bottles, inseparable from their greasy shop-ping bags. Across the road from Hardenbergplatz, next to the Presse Café, is a shadowy arcade where illegal cigarette-sellers trade beside gaudy bars and sex-caverns. It's one of the nastiest places in the area (*eine Pisspassage*, a friend kindly volunteered), but it also contains the International Presse, by far the best shop in Berlin for newspapers from all over the world.

Visitors looking for the 'other' Zoo, the one with the caged animals, will find an entrance on the far side of Hardenbergplatz, past the bus station. (For a free preview, through the fences in Tiergarten Park, see *Walk 2.*)

Once through the railway bridge in Hardenbergstrasse, the atmos-phere clears. On the left is Amerika Haus, and next door at No.20 its cultural equivalent, the British Council (first floor).

Walk on to Steinplatz. On the right stands the Academy of Arts (*Hochschule der Künste*) and beyond lie the modern blocks of the Technical University which blanket the ground from here to the other side of Ernst-Reuter-Platz, named after West Berlin's first Mayor in the Cold War years. In Steinplatz is a monument to the concentration camp (*KZ* or *Konzentrationslager*) victims of National Socialism, 1939-45. At the next corner is another monument, to the victims of Stalinism; unlike the former, this has been left undated.

Around the corner in Goethestrasse is a main post office (*Postamt*). Call in here for a phone card, particularly useful now so many call-boxes have been converted to card operation. Perhaps load up too with stamps, though these are easy enough to buy from coin machines on the street. Now fully supplied with travel pass, maps and so forth, head down Knesebeckstrasse to the gardens of Savignyplatz.

In these pleasant streets, their broad pavements a gift to extended lunching and open-air suppers at twilight, the traces of war have long been built over and painted out. And yet they must remain in the minds of many an elderly face glimpsed behind lace-curtained windows. In Knesebeckstrasse, part of the house at No.17 was once Frau Gumz's Laundry. She was one of the silent heroines under Hitler's dictatorship. Moved by the plight of Jewish people in the neighbourhood, she found safe homes for them to hide, secure from the knock on the door that meant a train-ride to extermination. In this way Frau Gumz and fellow-sympathisers rescued around 1,200 Berlin Jews from the horrors of the Final Solution.

Savignyplatz

The large open square is bisected by Kantstrasse – noted for retail bargains – and bordered on the far side by the *S-Bahn* line linking Zoo Station and points west to Potsdam. The square was laid out in 1926 and named after Friedrich Carl Savigny (1779-1861), a prominent lawyer and minister.

In the square, and in streets radiating from its northern end, are some of Berlin's best café-bars and a score of good, middle-range restaurants. I recommend a lazy half-hour at the Zwiebelfisch ('Onion Fish') by the junction with Grolmanstrasse. At Carmerstrasse 9, the Dicke Wirtin ('Stout Landlady') is usually crowded and sometimes raucous. In between these two, the Cour Carrée has a pretty terrace and an interesting menu; in the evening, here and elsewhere, it's best either to reserve or turn up before 19.30 to secure a table. Nearby, a plaque on the wall of No.5 records that the artist George Grosz died in this house in 1959.

On the south side of Savignyplatz, beneath the railway arches, Bücherbogen has an appetising selection of books on art and architecture, the prices of which spiral into the blue beyond of DM 400 and more. Good window-shopping, all the same.

Turn along here, past a row of galleries and pavement cafés by the *S-Bahn* station. To the left in Bleibtreustrasse are more cafés and smart boutiques. Café Zillemarkt is an established favourite for breakfast at all hours, with a shady terrace and back garden in summer. Further on, Café Bleibtreu also has its faithful regulars.

Bleibtreustrasse leads down to Kurfürstendamm, and indeed beyond. At Nos. 15-16 on the right is a pale stone building, gabled and turreted and faintly Ruritanian with reliefs of cherubs, shields and animals. Here, from 1966-71, lived the celebrated actress Tilla Durieux, whose long line of credits goes back to Twenties Berlin and the theatre productions of Max Reinhardt.

Kurfürstendamm

Arrive in a reasonably muted section of the great boulevard. This is Kurfürstendamm at its opulent best, shaded by plane trees and much less crowded than at the Memorial Church end.

Quieter it may be, but there is no shortage here of luxurious shops and gleaming showcases on the pavement, and prices to be wondered at. In a jeweller's window, this message: *'Ein bisschen Gold sagt doch alles'* (A little bit of gold says everything). The *bisschen* includes an unpretentious little choker, nestling there with its price tag of DM 51,400.

Continue past the Hotel Mondial and its agreeable terrace. Next, all in a row, are fashion at Jil Sander, art at Galerie Binhold, hair styling at Anita Leütner and ritzy furniture at Robbe & Berking. Across Schlüterstrasse is Mientus for men, ladies' shoes at Scarpa Moda, then Yves St Laurent Rive Gauche and rich plate and antiques at G. Bustert. Who buys these desirable things I cannot say. I asked a friend, always suavely turned out, if she ever bought clothes or shoes on Kurfürstendamm. 'No, never,' she said, 'I get mine at the little shops round the corner, or the Flea Market.' (By Flea Market she meant the neighbouring Art Market which flourishes near Tiergarten at the weekend – see *Walk 2* for details.)

Ku'damm strides on. And so may you, all the way past Adenauerplatz and up as far as the Ring Road. The pavements remain broad and handsome throughout, like those of the Champs Elysées in Paris which served as the original model. At the close of the Franco-Prussian War (1870-1), Chancellor Bismarck ordered the building of a grand boulevard here, a place where the rich could build mansions and ride their horses along a central reserve to the forest paths of Grunewald. Trams for the masses took over as Berlin exploded westward, and public transport is now supplied by the square-fronted double-decker buses (Nos. 119, 129 and 219) which yaw in and out of the traffic lanes, like docking ships, rarely more than a couple of minutes apart.

After Olivaer Platz, the character of Kurfürstendamm grows a little more domestic. The cafés and inevitable banks continue, but in between the mixture changes – a locksmith, a photo shop and a supermarket in place of the de-luxe outfitters, and broad street corners bright with flower stalls.

I write these lines not far from here, in a deep-windowed room overlooking a courtyard shaded with tall silver birch and sycamore trees, loud with birdsong at dawn and until well after sunset. The trees strain narrow trunks upwards to secure their patch of light. On the third floor I sit level with an old bird's nest which has survived the winter and in May still awaits dismantling, if not new occupants. The courtyard issues onto a street running north from Kurfürstendamm, just at the foot of what Christopher Isherwood called 'the last dreary stretch which rises to Halensee'. That was more than sixty years ago, of course, and he might find it a little livelier now. Hereabouts, in *Goodbye to Berlin*, he located Sally Bowles's first landlady, Frau Karpf, fat, scruffy and dishonest 'with a pouchy sagging jowl like a toad'. Rereading his text, here in this green courtyard, surrounded by quiet and courteous neighbours, I am struck by the thought that Isherwood did not like Berlin at all. If so, the 'I am a camera' line – its shutter open, quite passive, recording, not thinking – need not be taken as something he did all the time, or even much of it.

Pariser Strasse

At Olivaer Platz, take to the hinterland on the south side of Ku'damm.
In Lietzenburger Strasse, facing the gardens, is Café New York, marking the start of a laid-back café culture which continues in Pariser
Strasse. The tone is smart and designerish, in concord with the many
art galleries and boutiques which line the street in haphazard fashion.
Nothing much happens here, compared with the unending street-
theatre of Kurfürstendamm, but this is where locals come to browse
and take a coffee in their lunch-break – usually a brief half-hour pause,
then back to the office desk or shop counter.

Keep on to the Catholic church in Ludwigkirchplatz, and return along
Pfalzburger Strasse towards the buzz of metropolitan Berlin.

Ku'damm 2

Shopping malls have multiplied like mole tunnels in these parts, there
being no longer enough on-street space for all the clothes and accessory
shops which feel they must trade here. Ku'damm Karree, on the far
side of Lietzenburger Strasse, opens at its southern end with an arcade
of seedy bars known as *Kneipen Stadt* or Pub City; then boutiques
crammed with shimmering knick-knacks lead out to Ku'damm.

To the left is the Komödie Theater and to the right the Theater am
Kurfürstendamm. Both are in the business of broad-humoured boulevard comedy, and battle nightly to keep the war of the sexes alive, to
the loud consternation of Berlin's feminists. (Which of these factions
now outnumbers the other would make an interesting social survey.)

At the junction with Uhlandstrasse is the reassuring sight of Café
Möhring, a famous rendezvous for gossip and cakes in the 'Old Berlin'
manner; warm, conspiratorial, eyes darting this way and that while
waistlines slowly thicken. Waitresses in crisp white blouses are there
to repeat the dosage according to desire, ferrying cakes from the show-
counter with an understanding smile.

On the opposite corner of Ku'damm is the residence-without-walls of
'Tüten-Paula', Berlin's best known bag-lady. Most of the time she sits
and broods on a garden chair next to the telephone boxes, surrounded
by heaped-up shopping bags (*Tüten*). In summer and winter she wears
a crash helmet, a heavy coat and boots without laces. She is a proud
woman who regularly sweeps the area round her pitch, and she does
not like to be interrupted in her thoughts. Approaches are met with

fierce abusive cries, on the lines of 'Shove off, you cheeky snotrag!' Having seen off the intruder, she nods back into her one-person world.

Keep on to Fasanenstrasse, noted for its charming urban villas. A resident of Wilmersdorf, the district to which this part of Berlin belongs, assured me that Fasanenstrasse was the most beautiful street in the city. Allowing for local bias, and the fact that she had probably not even considered candidates from East Berlin, she could make a strong case. Many of the street's best buildings date from the 1890s, and one group commands particular attention.

The scale of the broad garden at No.23, the Literaturhaus, is a splendid surprise. The house is divided between the Kohlhaas & Company bookshop, the Literaturhaus – whose events are described on the noticeboard attached to the front railings – and the atmospheric Wintergarten Café.

The other components of this architectural group are the Käthe-Kollwitz Museum, which we go into shortly, and the Villa Grisebach on the far side. Artfully designed by the architect Hans Grisebach, and built in 1891-5, the villa is a Jugendstil magician's castle squeezed into the frontage of a town house: a flat, high-gabled main façade and a corner turret with a steep crown, its recessed front set off by a balconied porch. The villa now partly serves as an art gallery, the Galerie Pels-Leusden.

Käthe-Kollwitz Museum

This great Berlin artist was born in 1867 and died shortly before the end of the Second World War at the age of 78. In 1891 she married Karl Kollwitz, a doctor practising in the working-class district of Prenzlauer Berg, and settled there, drawing extensively on the grim conditions of the neighbourhood. In 1931 she fell foul of the Nazis and was removed from her post as head of graphic arts at the Academy of Arts. In 1936 she was barred from holding exhibitions and her work was withdrawn from museums and galleries.

On the four floors of the museum her lifelong themes emerge with resounding clarity: unemployment, the misfortunes of women, poverty, drunken men, the horrors of a totalitarian regime, the threat of war, sickness and death. The subjects are handled straight, as portraits from life in charcoal or woodcut, or massed to form an image of simple symbolic power – mothers, for example, pressed together in a tower-like huddle to withstand unseen forces.

On the top floor the larger sculptures include her own *Muttergruppe* and a bronze portrait of her by Gustav Seitz. (In *Walk 11*, see the memorials to her in Kollwitzplatz, Prenzlauer Berg.)

In the garden, the gracious turning mobiles are by George Rickey, and there is a version of *The Crier* ('Der Rufer') by Gerhard Marcks. Six of these were made, and the most prominent stands in Strasse des 17. Juni near the Soviet War Memorial (see *Walk 2*).

Ku'damm 3

Return to Kurfürstendamm, and keep on to the overhead attractions of Ku'damm Eck – from the outside ablaze with neon signs, on the inside a forgettable collection of gaudy shops, porno cinemas and restaurants. Across the street, on the sunny side, the red and white awnings of Café Kranzler attract countless visitors to the city, though few locals go there and the interior has none of the charm of Café Möhring.

From Ku'damm Eck to the bend at the Memorial Church is the tacky end of the boulevard. Tourists drift aimlessly on the broad pavements, buskers busk, and some days a Fujicolor Zeppelin circles overhead, as though pinpointing the target for the next arrivals, funnelling in from Zoo Station and the scores of surrounding hotels.

Kaiser-Wilhelm-Gedächtniskirche

Few purpose-built memorials are as huge as the chopped-off former West Tower of the Kaiser Wilhelm Memorial Church; or quite as ugly. The original ensemble was a six-towered neo-Gothic monster, erected in 1891-5 with the dual aim of glorifying God and the memory of the departed Emperor, Kaiser Wilhelm I, under whose rule Prussia rose to become the most dangerous war-machine in Europe. In the Second World War, particularly on the night of 22 November 1943, Allied bombs destroyed the church. After a long debate, the city authorities decided to leave the former entrance tower as it stood. Henceforth it was to be seen as 'an admonition against war and destruction, and a call to reconciliation in Jesus Christ'.

The sentiments are admirable, though it was naive to imagine that this gloomy stump would be automatically transformed, as though by senatorial edict, into a visually moving testament. War *is* brutal and ugly, and so is the stump, but the stump is not *like* war, only one of war's many thousand manifestations which by May 1945 had levelled Berlin to a wasteland of rubble.

Inside the tower is the Memorial Hall (*Gedenkhalle*), decorated with reliefs celebrating the Imperial family and chronicling Prussian military triumphs. Also on view is a photographic history of the old church and the Cross of Nails presented by the congregation of Coventry Cathedral, which itself was destroyed in the Second World War.

Beside the surviving wreckage of the old church stands a new, uncompromisingly modern complex built in 1961-3. The main building is the new church, a low octagonal slab assembled like the others in a series of honeycomb frames; despite the thousands of blue stained-glass panes which fill the spaces of the honeycomb, comparisons with a military pillbox are inescapable. A matching hexagonal tower 53m (174ft) high contains a peal of six bells. At its foot is a bookshop and souvenir store dedicated to helping the Third World. The low square chapel nearby is open for services only.

Europa-Center

Next to the church is Breitscheidplatz, one of those appalling public spaces adored by police chiefs and ministers of culture – but who else? – where the young, the dim and the footloose are encouraged to hang out and let off steam. In summer, up to three primitive rock bands compete for attention, flanked by portrait scratchers, bead merchants and beer sellers touting cans of lager stacked in pyramids on the ground. Skateboarders tack the concrete ramps around the arena's centrepiece, a vaguely spherical beige fountain known officially as the *Weltkugelbrunnen* or 'Globe Fountain', and unofficially as the *Wasserklops* or 'Water Dumpling'.

Pass quickly by to the Europa-Center, a grandiose vertical shopping mall with sculptural sideshows. In the front inner court is the lofty 'Clock of Flowing (or Vanishing) Time' (*Uhr der fliessenden Zeit*) by B. Gitton. Green liquid, like the stuff I associate with washing-up, flows along plastic tubes and fills hollow globes and smaller discs to mark the hours and minutes of the day. In the back court is a slightly more sympathetic *Lotus Fountain* by Bernard and François Bachet. This waves slender stems of stainless steel in the air as water tips onto the lower petals and leaves; above it are the (real) palm-hung terraces of Tiffany's Café, where no doubt girls with names like Tiffany are to be found. (In Berlin, girls with names like Tiffany are collectively known as *Tussis* after the German girl's name Tusnelda, commonly linked with someone who is *doof* or brainless. *Tussis*, I am told, are usually blonde, wear leggings and high heels '*damit der Hintern wackelt*' – to make their bottoms wiggle – and use this successful formula to catch the passing male.)

For views of the city from on high, take the express lift to the twentieth floor and walk up to the outdoor, caged-in *Aussichtsplatform*. Although lacking the height of its former rival, the TV Tower in East Berlin (see *Walk 5*), it offers a good introduction to the sprawling city. Beneath the Star of Mercedes, look along the tree-lined avenue of Kurfürstendamm, then northward over the plump green duvet of the Zoological Gardens and Tiergarten Park, out of which the *Siegessäule* (Victory Column) pokes its tiered shaft and gilded Victory. Then comes the saucer roof of the Kongresshalle, panning round to the Eastern centre. This is dominated by the chimney and globe of the TV Tower and the Berliner Dom (Cathedral) at its foot, and the flat-faced blocks of Alexanderplatz, which not so long ago were emblems of progress in an alien land.

Kaufhaus des Westens

The Europa-Center debouches its visitors in all directions: southward, into Tauentzienstrasse. With Kurfürstendamm, this street is the main shopping axis, and has been since the turn of the century when the bursting city needed to expand, and thrust out to form the New West. At the far end of Tauentzienstrasse is Kaufhaus des Westens (or KaDeWe, pronounced 'Kaa-Day-Vay'), the biggest department store on the Continent.

Before we reach it, note the tangled eminence in the centre of the road. It was put up to celebrate Berlin's 750th anniversary in 1987. Designed by Matschinsky and Denninghof two years before the Wall came down, its vast bendy limbs are like a 3-D transport map, showing the city hooked up as one historic entity, but with all connecting lines severed.

The charms of KaDeWe are often exaggerated. As stores go, it is not so special, and years behind the best of Paris and London. Visitors might skip it altogether – but for the Food Hall. The Food Hall is on the sixth floor and it is a marvel, combining the chance to goggle at the spectacular delicacies . . . and indulge in some serious sampling too. Wander among the specialist counters – the *Gourmet Fischkutter*, flanked by lobsters and trout in tanks; the *Oysters and Champagne Bar*; *Specialities from Bavaria*; or pause for a quick one at *PilsnerUrquell*, or a flying snack at the *Geflügel (Poultry) Grill*, or a schnitzel at the *Grill & Pfanne*. Or a more thorough investigation of German sausage-types, a diploma-long exercise that need never end.

The Food Hall at KaDeWe is the flagship of a carnivorous city. Its public invitation to snack, swig and shop at the same time strikes an obvious common chord. People who on the street may seem over-earnest or remote are here restored to their better selves – pink-faced and smiling – after just a few minutes at one of the magic counters. It's a slice of Berlin that few can resist. And where better to end this walk?

Walk 2

Tiergarten

Berlin's great central park. Follow its shady paths to the Victory Column, see the Schloss Bellevue and Congress Hall, then the Soviet War Memorial and the Brandenburg Gate, triumphal entrance to Unter den Linden.

Allow 4-5 hours.

Best times Any day, though Victory Column closed on Monday.

ROUTE

Begin at ⑤ Tiergarten; Bus 123. At station exit, turn left to the **Berlin-Pavillon** (exhibition of city building projects) 👁 ; open 11.00 to 20.00, closed Monday. Continue to Klopstockstrasse and cross Strasse des 17. Juni to the **Tiergarten**.

In park, bear left to Grosser Weg which runs beside the lake of Neuer See. To right of path see brick pillar marking site where Socialist leader Karl Liebknecht was shot after being captured with Rosa Luxemburg in January 1919. Her memorial stands some 200m away (right at Lichtensteinallee and across canal bridge).

At Lichtensteinallee, turn left through Fasanerieallee to the Grosser Stern and **Victory Column (Siegessäule)** at centre of circus 👁 ; open April to November 09.00 to 18.00, December to March 11.00 to 16.00, closed Monday (these times may vary). *Admission*. Access via tunnel under road; 285 steps to viewing platform.

Note To save a little energy on the next stretch, hop on a Bus 100 at Siegessäule and ride to the Kongresshalle. On foot: cross to N side circus and turn in at massive Bismarck monument. Walk round to back and follow path to right which leads to Spreeweg. Turn left to **Schloss Bellevue**, a classical palace begun in 1785, now the official residence of the German President.

Turn right along John-Foster-Dulles-Allee to the saucer-roofed **Congress Hall (Kongresshalle)**, now the House of World Cultures (Haus der Kulturen der Welt) and open at various times for special exhibitions and concerts 👁. To rear of building, try airy Restaurant in der Kongresshalle, overlooking River Spree.

From Kongresshalle, turn left past square tower of Carillon to Grosse Querallee and cross John-Foster-Dulles-Allee. Walk down through woods of Tiergarten to Strasse des 17. Juni and turn left to **Soviet War Memorial (Sowjetisches Ehrenmal)**.

Walk on to **Brandenburg Gate (Brandenburger Tor)**, where this walk ends among stalls selling old Soviet military ephemera, Berlin bears, T-shirts and usual junk. Nearest refreshments meagre (at an *Imbiss* behind Pariser Platz) or follow Unter den Linden to Café Kisch (on left) or to corner Friedrichstrasse (La Petite Fleur Café at Grand Hotel). Nearest ⑤ Unter den Linden; or Bus 100.

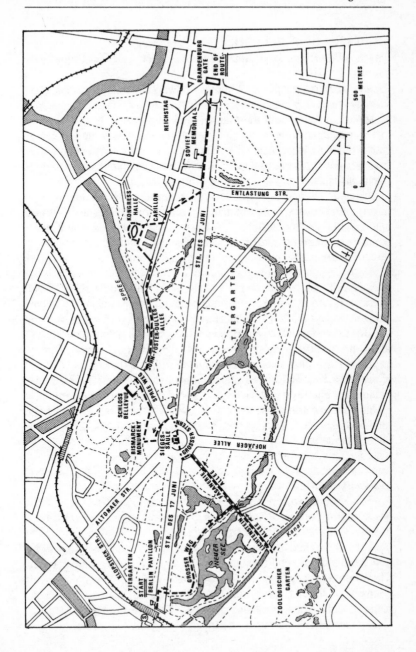

On the edge of the park

Question What has a steel pedestal, a swan neck and four-burner hanging lights?

Answer The first of a parade of old gas-powered street lamps, each one lovingly labelled, which runs from S-Bahnhof Tiergarten into the park and down to the bank of the Landwehrkanal.

The collection is known as the Open Air Gaslight Museum. It was installed in 1978 and has many fine examples gathered from far and wide – from Brussels, Zürich, Budapest and The Hague as well as from various Berlin districts (*Bezirke*) and other German cities.

Before crossing to the park, look at the Berlin-Pavillon nearby. The building reopened in 1991 and has fascinating exhibitions about future building schemes for the city. The displays are organised by the ruling Senate's architectural department and handle a different theme every three months. Look out for copies of an attractive free magazine, *Berlin Foyer*, published by the Senate.

Another minor attraction in this area is the showroom of KPM, the royal or (since 1918) state porcelain manufacturer (*Königliche Porzellanmanufaktur Berlin*). This stands on the other side of the railway bridge at the foot of Wegelystrasse. Though really only a shop (no factory tours on offer), the showroom has an interesting display of coffee and dinner sets introduced in the reign of Frederick the Great (1740-86) to serve the King and make suitable gifts for visiting nobility. The showcases are well baited with collectables – white figurines, topographical plates, bright harlequins and columbines. By contrast, some of the modern designs are quite horrid, best reserved for a crockery-smashing competition.

Weekend extra

For a morning stroll at the weekend, try the Arts/Crafts and Flea Markets (the biggest in Berlin) on Strasse des 17. Juni; open Saturday to Sunday, 08.00 to 15/16.00.

Begin at Ⓤ Ernst-Reuter-Platz. Walk along the broad avenue between the blocks of the Technical University. The first group of tented alleys on the left houses the so-called *Kunstmarkt* or Art Market, in reality a not-so-cheap assortment of hats, dresses, scarves, jewellery, pictures and frames, glass and pottery. Continue to the Flea Market (*Flohmarkt*) which runs up to the railway bridge by S-Bahnhof Tiergarten. Here you will find a full range of antique to junk furniture, ephemera and knick-knacks – a vintage doll's pram, brass door handles, kitchen gadgets, tiles, games, and such oddities as sable collars, complete with head, just like Kirchner's Berlin ladies wore in the Twenties, but which today provoke snarls from humans as well as dogs, and waspish retorts like this true specimen, overheard at a social gathering: 'How *could* you? You have about you the aura of a dead animal!'

To finish, take in the small market under the railway arches and seek refreshment in the agreeable, typical Berlin *Kneipe* nearby – the Tiergarten-Quelle – there to review treasures bought to the spasmodic drum of iron wheels passing overhead.

Tiergarten

Follow the antique lampposts into the park, then cut away left along Grosser Weg which tracks the northern bank of Neuer See, here and there overhung by willows. In moments, the great wood closes off the city, the blast of cars replaced by the occasional whirr of bicycle wheels or the thump-thump of an overtaking jogger.

On a weekday the paths are almost deserted; at the weekend they will certainly not be. Couples and families stroll in line abreast, some of the elders in stern Sunday finery, and cyclists must thread a serpentine route between them.

By night, this entrance to the park is not so pleasant. It is a renowned pick-up spot for a *lichtscheues Gesindel* (light-shy rabble) of down-at-heel homosexuals, and girls practising *Autostrich* with kerbcrawlers who drive along Strasse des 17. Juni. Best avoided, therefore, after dark.

For the daytime walker, noticeboards with maps point out the footpaths and the *Liege-Spielwiese* where you may lie and sunbathe or otherwise relax – but not play ball-games! Marked in dark green are the more fragile plantations, lawns and flowering meadows onto which you *may not go at all*!

To the right of the pathway stands a brick pillar, vertically lettered with the words 'KARL LIEBKNECHT'. At this spot, on the evening of 15 January 1919, the Socialist leader Dr Karl Liebknecht was shot after being captured by members of the right-wing *Freikorps* and his body thrown into the lake.

Also seized and murdered that night was Rosa Luxemburg, an eminent force among left-wing thinkers. She was then beaten to death, or close to it, and flung into the Landwehrkanal. To find the Luxemburg monument, turn right at the next crossing and follow Lichtensteinallee to the canal bridge. On the far side is a bronze plaque and, tilted dramatically over the dark waters of the canal, a metal block forming the letters of her name.

Close to the Luxemburg memorial, a scribbled slogan urges people to get rid of cars by the novel method of burying them underground, and so help the fight against the greenhouse effect, smog and polluted streets:

> 'Gegen Treibhaus, Smog und Strassen
> hilft nur AUTOS – UNTERN – RASEN!'

The plea is typical of graffiti in middle-class (*bürgerlich*) West Berlin – preoccupied by the *Umwelt* (environment) and the search for cultural improvements. In the East, the messages on the wall are fiercer and more immediate, attacking Neo-Nazis and the spectral prospect of another Greater Germany. Berlin may now be one city, but the minds of the people are ruled by two very different thought processes.

Flanking this part of Tiergarten is an extension of the Zoo. Peer through the vines which climb the perimeter railings to find zebra and antelope munching grass. (The main entrance to the Zoo, which is large but not all that astonishing, is in Hardenbergplatz, next to Zoo Station.)

Return to the other side of Neuer See and keep on up Fasanerieallee, first laid out in 1698. Pass a set of vigorous if not downright bloodthirsty statues dedicated to the hunt – baying hounds and dead game, and semi-naked figures spearing boars and bulls. Such was the Tiergarten (literally, Animal Garden) in earlier times: a hunting ground set up *c*. 1530 by Joachim I where Prussian rulers sported and entertained their guests. Later, G.W. Knobelsdorff converted the land into a park with broad Allees, and then in the nineteenth century the Tiergarten took on its present form. This was largely the work of Peter Joseph Lenné, who between *c*. 1815 and the 1850s was also responsible for landscaping the Zoological Gardens, Mariannenplatz in Kreuzberg,

Park Kleinglienicke, the gardens on Pfaueninsel and several other open spaces in the city.

The next great change to the Tiergarten was born of catastrophe. By the end of the Second World War, bombs had made a wasteland of its 200 hectares (494 acres). Cold and starving Berliners chopped up the remaining trees to fire their household stoves and grew potatoes and root crops in the clearings. A picture book published in 1956* shows an astonishing transformation. On one page is a view of the old pre-war Tiergarten. It is summer, and four visitors to the park, all wearing hats, sit stiffly on a bench near an equestrian statue. All around is a rich growth of formal clipped hedges and overhanging trees, densely interwoven. Facing this picture is another from the same viewpoint, taken soon after the war. Only the statue has survived the Allied blitz. It stands at the edge of a barren field, the rider looking clear across to the Soviet War Memorial and the shattered Reichstag building. In the foreground, rows of kale stand ready for harvesting.

The present rehabilitation of the park was led by Ernst Reuter, first Mayor of West Berlin. More than a million trees and shrubs were planted and new paths laid out in a free adaptation of Lenné's designs. Today the park is once more complete, mellow and mature, a wonderful retreat for city-dwellers in need of green leaves and a certain solitude.

Victory Column

The *Siegessäule*, dripping with gilded cannon, shoots massively upwards at the centre of Grosser Stern, a circus fed by five broad avenues. The greatest of these is Strasse des 17. Juni, linking Ernst-Reuter-Platz and the Brandenburg Gate.

The column stands on a square pedestal of red granite, ringed at its base by columns. Here on the inner wall is a set of mosaics by A. von Werner celebrating the military victories of 1870-1 which laid the French low and brought national unity to Germany. The fluted shaft of the main column is topped by an over-sized *Viktoria* grasping laurel and staff and turned to face triumphantly in the direction of France. At 35 tons she is the heaviest woman in Berlin, and sometimes referred to as *'Gold-Else'*. Until 1939 the Victory Column stood in front of the

*Otte Hagemann, *Haupstadt Berlin: gestern – heute – morgen*, Arani, 1956.

Gold-Else on the Victory Column

Reichstag building, where it was inaugurated in 1873. Under Hitler's rule it was dismantled in 1938-9, a fourth drum was added to the shaft and the new column was erected in the centre of Grosser Stern, a focal point in the Nazis' grand east-west axis road, much used for strutting military parades.

The spiral climb up 285 steps to the viewing platform is hard work, though there are occasional iron seats fixed over the well. From the top, broad views over Tiergarten and down the plumb-straight Strasse des 17. Juni make the effort worthwhile. Up there on the cramped, caged-in platform, the wind can be surprisingly sharp.

From the exit tunnel, cross to the north side where the Bismarck Memorial is set back on the fringe of the *Englischer Garten*. The Great

Unifier stands high on his plinth, dressed in military topcoat and spiked helmet (*Pickelhaube*), his sword at the ready. Around the base of the memorial are four bronze groups. These include Atlas bearing the globe and, to the rear, Siegfried forging the Sword of Empire. The Bismarck Memorial dates from 1901; until 1938, like the Victory Column, it was sited close the Reichstag.

A charming facet of these gardens is the rabbit population. Berlin, with its sandy soil and numerous parks, is ideal for rabbits. They pop up everywhere, in car parks, on canal banks and any small expanse of green; and seem remarkably tame. In Berlin the rabbit is generally looked upon as too tough and stringy to eat. The animals, in their turn, seem more tolerant of human company than they might otherwise be.

Schloss Bellevue and Kongresshalle

This tour through the Tiergarten makes a longish walk, and Bus 100 is ideally routed for a foot-soothing ride between the Victory Column and the Kongresshalle. On the way, look across to the elegant front of Schloss Bellevue, a classical palace which now serves as the official residence of the Federal President. It was designed by Philipp Michael Boumann and built in 1785-6 for Prince Ferdinand, brother of Frederick the Great. Later it served the Nazis as a lodge for receiving esteemed guests of the regime; in the war it was shattered by bombs and not fully restored until 1959.

The Kongresshalle, designed by Hugh A. Stubbins, was opened in 1957, financed by the Benjamin Franklin Foundation to mark German-American friendship during the Cold War years. In the garden to the front, the huge shell of the roof is mirrored by Henry Moore's statue, *Large Butterfly*, with its upswept wings. After 1980, when the hall's ambitious roof collapsed, restoration was again financed by the original sponsors and the building reopened in 1987. In the rectangular ponds leading to the hall, ceramic geese peck at the waters, and, standing on a raft, a group of multi-ethnic figures proclaim the building's present function as the House of World Cultures (*Haus der Kulturen der Welt*), mounting a series of exhibitions on life in the lands of Africa, Asia, Latin America and Oceania.

At the back of the building, overlooking the River Spree, is the large high-ceilinged Restaurant in der Kongresshalle, which offers restful views through enormous windows. On the waterfront a boat station connects with the river trip 'Under the Bridges of Berlin' and the occasional gigantic barge chugs through, filling the middle ground with its hull and vast holds, then about half a minute later the low wheelhouse veers slowly past.

Refreshed, head for the woods once more, passing the new Berlin Carillon in its square tower. Inaugurated in 1987, it has a peal of sixty-eight bells and plays a brief melody each day at 12.00 and 18.00.

Soviet War Memorial

Emerging from a woodland path beside the Grosse Querallee, the walker suddenly meets a dramatic view of the Brandenburg Gate straddling the far end of Strasse des 17. Juni. Closer to, a pair of Russian T-34 tanks, Nos. 200 and 300, mark the entrance to the garden of the Soviet War Memorial (*Sowjetische Ehrenmal*). At the centre of a seven-pillared
arc stands the colossal figure of a Soviet infantryman, rifle over his shoulder, bayonet mounted. The central inscription, in Russian, carries this message:

ETERNAL GLORY TO THE FALLEN HEROES IN
BATTLE WITH THE GERMAN FASCIST
AGGRESSOR FOR THE FREEDOM AND
INDEPENDENCE OF THE SOVIET UNION
1941
1945

In gilded wreaths on each inscribed pillar are crossed rifles, cannon, an axe and shovel, a propeller, a tank. The memorial was erected in 1945 from marble taken from the ruins of Hitler's Chancellery.

Brandenburg Gate

Walk on towards the Brandenburger Tor, so long the chief symbol of the divided city. In the centre of Strasse des 17. Juni stands the dramatic statue of *Der Rufer* ('The Crier') by Gerhard Marcks. A robed figure calls for peace through cupped hands. Around the four sides of

the base is this inscription:
'I GO/THROUGH THE WORLD/AND CRY:/
PEACE PEACE PEACE'

The Brandenburg Gate was built in 1788-91 by Carl Gotthard Langans in a classical style with two side pavilions facing into Pariser Platz on the eastern side. It is crowned by a triumphal bronze Quadriga, a copy of Gottfried Schadow's original. This too faces east, not for recent political reasons but because the *Tor* was originally a town gate in the eighteenth-century line of fortifications, built to ensure that entrants to Berlin paid their customs dues and that soldiers of the town garrison were deterred from deserting at whim from their sometimes intolerable occupation. It is the city's most splendid gate, sited to close the long straight avenue of Unter den Linden which originally led away from the Royal Castle (Schloss) at its eastern end. The Schloss was demolished in 1950.

In the post-war years, when it fell within the Russian zone, the Brandenburg Gate became *the* arena for ideological conflict. In the popular revolt of 17 June 1953, from which the avenue on the western side takes it name, East Berlin workers pulled down the Red Flag from the top of the Gate and marched through to the West carrying flags in the Federal colours of black, red and gold.

When the Wall was built in 1961, and visiting Western politicians came to view the Communists' handiwork, they did so from a raised platform facing the Brandenburg Gate. On the other side, the GDR authorities responded by lowering gigantic red banners between the columns of the Gate to obscure their opponents' view. The banners also served usefully to prevent East Germans from seeing what was happening.

When at last the border was opened in 1989, it was to the Brandenburg Gate that people poured in their thousands. Perhaps up to a million gathered there during the amazing days of 9-10 November, to stand on the hated Wall, to dance on the bones of Erich Honecker's corrupt state – even while it still lived – and to sing, embrace, and weep from simple joy.

To close this walk, make a symbolic pilgrimage through the Gate, and look back along the triumphal way. To the east, the immediate scene is unpromising. War blasted away the villas which once stood on Pariser Platz. Now in their place are rows of souvenir sellers. Old Soviet army caps are a speciality, and fur hats in winter, and other treasures from the quartermaster's store: badges, belts, naval binoculars, epaulettes and daggers, Russian dolls and hideous Checkpoint Charlie plates. There are model Trabants (wind up the back wheels and they go faster than the real thing). And there are (still!) paint-sprayed chunks of concrete purporting to be genuine *Mauer* (Wall), as likely to be authentic as they are rocks from the moon.

Today the Wall, where it has survived the hammers and chisels of private enterprise, is seen as a public monument, to be protected from extinction. The wheel of circumstance has turned full circle and now in some places there are walls to guard the Wall. One day, I sometimes think, the world will become a single state called Heritage, governed by a Praesidium of former museum curators.

Walk 3

Third Reich and the Wall

Fifty years of history and conflict at the heart of the once divided city. Visit the Reichstag, again to be the home of Germany's Parliament. Stand over the remains of Hitler's Chancellery, then follow a segment of GDR Wall to a war museum in the cellars of the old Gestapo HQ. Finish at the former Checkpoint Charlie border-crossing.

Allow 5 hours.

Best times Not Monday.

ROUTE

Begin at Ⓢ Lehrter Stadt Bahnhof; Bus 248. From the train platform, leave by the eastern exit and turn right down Friedrich-List-Ufer. Beside the river, turn left over Moltke Bridge and bear left across a corner of Tiergarten park towards **Reichstag** ☞; open 10.00 to 17.00, closed Monday.

At exit, turn right. Next to River Spree are memorials to those who died trying to cross the Berlin Wall (1961-89). Walk S to Brandenburg Gate and through it to Pariser Platz.

At end Pariser Platz, turn right down Toleranzstrasse (*Otto-Grotewohl-Strasse*). On left, sites of Nazi Ministry of Justice and Goebbels' Ministry of Propaganda. Turn right along Voss-strasse to large triangle of wasteland. The mound here probably marks site of liftshaft leading down to Hitler's apartments in **Reich Chancellery (Reichskanzlei)**.

Turn SW towards Esplanade Hotel, next to which was People's Court (Volksgerichtshof). Cross Potsdamer Platz and bear left to section of GDR **Wall (Mauer)** flanking Stresemannstrasse. Turn left along Niederkirchnerstrasse. Here visit **Martin-Gropius-Bau** (Jewish Collections and temporary art exhibitions) ☞; open 10.00 to 20.00, Friday and Saturday closes 22.00. *Admission*.

At exit, turn left to **Topography of Terror** exhibition, partly housed in cellars of former Gestapo HQ ☞; open 10.00 to 18.00, closed Monday. Go out to grounds and climb mound to viewing platform; photoboards pinpoint key Nazi buildings.

At far side of museum grounds, go through turnstile to Wilhelmstrasse. Cross road to Kochstrasse. At corner Friedrichstrasse, visit **Haus am Checkpoint Charlie Museum** ☞; open 09.00 to 22.00. *Admission*.

At exit, turn right to former Checkpoint Charlie crossing-point, where red and white barrier poles are still in place. Walk ends here. Nearest refreshments on left at Café Adler or further up at Alte Julius Kahlbaum-Stube. Nearest Ⓤ Kochstrasse, or walk N to Ⓤ Stadtmitte; Buses 129, 142.

To the Reichstag

In the last war the goodsyard at Lehrter Stadt Bahnhof was a starting-point for trains carrying Jewish citizens of Berlin to extermination

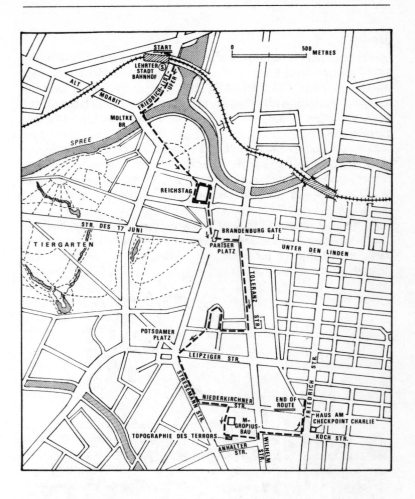

camps in the east. Between October 1941 and the end of the war, 63 death trains left from here, and from similar assembly stations at Grunewald and Putlitzstrasse. Packed into the trains were more than 35,000 Jewish victims.*

* See *Stätten des Widerstandes in Berlin 1933-45* (Resistance Sites in Berlin 1933-45), published by the Gedenkstätte Deutscher Widerstand, Stauffenbergstrasse 13-14, 1000 Berlin 30.

In the recent bout of station and street renaming, hitherto confined to locations in the former Communist territory of East Berlin, it came as a surprise to find that U-Bahnhof Putlitzstrasse, in the former Western district of Wedding, had been quietly renamed Westhafen. It remains to be seen whether the authorities now intend to start rewriting history on a larger scale.

From the station it is a short walk down Friedrich-List-Ufer to the hundred-year-old Moltke Bridge. Beside the road is a group of buildings being prepared for the Bundesgartenschau 1995, which promises to be an occasion of high horticultural splendour, proving for all time that Berlin is *grün*!

On the pink sandstone bridge, briefly admire statues of griffins and child warriors in Roman armour. Then turn into the Tiergarten and follow a well trodden path across the grass in the direction of the Reichstag.

Watchtower with angels, near the Reichstag

The S-Bahn station at Unter den Linden is much nearer to the Reichstag than our point of departure, but the approach from that side cannot match the grandeur and pageantry of the view from the park. Here, seen at its best angle, stands the weighty front of the German Parliament building, four-towered and beflagged in the colours of the Bundesrepublik, seldom admired for its beauty but respected for its mottled past.

The Reichstag is in many ways an odd building, one which in effect has been lost to the outside world for fifty years. Anyone living in Berlin during that time could see it every day, for example from the S-Bahn curving into and out of Friedrichstrasse Station. During the Cold War the Reichstag was in the West and always on view, but its global relevance faded soon after May 1945. Its secondary status was confirmed in 1949 when Bonn was appointed capital of the new Federal Republic of Germany.

Now Berlin is again capital of Germany. In readiness for great days to come, the new lawn in front of the Reichstag glows with the verdant perfection that will be taken for granted in nineteen-ninety-something, when the Government at last comes back to the city and the Reichstag's monumental inscription 'DEM DEUTSCHEN VOLKE' (TO THE GERMAN PEOPLE) will once more have national meaning.

The Reichstag arose in 1884 to designs by Paul Wallot and was completed ten years later. In 1918, after the abdication of Kaiser Wilhelm II, the Social Democrat deputy Philipp Scheidemann proclaimed the Republic from this building. In 1933 it was set on fire, possibly by the Nazis but this has never been firmly established, and in 1945 it was wrecked by Allied weapon fire. Until 1954 the over-solid High Renaissance façade was lightened by a glass cupola which covered the central section, but this was eventually removed during renovation work.

Closer to, the gigantic double-columned portico, the florid capitals and doorway flanked by reliefs cannot conceal the distinctly shabby state of the exterior. Some of the stone is almost restored to its natural sand colour, while other parts remain virtually soot-black. Everywhere, filled-in shell and bullet holes are covered by rectangular patches in the masonry, quite clear to see like so many sticking plasters.

To visit the current exhibition – *Fragen an die deutsche Geschichte* ('Questions on German History') – go in through a door on the north side. Copious documentation is on hand in the front hall, and in several languages, though much of it is school-party fodder, a propagandising trot through the history of the German Bundestag since 1949 – who did what, how legislation is passed, and so on. The book of the exhibition is very reasonably priced, however, and worth getting for the pictures alone.

The exhibition itself is dull. In picture booths, on wallboards and free-standing towers plastered with illustrations, some poorly captioned and some not at all, the story of Germany's progress from 1800 is dutifully recounted. The March Revolution of 1848, the Industrial Revolution, the Revolution of 1918-19, the Crisis Year of 1923 . . . and on up to 1990 and Reunification. There is a pronounced lack of accent, as though the management wishes not to disturb its visitors with unpleasant reminders. The Third Reich is certainly not ignored, but the exhibit for that shameful period does no more than flick through some of the landmark events. Schoolchildren and students respond to the bland display by turning aside from it, preferring to gather at the windows and gaze out over the Tiergarten. Thus the Reichstag presently limps along in a vacuum. One day, but only then, the heated voices of politicians may bring it back to the life it was built for.

Tracing the Wall

On the ground, the cross-city route of the Berlin Wall is now difficult to follow. Most of the actual structure has disappeared. In places there are stretches of Wall (*Mauer*) and elsewhere swathes of open ground which clearly mark its former course and those of the flanking death strips. At the north-east corner of the Reichstag building, close to the River Spree, a shrine with a row of white crosses recalls just a few of those who lost their lives trying to cross to freedom. On the far bank of the river, on a piece of wall painted black and white, the cost in lives is counted, year by year, and totalled: 258 sacrifices, 18 drowned, 25 GDR border guards. This memorial stands beside a new plantation known as the Parliament of Trees; on the ground nearby, carved stones represent the graves of those who perished.

Throughout the Cold War, Berlin was a political island. When the Wall was built in 1961, it surrounded the Western sector and carved a jagged path across the city. Its brutal function was to stop East Germans from pouring to freedom and depriving the GDR of badly needed manpower. Its effect on families living on both sides was devastating.

In Bernauer Strasse, between the districts of Prenzlauer Berg in the East and Wedding in the West, the border split the street in two. When guards and a squad of masons arrived to wall up apartment windows on the GDR side, people started jumping out of the windows and into firemen's sheets held below. There were tragic accidents, and several died.

Over the years the GDR strengthened and realigned its defences until a tight network of 3m (10ft) wall, fencing, barbed wire, open death strips, guard towers and searchlights extended for 160 km (100 miles) around West Berlin. Houses close to the border were pulled down to improve firing lines. Guards had orders to shoot to kill, and mostly obeyed them. For twenty-eight years, German was turned against German. Eastern leaders justified the Wall with ludicrous rhetoric that could never excuse the inhuman means they relied on to make it effective.

From the River Spree, the Wall pressed close against the back of the Reichstag, running south to the Brandenburg Gate – the history of which is described in Walk 2. In the context of the Wall, which passed directly across its face, the Gate served the West as a constantly evoked symbol of what had been lost. In the East, its possession and retention were everything. It was the Gate which guarded the straight way to the GDR's power centre in Marx-Engels-Platz. At times of particular stress, armed officers stood on top of the Gate, glaring down through binoculars at the crowds of so-called 'militarists and imperialists' who roared their protests on the free side of the Wall.

From the end of Pariser Platz, the newly named Toleranzstrasse (*Otto-Grotewohl-Strasse*) runs south to the heartland of Hitler's former police state. In those days (1939-45), it was called Wilhelmstrasse and it contained the Ministry of Justice and Goebbels' Ministry of Propaganda (which still stands). There is little to see now, save the classier blocks of flats reserved for GDR dignitaries. One day, standing on the wasteland at the end of Voss-strasse, I was joined by a stout middle-aged cyclist wearing *Lederhosen*. He gestured up at the apartment block. 'Yes,' he almost shouted, 'there were some right shits living up there, I can tell you.' He may also have been a little drunk, but his observation was not the product of alcoholic fantasy.

Hitler's Bunker

Around Voss-strasse, or where building works allow, turn towards the great triangular field where Hitler's Reich Chancellery once stood. Before the Second World War, the far side of this extraordinary barren expanse was occupied by the old Potsdamer Platz, one of Berlin's busiest thoroughfares. In the distance, the Esplanade Hotel is a forlorn survivor. During the war the square was razed by bombs. In the years of partition it was left empty, and eventually walled off on all sides by the GDR authorities. The flat terrain is broken by a single mound. This probably marks the site of a liftshaft leading down to Hitler's bunker in the Chancellery complex. It was here on 30 April 1945 that he committed suicide with Eva Braun. After the war, Soviet engineers blew up the ruined buildings, salvaging marble and other materials to build the Soviet War Memorials in Strasse des 17. Juni and at Treptower Park, and to refurbish the former Kaiserhof U-Bahn station (now Mohren-strasse).

In recent times, politicians have been conspicuously unwilling to disclose the nature of the war remains lying beneath this battered field. Despite further Soviet-organised explosions in 1988, it is still possible that several underground structures on the Ebertstrasse side may be in some measure intact. These may include SS garages and workshops, and the office of Kempka, Hitler's chauffeur. Another point of view maintains that there can be little worth recovering; below ground, the area is so full of pipeways and transport tunnels, it must look like a Gruyère cheese in cross-section. Meanwhile, the Federal Government is determined not to allow the place to be turned into a Nazi shrine, frequented by gangs of skinheads flaunting the swastika, egged on by devious politicians of the Extreme Right. Already, as recent elections have indicated, they are enough of a threat to Germany's precarious stability.

From Potsdamer Platz, turn along Stresemannstrasse to find gaudily painted remnants of the Berlin Wall. At the corner of Niederkirchnerstrasse, a sign on a lamppost explains that the street was renamed in 1951 after an anti-Nazi resistance fighter. Its previous name was Prinz-Albrecht-Strasse, which between 1933 and 1945 was the most feared address in Berlin, for here stood the headquarters of the Gestapo.

Martin Gropius Building

This attractive and colourful building currently performs double duty as a venue for temporary art exhibitions and as a home for much of the Berlin Museum's Jewish Collections. One day, it is hoped, the collections will find their own permanent home.

Martin Gropius was a pupil of Karl Friedrich Schinkel, Berlin's greatest architect, and an uncle of Walter Gropius, a founder of the Bauhaus. His red sandstone building, designed in 1877, revives the *palazzo* style of the Italian Renaissance and derives also from Schinkel's warehouse-like Bauakademie, later demolished. The building suffered badly from bombing in the Second World War and restoration began in 1979. The museum's café has a pleasant terrace on the south side, a welcome rest-stop in an area bereft of decent watering holes.

Topographie des Terrors

Across the cobbles from the Martin-Gropius-Bau stands a war museum partly housed in the cellars of the former Gestapo HQ. Although the exhibition is no more than a competent survey of the war and of atrocities committed by the SS and the Gestapo, it is chilling to stand in those cells and interrogation rooms where so many were once dragged in and tortured.

The museum's title and purpose are more truly reflected in the outdoor exhibition in the adjoining field. Here steps lead up to a viewing platform on top of a weed-strewn mound. Visible from here are numerous buildings which during the Third Reich were dedicated to the pursuit of war and terror. Opposite the Gropius building, in Niederkirchnerstrasse, is the former Prussian Chamber of Deputies which Field Marshal Goering took over and turned into the House of Fliers. Nearby is his vast Air Ministry complex, which later became the GDR's House of Ministries (Haus der Ministerien). Now it is the head office of the Treuhand, the agency charged with selling off, or shutting down, some 10,000 businesses in former East Germany. To the rear of the *Topographie* site is Hedemannstrasse. At No.10 were the editorial offices of *Der Angriff* ('The Assault'), a propaganda paper run by Goebbels. No.31 was the headquarters of the SA (Stormtroopers) Group for Berlin-Brandenburg.

In the surrounding wasteland are further viewing points, flanked by a long section of Wall in Niederkirchnerstrasse. In the opposite corner, by Wilhelmstrasse, the SS established their central offices between 1934 and 1945 in the Prinz-Albrecht-Palais; nothing remains of the building.

Haus am Checkpoint Charlie Museum

After the grey Eastern blocks of Toleranzstrasse and the grim surrounding vistas, Kochstrasse is resolutely Western in character; houses and offices are brightly painted, the food shops revealing a Turkish influence. This is the fringe of Kreuzberg, the enclave which in the Cold War sheltered beneath the curtain of the *Mauer* on East Berlin's southern perimeter. At the junction with Friedrichstrasse is the Museum of Checkpoint Charlie.

The collection tells the story of the Wall. It does so in, to me, a disconcertingly breezy style, a tabloid approach which comes close to trivialising its subject. The target audience seems to be visiting students, who cluster round the more sensational exhibits – the tiny Isetta car, for instance, its heating system and battery removed to make a compartment where a refugee could hide and be driven across the border. The museum has collected an admirable series of documents and objects, but the emphasis on 'learning by adventure' may disappoint serious visitors.

The Border Crossing

Continue to the site of the Checkpoint Charlie crossing-point. Red and white border poles mark the edge of the old American sector.

When the GDR ruled East Berlin, precise regulations governed entry and exit from the West. Visitors could go in for a single day and had to be out by midnight. On production of a passport, West Germans and non-Germans were issued with a visa costing DM 5, free to children under sixteen. Residents of West Berlin had to buy their visa at least three days in advance from a booth near Zoo Station. Waiting time at the crossing-points might run into hours, especially at Christmas or Easter.

There were two permissible crossing-points, and other rules about opening times and currency. Here are brief extracts from one official account:

'Crossing-points

Non-Germans using the S-Bahn or U-Bahn must use Friedrich-strasse Station. Non-Germans travelling by car must use Check-point Charlie. You are free to use either crossing-point, but you must return by the same crossing-point.

Times of opening

Friedrichstrasse Station: 7 am – midnight.

Checkpoint Charlie: 7 am – midnight.

You may stay no later than midnight on the day of entry.

Minimum exchange of D-Marks

You are required to exchange a minimum amount of money. D-Marks are exchanged into marks of the GDR at the rate of 1 to 1. The minimum exchange requirement per day is as follows:

- for people aged fourteen, DM 7.50 [Children aged under fourteen were exempt from this requirement.]
- for people over fourteen and up to pensionable age, DM 25.
- for people of pensionable age, DM 15.

The minimum exchange is completed at the crossing-point immediately after the visa has been issued.

Spending the minimum amount exchanged – no changing back

You must spend the marks of the GDR you obtain from the compulsory exchange.

You cannot change back any amounts you may have left over, but you may deposit these at an exchange-office of the state Bank of the GDR . . . You are not allowed to have with you Marks of the GDR or currencies of other East European states on entering or leaving.'

In reality, an East Mark was worth one quarter or less that of a D-Mark. You could buy little with your twenty-five East Marks, and would certainly not be able to eat at the Communist sector's more lavish restaurants. West Berliners balanced up the inequity by buying cheap East Marks in the West and smuggling them past the guards. In the early years there were regular body checks at the border but these became less and less frequent.

The huts and control posts are gone but this most famous of crossover points is an eerie place. On the former Eastern side the road enters a featureless square backed by shabby apartments and offices. The invasion of the developers is yet to come but cannot be far away, for this prime site lies close to the prestigious streets of Unter den Linden and Leipziger Strasse.

Meanwhile a family of Berlin's intrepid rabbits make the most of their temporary solitude, feeding off the rough grass and retiring beneath cars and trucks standing in the vacant lots.

Walk 4

Unter den Linden

'Under the Lime Trees' – one of Europe's most famous avenues, magnificently restored and now open for all to see. Superb baroque and neo-classical buildings include the domed French and German churches, the Schauspielhaus (Playhouse) and Neue Wache (the former Royal Guardhouse). Visit the German State Opera House and the first neo-Gothic church in Berlin, now a museum dedicated to Karl Friedrich Schinkel, the architect who shaped the lines of the modern city.

Allow 6 hours.

Best times Not Monday-Tuesday, when Schinkel Museum closed. (Huguenot Museum also closed Friday, and Zeughaus closed Wednesday.)

ROUTE

Begin at Ⓢ Friedrichstrasse; Buses 147, 157; Trams 22, 46, 70, 71. Exit on S side (*'Ausgang Friedrichstrasse'*) and turn right and right to weed-infested riverbank road (Reichstagufer). Walk towards Reichstag and turn left down Toleranzstrasse (*Otto-Grotewohl-Strasse*) to Pariser Platz. On right the **Brandenburg Gate (Brandenburger Tor)**.

Turn left along **Unter den Linden**. On right the grand recessed front of the former **Soviet Embassy**. Continue along Unter den Linden or turn right down Glinkastrasse and left along Behrenstrasse to find the **Comic Opera (Komische Oper)**; box-office in building opposite, open 12.00 to 18.00 and one hour before evening performances, closed Sunday.

Return to Unter den Linden via Friedrichstrasse; refreshments in La Petite Fleur Café at Grand Hotel. Continue along Unter den Linden and turn right down Charlottenstrasse to **Gendarmenmarkt** (*Platz der Akademie*), the city's most gracious square. On N side, the **French Church and Dom (Französischer Dom)** 👁; 240 steps up tower to viewing Balustrade, closes 17.30; on ground floor **Huguenot Museum (Hugenottenmuseum)**, open 10.00 to 17.00, Sunday opens 11.30, closed Monday, Friday. *Admission*.

At centre of square see the **Schauspielhaus**, now a concert hall; go in at side to box-office and foyer for brochures and bookings.

On S side square is domed **German Church (Deutscher Dom)**, a matching companion to the French Church.

On E side square, walk up Markgrafenstrasse (*Wilhelm-Külz-Strasse*) and turn right along Französische Strasse, then next left up Hedwigskirchgasse to front of **St Hedwig's Cathedral** 👁; open 10.00 to 17.00, Saturday closes 16.30, Sunday opens 12.30.

Exit to Bebelplatz and the **'Forum Fridericianum'** at the heart of Frederick the Great's Berlin. On left the curving façade of the **Old Library (Alte Bibliothek)**, on right the **German State Opera House (Deutsche Staatsoper)**; box-office at front of building open 12.00 to 18.00 and one hour before performances.

Cross Unter den Linden to Frederick the Great statue. On far side is **Humboldt University**, and to its right the **Neue Wache**, where a flame burns to the 'Victims of Fascism and Militarism'.

Beyond Neue Wache stands the **German History Museum (Deutsches Historisches Museum,** housed in former **Arsenal**

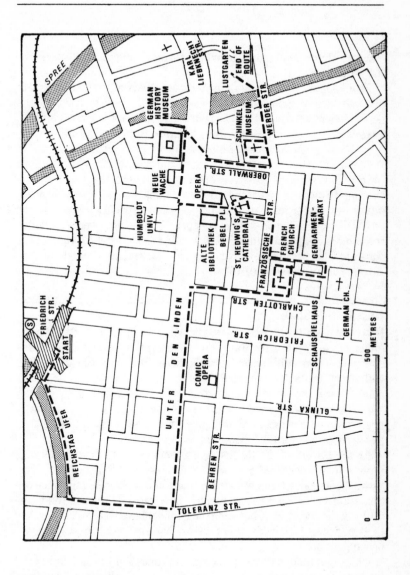

(Zeughaus)) 👁 ; open 10.00 to 18.00, closed Wednesday. *Admission to temporary exhibitions*.

Cross Unter den Linden to find the terrace and sparkling interior of the **Operncafé**.

From Unter den Linden, turn down Oberwallstrasse and walk beneath arches connecting Operncafé to main wing of Palais Unter den Linden. Arrive beside red-brick neo-Gothic church, the **Friedrichswerdersche Kirche**, home of **Schinkel Museum** 👁; open 10.00 to 18.00, closed Monday-Tuesday. *Admission*.

At exit, turn left along Werderstrasse and cross bridge to Lustgarten (*Marx-Engels-Platz*), a barren open space where the Royal Palace (Berliner Stadtschloss) stood until its demolition in 1950-1 following heavy war damage. Cross to Palast der Republik, former home of GDR's *Volkskammer* (Parliament). Walk ends here. Nearest refreshments at Café am Palast beneath Palast Hotel (to right along Karl-Liebknecht-Strasse). Nearest Ⓢ Hackescher Markt (*Marx-Engels-Platz*); Buses 100, 157.

Beside the Spree

Little has been done to beautify the banks of the Spree in central Berlin, either in the West or the East. The pavement of Reichstagufer is uneven and edged with weeds; few walk there. The river, though, is alive with barge traffic and pleasure boats in season, the barges huge and cumbersome on the less than broad waterway, urged on by pusher tugs. They are in effect the monarchs of the Spree, which has always been first and foremost a thoroughfare for water traffic rather than a pleasure ground for the inhabitants of the city.

As the towers of the Reichstag draw nearer, turn down Toleranzstrasse (*Otto-Grotewohl-Strasse*) to the hawkers of Pariser Platz. Fine town houses once faced onto this square, formerly called the Quarré. Some form of elegant replacement is now urgently needed to fill the flanks of the scruffy void between the Brandenburg Gate and Unter den Linden. Some good cafés, *à la* Champs Elysées, would be a great improvement on the present dismal scene.

Unter den Linden is one of the grand avenues of Europe, and since 1989 its potential has been revived. The central *allee* under the lime trees is the best place to walk. Limes were first planted at the beginning of the avenue (the far end) in 1674, and gradually the street acquired a double line of urban palaces flanking its length.

The buildings at this end are GDR-shoddy, made even less appealing by the new *Wessi* window displays of Yamaha and Volkswagen – these days, though, who else can afford the rent? Then on the right is a wonderful museum-piece, the recessed front of the old Soviet Embassy, built in 1950-3 with many of the hallmarks of Totalitarian Palatial: flat-topped and massive, crowned by a pillared cubic lantern, the lower front studded with gleaming lamps and iron-panelled doors. Although showy and pompous, it is not over-large for the site, and the front courtyard and a screen of trees preserve a discreet distance between building and street.

Around the corner in Behrenstrasse is the Comic Opera (*Komische Oper*), a fine old Berlin institution which consistently puts on productions of high quality. For this and all other opera houses and concert halls, it is best to book as early as possible. Many of the seats are taken up by season-ticket holders and the rest sell out quickly in this culture-conscious city.

The corner with Friedrichstrasse was once a centre of café life, and one day may be so again. Beneath the Grand Hotel, the Petite Fleur Café is well-mannered and quiet, serving coffee and *Torten*, and tables in the window bays offer a good view of Unter den Linden. On the next corner, Lindencorso is currently a joyless place, though a considered facelift could work wonders.

Along with the old cafés came Friedrichstrasse's reputation as the city's number one street of sin. 'Friedrichstrasse swarmed with whores,' wrote George Grosz of the period before 1914. 'It was the time of big feather hats, feather boas and breasts strapped up high. The handbag swung backwards and forwards was the trademark of the guild. The most famous whores' café was the Café National . . . People worshipped Zola, Strindberg, Weininger, Wedekind – naturalistic enlighteners, anarchistic self-torturers, death-lovers, erotomaniacs. It was shortly before the war.'

Since 1989, some of the girls' great-granddaughters have returned to Oranienburger Tor, on the far side of Friedrichstrasse Station, but that is another story (see *Walk 8*).

Gendarmenmarkt (Platz der Akademie)

The grand architecture of Unter den Linden is a little way off yet, but

Schinkel's Playhouse and

French Dom, Gendarmenmarkt

Berlin's most perfect square is just around the corner. In the broad piazza of Gendarmenmarkt the two matching cathedral domes – the French and the German – stand in harmonious balance to either side of Schinkel's Playhouse which projects its mighty stone staircase into the square. In front of the theatre, now a concert hall, the statue of Friedrich Schiller, second only to Goethe among the 'heavies' of German literature, leads the eye further outwards.

Originally the square provided stables and a guardhouse for the Gens d'Armes Regiment. Elector Friedrich Wilhelm then granted asylum to Huguenots in flight from France, after Louis XIV had revoked the Edict of Nantes in 1685. The French Protestant community settled in this area – the new suburb of Friedrichstadt, founded in 1688 – and two churches were built, one for the Huguenots and one for Lutheran worshippers – the German church in Mohrenstrasse.

The French Friedrichstadt church (1701-5) stands modestly next to the late baroque *Dom*, which arose in the next phase of development. Under the patronage of Frederick the Great, who wanted to create a square like the Piazza del Popolo in Rome, Karl von Gontard designed the two domed towers in 1780.

Views from the Balustrade near the top of the French *Dom* are well worth the climb – two hundred and forty steps up to the vast *Glockenspiel* which hangs inside the dome. Lower down is the *Turmstube*, a rather expensive French restaurant in an enviable setting – even if it *is* eighty steps up to your table. At the base of the dome, the history of Berlin's Huguenots is traced in a group of small rooms. The French community in exile grew to a strength of some 20,000 and came to exert an increasing influence on Berlin culture. Things French, beginning with the language, became fashionable and in pre-Enlightenment times were widely adopted. The Huguenots set up model schemes of education and caring for the poor, and individuals rose to high office in both state and army.

All the great buildings of Gendarmenmarkt suffered heavy damage in the Second World War. A photograph of 1945 shows both domes completely sliced off, and rubble lying where it fell. The basic structures were spared, and under the GDR were painstakingly restored. Work continues at the Deutscher Dom, which is due to reopen for religious services in 1995.

The first theatre in Gendarmenmarkt had a remarkably short life.

Carl Gotthard Langhans built his Nationaltheater in 1801 to complete the square's monumental plan. It was badly destroyed by fire and replaced in 1818-21 by the present building, Schinkel's Königliches Schauspielhaus or Royal Playhouse. This is now the home of the excellent Berlin Symphony Orchestra. The auditorium is light and beautifully decorated, surrounded by busts of the great composers, and in the elegant refreshment rooms season-ticket holders promenade and seek out familiar faces.

Cafés and shops are now making their mark in the general revitalisation since the *Wende*, and the Café Arkade beneath the Charlottenhof Hotel is pleasant and reasonably priced. On the far side of Gendarmenmarkt, the G.W. Leibniz bookshop has an interesting Jugendstil façade, decorated in cream speckled with red.

St Hedwig's Cathedral

At the top corner of the great open square of Bebelplatz, St Hedwig's Cathedral spreads its stout rotunda and copper dome, broad and low like a planetarium. Or is it a teacup? This is what Frederick the Great, an admirer of porcelain products, is said to have ordered from the architect Georg von Knobelsdorff: a dome like an upside-down teacup, that was what he would like to see. On the other hand, the 'teacup' could be but a Berlin nickname, tagged on later when the new building became visible. Whichever version is true, it is clearer still that the cathedral is modelled on the Pantheon in Rome.

St Hedwig's was built between 1747 and 1773 to serve the city's Catholic community. Destroyed in the last war, it was virtually rebuilt in 1952-63. The remodelled dome now sits uneasily over the pediment and thoughts of a soup bowl, rather than a teacup, are hard to suppress. The interior consists of a great circular room with a simple modern altar. An open stairway leads down to the Underchurch; in a niche in the altar is a seated fourteenth-century figure of St Peter. The early Catholic Bishops of Berlin are buried in the crypt.

'Forum Fridericianum'

The 'Forum Fridericianum' was built to enhance the expanding city when nearby medieval ramparts were pulled down. Its planning was entrusted to Knobelsdorff, and the Deutsche Staatsoper was the first building to occupy the site. It stands directly on Unter den Linden, was built in 1741-3 and features a monumental pedimented portico entered from steps to the side. To Frederick the Great it was a 'Temple of Apollo'. As Berlin's first theatre, it drew wide admiration from actors, architects and audiences. In the last war it was destroyed twice, and is now magnificently restored – one of the many prestigious projects which the GDR completed in and around Unter den Linden (at the expense of just about everywhere else in East Berlin).

Facing the Opera House across Bebelplatz is the curved front of the Alte Bibliothek (Old Library), built in 1775-80 by Georg Unger and nicknamed the *Kommode* after the outer wings which bulge like a chest of drawers. A plaque at the front records that Lenin worked here in 1895.

The Forum was renamed Opernplatz before the GDR ordered a second renaming to honour August Bebel, a nineteenth-century workers' leader. It was here, on 10 May 1933, that students in SA (Storm-trooper) uniform burnt some 20,000 books in a so-called symbolic act. The burning was inspired by Josef Goebbels, and the 'crime' of the books chosen for burning was that they ran counter to Nazi thinking. This one piece of literary terrorism outlawed many respected German authors who shortly escaped into exile. Among them were Thomas Mann, Heinrich Mann, Einstein and Stefan Zweig.

At the centre of the Forum, and of Unter den Linden, is a famous if poorly maintained statue of Frederick the Great. It was designed in 1840 by Christian Rauch, a pupil of Schadow. The king is portrayed riding towards the old centre of Berlin, and around the pedestal is a lively frieze of his generals and civic officials.

Across the avenue stands the courtyard and principal block of Humboldt University, in recent years the university of East Berlin. This building was also conceived as part of the Forum Fridericianum and was designed by Johann Boumann the Elder and built in 1748-53. It was originally intended as a palace for Prince Heinrich, brother of Frederick the Great, and became part of the university when it was founded in 1809 by Wilhelm von Humboldt. Former lecturers include J.G. Fichte, the first rector, Hegel, the Brothers Grimm and Einstein.

Neue Wache and Zeughaus

To the east along Unter den Linden, a noticeboard advertises the repertoire of the Maxim Gorki Theater which stands back from the road at the end of an avenue of chestnut trees. The next building is the Neue Wache, the former Royal Guardhouse. One of Schinkel's finest creations, it dates from 1816 to 1818.

Karl Friedrich Schinkel is undoubtedly Berlin's greatest architect. The broad adventurous lines of his neo-classical buildings continued the spirit of what had gone before and gave the city a model profile to which it has since largely adhered. From 1800 Schinkel was the chief inspirational force, his legacy much helped by a planning law which until the 1930s prohibited any building in the city centre from rising higher than the lantern on the dome of the Stadtschloss.

Berlin, conforming to the Brandenburg Plain on which it stands, is a low-built city of long, flat-topped rooflines. It has its spires and towers also, and high-rise blocks dating mainly from the 1960s. It is reasonable, nonetheless, to argue that through Schinkel a perceptible line of architecture has evolved. Borrowed at first from Greece and Rome, it was preserved after Schinkel in the ubiquitous apartment blocks of the late nineteenth century, in the Bauhaus style, in Modernism and in much of the post-war reconstruction programme.

Schinkel's work is chronicled in some detail in the Friedrichswerdersche Church, which we shortly visit. There it becomes clear that he was a master at adapting classical forms to design a variety of pavilions, temples and public buildings. For the Neue Wache he planned a low cube and a wide portico bonded by the shallowest of pediments. In the entablature, a row of Victory figures gives emphasis to the lateral energy that is so characteristic of his work.

Under the GDR the Neue Wache became a memorial to the 'Victims of Fascism and Militarism' and was guarded by goose-stepping soldiers. In the sombre interior, flames burn in a chest of burnished bronze and heatproof glass. Plaques in the floor commemorate an Unknown Soldier and an Unknown Resistance Fighter.

Next to the Neue Wache is the German History Museum, housed in the old Zeughaus or Arsenal, a gracious baroque structure designed in 1695 by Johann Nering. In the inner courtyard, the Schlüterhof, the walls are adorned by a famous series of stone masks of dying warriors sculpted by Andreas Schlüter. The museum offers temporary exhibitions on German themes such as 'The Last Emperor – Wilhelm II in Exile' and 'German Posters – 1888 to 1933'. There is a smart café in brasserie style where long-aproned waiters and waitresses nip about balancing trays on the palm of one hand.

Best of all, though, for light refreshment in the 'Old Berlin' manner is the Operncafé across the road in the former Princesses' Palace. At the front of the long glittering room is one of the city's most succulent cake counters.

Schinkel Museum (Friedrichwerdersche Kirche)

Karl Friedrich Schinkel moved some way from his neo-classical mode when in 1824 he designed this church, the city's first neo-Gothic brick building. The plan is still box-like and symmetrical, with a rectangular nave and towers formed from two superimposed cubes. Along the roof of the nave the buttresses yield to tall pointed pinnacles. The view over Berlin from this roof was the subject of a fascinating *Panorama* by Eduard Gärtner, now in the Schinkel Pavilion at Charlottenburg (see *Walk 14*).

The church, fully restored after receiving heavy bomb damage in the war, reopened in 1987 as a museum of Schinkel's work. In the nave are sculptures by contemporaries and architectural drawings by Schinkel; these continue around the gallery. Schinkel extended his range to include shops as well as temples, houses as well as grand public buildings. Among the designs on view are those for the Pomonatempel in Potsdam (1800); alterations for the Berliner Dom (1820-22); the Altes Museum (1825-30) and the Schauspielhaus (1818-21).

Last of the New

From the Schinkel Museum it is a short walk across the Schleusen-Brücke to what, until 1990, was the centre of decision-making in the German Democratic Republic.

Three buildings overlook a vast open space, the former Marx-Engels-Platz, now renamed the Lustgarten. This was the former site of Berlin's Royal or Imperial Palace, the Stadtschloss, which in its earliest form dated back to 1538. In the last war it was reduced to a shell of shattered façades, and in 1950-1 it was demolished.

Overlooking the site is a gleaming white building, the former Foreign

Ministry, and to the right the Council of State or Staatsrat which incorporates a portal of the old Schloss. From this balcony, Karl Liebknecht proclaimed his socialist republic in November 1918.

Ahead stands the Palast der Republik (1973-6), its façade 180m (590ft) long and dimly ablaze with acres of bronzed glass. Here sat the *Volkskammer*, the GDR's Parliament, which earned the building the nickname of *Ballast der Republik*. It was also attacked for its flamboyant ugliness, and in that context was known as the *Palazzo Protzi* or Showoffs' Palace.

As the present German Parliament prepares to move to Berlin from Bonn, this redundant sector is seen as the most likely future site for key ministry buildings. The Palast der Republik may be doomed to demolition or, at the very least, an extremely expensive refurbishment. There is asbestos in its fabric and it has been closed. One conservationist group is anxious to preserve all the old Marx-Engels-Platz buildings as 'an ensemble, a monument to the Centre of Socialism'. To do so would be 'extraordinarily significant for a better understanding of GDR history'.

All is still to be decided at the time of writing. Whatever happens, expect thick clouds of builders' dust to gather over the former Marx-Engels-Platz, and to remain there for most of the 1990s.

Walk 5

Alexanderplatz

'Alex' – the huge if dismal commercial centre of East Berlin. Ascend the TV Tower for excellent all-round views (coffee and cakes in the revolving café), walk over to the Red Town Hall (Rotes Rathaus), see the 'Rubble Woman' statue and the 14C Marienkirche, second parish church of medieval Berlin.
Allow   3-4 hours.
Best times   Any day, though TV Tower closed 09.00 to 13.00 on 2nd and 4th Tuesday of each month.
Note   The end of this walk connects with the beginning of the next (Nikolai Quarter).

ROUTE

Begin at Ⓢ/Ⓤ Alexanderplatz; Buses 100, 142, 157, 257. At station exit, walk S to piazza in front of **TV Tower (Fernsehturm)** ◉ ; open 09.00 to 24.00, closed 09.00 to 13.00 on 2nd and 4th Tuesday each month, last admission to Panorama viewing platform 23.30; to Telecafé 23.00. *Admission*.

At exit, turn right to find **Tourist Information Office (Verkehrsamt)** in complex at base of tower; some books and booklets, large table model of East Berlin and free Multivision show, open 10.00 to 17.00.

Continue to **Berliner Rathaus**, where lunch in Ratskeller a good possibility. Return across square to **Rubble Woman** statue, **Neptune Fountain** and **Marienkirche** ◉ ; church open Monday to Thursday 10.00 to 12.00, 13.00 to 17.00, Saturday 12.00 to 16.30, Sunday service 10.30. See noticeboard for news of free organ recitals.

Walk up Karl-Liebknecht-Strasse and take pedestrian subway to **Markthalle** on far side – a modern covered market with a good variety of shops and stalls. Return to other side of road and turn left to **Alexanderplatz**. Explore square: Kaufhof department store (clothing bargains), fountain and World Time Clock.

Walk ends here. Nearest refreshments in square (selection currently poor). Nearest Ⓢ/Ⓤ Alexanderplatz; Buses 100, 142, 157, 257.

Television Tower (Fernsehturm)

Seen through the glass side wall of the arcade covering the platforms, it soars like a factory chimney, smooth-sided and thick, truncated from this angle by the station roof. Around the base, a set of sharp triangular roofs emphasise its alien presence.

The Television Tower is Berlin's tallest building, and likened by natives to an asparagus ('der Telespargel'). From apartments all over the central districts of former East Berlin – in Mitte (literally, 'Middle'), in Friedrichshain and Prenzlauer Berg – it is omnipresent, inescapable, Big Brother on a stick. Now, of course, it is no longer the totem pole of an all-caring regime but it retains its uses as a vantage point and daily weather guide. On bright days the globe sparkles like a space platform, the red and white mast piercing blue sky. On grey murky days, clouds descend and cover the tower, sometimes completely, at other times blanking out the top half and leaving just the great shaft and some of the

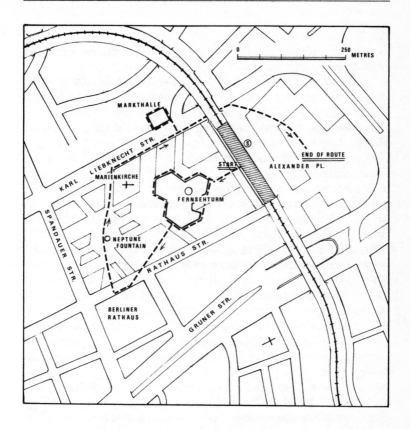

globe on view. This produces a remarkable effect, like the pillar of a giant wash-stand reaching heavenward for the convenience of passing gods and angels. Almost needless to add, if you intend visiting the tower but cannot see the globe from the ground, you will see nothing from inside it. Better to leave it for another day.

Many statistics are attached to the *Fernsehturm*, and the lift attendant raps them out. Forty seconds up to the Panorama – height of 203m (666ft) – whole tower 365m (1197ft) high – built in 1965-9, and so on. Meanwhile an illuminated needle marks the progress of the lift whizzing upwards.

The Panorama is a circular chamber with stupendous views over Berlin through tall, outward-leaning windows. Walk slowly round, or let the revolving tables of the Telecafé upstairs do the work for you, to the accompaniment of coffee and a soft cream-filled slice.

Tables take half an hour to turn through a full circle. In GDR days the tower was a major source of public amusement, attended by long queues, and time in the Telecafé was rationed; when theirs was up, honourable guests were flung down the stairs. No such fears now, although be prepared to share a table at busy times.

From such an exalted angle the segments of Berlin make a fascinating topographical parade, all the easier to decipher if you have a city map to refer to. Down below is the stout dome of Berlin Cathedral, then the treetops in Unter den Linden lead off to the Brandenburg Gate and the woods of Tiergarten. To the right (moving clockwise like the slowly turning ring of café tables) the River Spree winds past the flat-domed Bode Museum at the top of Museum Island; an S-Bahn train snakes away from Friedrichstrasse Station and gold ribbing shines on the dome of the Neue Synagoge in Oranienburger Strasse. In the north-west of the city, an airliner floats in to land at Tegel Airport, and from the strip another takes off and climbs hard into the western skies.

The table revolves to Alexanderplatz and the dominating slab of Hotel Forum Berlin. Karl-Marx-Allee reaches eastward to the circus of Strausberger Platz, a long line of high flat-faced apartment blocks, then continues on the long straight stretch to Frankfurter Tor. Twisting railway tracks flank the river, running into Jannowitzbrücke Station and on to Hauptbahnhof. In the far distance, factory chimneys send up plumes of smoke. Immediately below is the square clocktower of the city's chief town hall, the Rotes Rathaus, and the sharp twin spires of the Nikolai Church set aslant among the narrow streets of the quarter. Then the concentric paths and paved disc at the centre of Marx-Engels-Forum, and back once more to Berlin Cathedral.

Red Town Hall (Rotes Rathaus)

Berlin's Town Hall, seat of the Mayor and the ruling *Senat*, takes its popular name from the red clinker brick of its fabric, not from any political leaning or event. It stands on the site of the medieval town hall which it replaced in the 1860s. The city flag with its black bear flies from the spirelet on top of the neo-Renaissance clocktower, the most ornate and enjoyable part of Hermann Waesemann's palatial design. Between the first two storeys is the Stone Chronicle (*die Steinerne Chronik*), a series of thirty-six reliefs which depict outstanding moments in the history of Berlin and Brandenburg from the twelfth century to the unification of Germany in 1871.

In 1920, when the city expanded overnight to become Greater Berlin (*Gross-Berlin*), swallowing seven previously independent towns such as Spandau and Köpenick and many other urban and *Land* districts too, the Town Hall became the administrative centre for a population of nearly four million, larger even than today's (3.4 million, 1988 figures). The building was badly damaged in the Second World War, was rebuilt in 1951-6 and under the GDR served as headquarters of the East Berlin *Magistrat*. Until 1990 West Berlin was ruled from Rathaus Schöneberg. After the *Wende* there was further renovation, and at the time of writing the Ratskeller had yet to open its doors. When it does, it is likely to be a popular meeting-place. The German custom of having a bar and restaurant in the vaults beneath the town hall is both pleasant and widely cherished.

Statues in the gardens to the front show a *Rubble Woman* ('Trümmerfrau') and a male *Building Worker* ('Aufbauhelfer'). They were sculpted by F. Cremer in the 'heroic' mould of Socialist Realism and are a tribute to the people who helped to clear millions of tons of rubble from the city at the end of the Second World War. Much of this material ended up in rubble mountains (*Trümmerberge*) built in parks and outlying areas and then grassed over. Not so far away are the two hills of 'Mont Klamott' in Volkspark Friedrichshain; to the west of the city the 'Teufelsberg' in Grunewald has been turned into a winter sports centre.

Also in the open space between the Red Town Hall and the TV Tower is the Neptune Fountain (*Neptunbrunnen*), designed by Reinhold Begas in 1881. Serpents and crocodiles fire jets of water up into conches around the feet of seated Neptune. Four female figures around the basin personify the Rivers Elbe, Weichsel, Oder and Rhine. In his day Begas received many commissions for monumental works to enhance the Prussian city. He also designed the Bismarck monument for the Reichstag (now at Grosser Stern), and this fountain originally stood in front of the Stadtschloss (demolished).

Rubble Woman outside Red Town Hall

Marienkirche

This battered survivor is Berlin's second parish church after the Nikolaikirche. Rebuilt after the city fire of 1380, it has a fine tower by Carl Gotthard Langhans, added in 1789. Inside, the evident poverty of the foundation is reflected in the upkeep, although it was a victory in any case that it came through the atheist years. Among the church's treasures are the marble pulpit by Andreas Schlüter and the *Dance of Death* ('Totentanz') frieze which dates from the fifteenth century, alas much faded.

There are free organ recitals, at times which vary through the year. The noticeboard outside the church has details.

Markthalle

The modern setting is stark, like the rest of the buildings on this side of Karl-Liebknecht-Strasse. To reach it from the Marienkirche means taking the pedestrian subway, its tunnel lined with cigarette sellers waving packets of Marlboro and Lord, probably a busker too, and almost certainly a couple of beggars.

What this covered market lacks in visual charm it makes up for in vitality and range of goods – fruit and vegetables, kitchenware, cheap jewellery and flashy coloured glass, wines and spirits in curious-shaped bottles, flowers, china, fish, and ready-made salads in pots. Take the exit door on the north side to find an unusual fountain which celebrates Berlin's old street traders – the sausage seller and the flower lady, and the butcher with a piglet in one arm and a goose in the other.

Alexanderplatz

'Alex' is the central gathering-point in East Berlin. In 1989 hundreds of thousands packed its usually windy pavements to hear and applaud protest speeches which prepared the way for the end of the German Democratic Republic. It has long been a natural venue for public meetings; otherwise, it is a desert and has no life of its own. When the German Parliament eventually arrives in the city, occupying new ministries just down the road, Alexanderplatz in its present form will have to go. It is not good enough for the next Berlin.

Murals in the U-Bahn tunnels beneath the square, supplied by the Meissen and Berlin porcelain factories, show Alexanderplatz when it was an old wool and cattle market and reveal how radically it has been changed. In the 1920s, when Alfred Döblin wrote his Expressionist novel *Berlin Alexanderplatz*, it was a thumping noisy place, shuddering with trams and horse-drawn traffic, thronged with traders and businessmen, shoppers, office workers and out-of-work drifters. Even allowing for Döblin's exaggerated, neurotic style, the square undoubtedly had an attractive vitality. To some extent this was sabotaged in 1928 when the traffic was redirected and the Berolinahaus and Alexanderhaus were built, backing up to the railway station. The design of these blocks, by Peter Behrens, has been widely praised ever since, but to me they seem drab and as superfluous as most of the taller developments in the neighbourhood.

Perhaps the worst of these is the dauntingly huge Forum Hotel, (formerly the Hotel Stadt Berlin), which makes much of the fine views from its restaurant on the 37th floor, but has little else to commend it. The problem for the planners, when they come to redraw this massive square, is what to leave in place. Zero would be the best option, if they have the courage.

For more than twenty years, two small monuments gave the inhabitants of East Berlin somewhere to meet if not to linger. The *Well of People's Friendship* ('Brunnen der Völkerfreundschaft') by Walter Womacka, built in 1969, is a spiral fountain of seventeen copper pillars and basins, formerly noted as a tarts' pick-up point. And in front of the Alexanderhaus stands the *World Time Clock* ('Weltzeituhr') by Erich John, also 1969 – a drum on a pillar surmounted by a revolving celestial sphere. The drum carries assorted place names and a twenty-four-hour clock. From it we may learn that, at 14.00 for example, it is 05.00 in Edmonton and Denver, and 18.30 in Rangoon. The *World Time Clock* must have been a great comfort to a population denied the right to travel where they wanted.

Anywhere within a sausage-throw of the station is spotted with *Imbiss* stands, around which knots of drunks and the discontented gather, and the three-card trick is feverishly played using small blocks of wood.

That is Alexanderplatz, and that is how it may remain – until such time as the new owners delegate somebody to blow it up.

To finish on a fairly trivial but not altogether negative note: the old Centrum department store, famous for its shoddy goods and lack of choice, has gone. In its place is a branch of Kaufhof. By Western standards, Kaufhof is just one of the several middle-of-the-road stores, like Hertie and Karstadt. And if you lived in the West within range of the multi-bargain shops and stores in Wilmersdorferstrasse, you would not give it a second thought. Here, though, at the centre of the old East, it must still seem like Eldorado. If you are looking, by the way, there are usually bargains and special offers in leather jackets, lingerie, shirts and skirts. Kaufhof is particularly useful for those little things you forget to bring with you or have run out of.

Walk 6

Nikolai Quarter

A picturesque 'village', remade in the style of Old Berlin. Museums, galleries, outdoor cafés and boutiques. Visit the Nikolai Church and glide through the galleries of the Ephraimpalais in a pair of giant slippers.

Allow   4-5 hours.

Best times   Not Monday, when museums closed.

ROUTE

Begin at Ⓢ/Ⓤ Alexanderplatz; Buses 100, 142, 157, 257. At station exit on square, turn right pass *Imbiss* stalls and right under railway bridge in Grunerstrasse. On far side of road see ruins of Franciscan Abbey Church and tall dome of the House of the Council of Ministers.

The Nikolai Quarter begins on the far side of Spandauer Strasse, the twin spires of the **Nikolaikirche** rising above the houses. Take next turning, Eiergasse, past Zum Paddenwirt pub and arrive in Nikolaikirchplatz. Walk round to front of Berlin's oldest parish church, now a museum of early Berlin history ◉; open 09.00 to 17.00, Saturday closes 18.00, Sunday opens 10.00, closed Monday. *Admission*.

At exit, bear left to **Knoblauch House** in Poststrasse ◉; open 09.00 to 17.00, Saturday closes 18.00, Sunday opens 10.00, closed Monday. *Admission*. Ticket desk on 1st floor, then tour rooms of the Knoblauch family (best-known member the architect Eduard).

Continue towards Mühlendamm. On corner, Tuscan columns and curly balconies of **Ephraimpalais**,now used for varied programme of art exhibitions ◉; open 09.00 to 17.00, Saturday closes 18.00, Sunday opens 10.00, closed Monday. *Admission*.

On far side of gardens, next to Zur Rippe pub, is the small **Handicrafts Museum (Handwerksmuseum)**; open 09.00 to 17.00, Saturday closes 18.00, Sunday opens 10.00, closed Monday and each day 12.30 to 13.00. *Admission*.

Walk up to River Spree and turn right along Spreeufer. At next square are statue of *St George and the Dragon* and terrace of Café Spreeblick.

Keep on beside river and turn right along edge of Rathausstrasse to Poststrasse. Here look out for 1st-storey frieze showing incidents in Berlin history; frieze continues in Poststrasse in café courtyard of Zu den Arkaden, where choice of places to eat.

Return to front of Nikolaikirche. Walk ends here. For final refreshment, try for a seat in Zum Nussbaum (left along Propststrasse). Nearest Ⓤ Klosterstrasse; Buses 142, 257.

Brief history of an enjoyable fake

The approach along Grunerstrasse, itself a featureless funnel for motor traffic, offers the chance to survey the Nikolai Quarter from a distance. Long ago it formed part of the original city, close to the Dairy Market

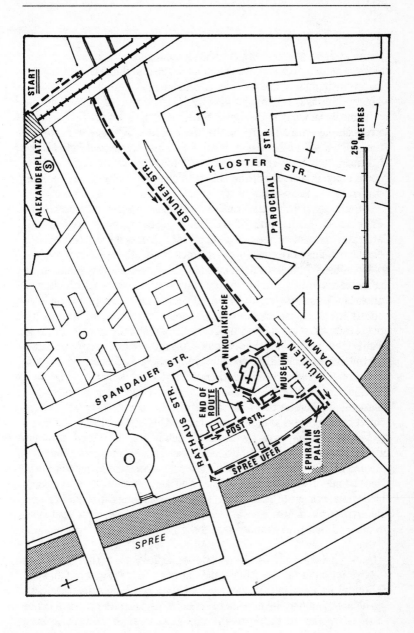

(Molkenmarkt) which in the thirteenth century lay at the centre of all things. The parish church was founded in 1232, and merchants' houses clustered round it in the narrow streets.

After the Second World War little remained of these ancient domestic buildings, and then in 1981 the GDR initiated a radical scheme to rebuild the entire quarter in the spirit of the past. The venture has succeeded well: an honest remake which has never pretended to be authentic. It is also very popular with tourists and an early start is recommended, arriving at the Nikolaikirche when it opens at 09.00 or 10.00 (see times above).

The varied styling of the front on Spandauer Strasse is typical of the new quarter. In this terrace are two pairs of narrow gabled houses flanked by rows of dormer-roofed buildings, some of them rendered in ochre to suggest a Berlin of former times. Beneath the windows of the gabled houses are sections of ribbed prefabricated concrete, and these are repeated in the clearly modern block to the right which contains a supermarket on the ground floor. There is no attempt to mask or prettify the materials used – though most are more comely than the concrete slabs. Another practical aspect, perhaps the most important, is that the blocks of the Nikolai Quarter contain very desirable apartments for some 1,500 people. In no sense is it a museum of the past, to be locked up at night when the last visitors have gone.

In Eiergasse (Eggs Alley), just beyond Spandauer Strasse, the character of the quarter is at once apparent: cobbled streets, subtly varied buildings and lots of visual charm. Outside Zum Paddenwirt, a traditional-looking Berlin *Gaststätte* (or pub with food), stands a well in brown marble.

'Ach, guck' 'mal, das ist schön!' cries a German lady visitor of pre-war vintage. She advances to the well and peers with enthusiasm through the iron grille on top, then steps back looking satisfied. Perhaps she was being polite, or was temporarily overcome with nostalgia, because all that is visible beneath the grille is a layer of foul-coloured sludge.

Nearby, at No.10 Nikolaikirchplatz, a plaque explains that in 1765, in a house on this site, the Enlightenment poet and playwright Gotthold Ephraim Lessing completed his play, *Minna von Barnhelm*.

The way round to the front of the church lies past an expensive dress shop, neighbour to the Nikolai Café. Across the next alley is Zum

Nussbaum ('At the Nut Tree'), a studious reconstruction of an old Berlin pub first built in Fischerinsel in about 1571, and earlier this century the haunt of the painter Otto Nagel and the caricaturist Heinrich Zille. Inside, the low taproom and small adjoining barrooms are invariably crowded.

Nikolai Church

The restored thirteenth-century parish church is now a division of the Märkisches Museum (see *Walk 7*) and in its nave, vestry and gallery presents an exhibition of Berlin's history up to 1648. The church is also used for concerts.

Outside in the courtyard the Berlin bear sits high on the pedestal of a stone and concrete fountain holding a shield emblazoned with the eagle of Cölln, the other half of the medieval township. On the ground nearby, a large wheel-shaped bronze monument frames the city seal of 1253 and this inscription:

> AROUND 1230 THE ASKANIAN MARGRAVE JOHANN I AND OTTO III GREAT-GRANDSON OF ALBRECHT THE BEAR GRANTED THE PRE-URBAN SETTLEMENT OF BERLIN THE RIGHT TO FOUND A CITY.

The church is the oldest building in Berlin, built in 1232-64. The Gothic choir dates from 1379 and the nave from the fifteenth century. In the Second World War it was badly bombed. Before rebuilding started in 1977, archaeologists uncovered remains of the early Romanesque stone basilica and more than seventy graves.

In the high white nave, whitewashed brick columns support the simple vaulted roofs; the painted ribs, coloured in green, brown, orange and blue, are the only decoration. Tall simple windows with three, four and five lights flank the nave and continue round the apse. Above the altar steps hangs a carved *Crucifixion* of 1485, originally in the Marienkirche, and to the left is an old stone font.

The survey of Berlin history begins on the south side of the nave with photographs of the church being rebuilt in 1981-7. There are models of the Romanesque basilica, the twin settlements of Berlin–Cölln in 1220-30 and another of the enlarged town of 1450, walled and moated.

Nikolai Church in its restored 'village'

Among the arms and armour, seals and staffs of the period is a boundary stone marking the fishery limits between the communities of Berlin and Spandau.

In the vestry is the Hunger Cloth, a long rectangle of embroidered lace which separated the choir and nave during Lent. In the brick-built west gallery is a collection of gravestones, epitaphs and burial plaques which decorated the church after the Reformation. Propst (Provost) Buchholzer proclaimed the Reformation in this church on behalf of Berlin on 2 November 1539, after which the altars were removed from all churches in the March of Brandenburg.

Among the paintings in the gallery is Michael Ribestein's *The Good Samaritan* ('Der barmherzige Samariter') of 1552. At some stage the four figures of the robbers, the priest and the Levite who passed by were scored through with a knife; no explanation is offered for this apparent fit of zeal.

Knoblauch Haus

The house of the Knoblauch family was built in 1759 by Johann Christian Knoblauch, and was one of the few in the Nikolai Quarter to escape the Allied bombing. In the 1980s it was extensively restored and is now a museum dedicated to the Knoblauchs who owned it for some 170 years. The family remained prominent in Berlin society during that period, supplying the university with several professors and also producing the architect Eduard Knoblauch, who designed the Neue Synagoge in Oranienburger Strasse (1859-66) and the Jewish Hospital in Auguststrasse (1858-60). Among the family friends who came regularly to the house were Gotthold Ephraim Lessing, Moses Mendelssohn, the Brothers Humboldt and Karl Friedrich Schinkel.

The Biedermeier Room is decorated with furniture from the Märkisches Museum, and in an alcove are details of the family's history from 1405, when Ladislaus Knoblauch, a judge, lived in the Upper Hungarian town of Kaschau/Kassa/Kŏsice. In the Yellow, Blue and Red Rooms are more family documents, including a group picture of 'Learned Berlin' which includes the Humboldts and the philosopher G.W.F. Hegel. The Blue Room has an exhibition on the Neue Synagoge (see *Walk 8*). The Red Room displays other designs by Eduard Knoblauch, among them drawings for Schloss Bomburg in Schleswig-

Holstein. Here too is a splendid tile oven (*Kachelofen*) covered in aquamarine ceramic tiles, a regal example of the coal-fired stoves which to this day heat thousands of Berlin apartments and keep the city's force of chimney sweeps in vigorous business.

Ephraimpalais

At the corner by Mühlendamm, Tuscan columns support the entrance to the Ephraimpalais (1761-4), one of Berlin's finest rococo buildings. Veitel Heine Ephraim was a wily entrepreneur who managed to combine several lucrative activities in a busy professional life. He was a banker, a manufacturer and Court Jeweller to Frederick the Great. He was also Keeper of the Mint, and automatically an unpopular figure with the citizenry who constantly faced extra levies to finance the king's wars.

The palace was built for Ephraim by Friedrich Wilhelm Dietrichs. Ephraim never lived there but rented it out on profitable terms. In 1843 the state bought the palace for use as an administrative building. In 1935, when the Mühlendamm was widened, the palace was pulled down but the best parts of the façade were preserved, including the columns of the portico. In the 1980s it was rebuilt on its present site, not far from where it stood in Ephraim's day, and skilfully merged with the surrounding architecture.

Today the palace puts on various art exhibitions, usually with a Berlin theme. It is worth the modest entrance fee just to climb the gilded spiral staircase carrying a pair of giant felt slippers, and then to put them on and glide about the shiny parquet floors, gently skating from one gallery to the next.

Around the Quarter

The sites described above are the main ingredients of a tour of the Nikolai Quarter. The Route section, above, offers a way to see the rest without doubling back or repeating your steps, but the quarter is small anyway and ideal for aimless wandering among the shops and cafés.

The Handicrafts Museum is also small, very small in fact, with a display of tools and crafts and three workshops fitted out for a woodcarver, a printer and a dollmaker. In Poststrasse is an attractive frieze above the arcades which describes events in the history of Berlin. At one end it terminates at Zu den Arkaden, a good place to pause and recollect the day, either at the large outdoor café terrace or in the neighbouring cool of the *Gerichtslaube*, the old court room, now a handsome vaulted café-restaurant.

Walk 7

Around Fischerinsel

Across the River Spree, tour the Märkisches Museum and find a charming row of 18C houses on the waterfront. See the last surviving section of the old city wall, and the ruined Franciscan abbey church, and call in at Berlin's oldest pub, Zur Letzten Instanz.

Allow 3-4 hours.

Best times Not Monday-Tuesday.

ROUTE

Begin at ⑤/Ⓤ Jannowitzbrücke; Bus 147. At station exit, cross road and walk over river bridge towards Berliner Congress Center. Turn right beside river along Märkisches Ufer.

Turn left at Am Köllnischen Park to **Märkisches Museum** (of Berlin history) ☞; open 10.00 to 18.00, closed Monday-Tuesday. *Admission*.

At exit, turn left to gardens and continue along Wallstrasse. At corner of Inselstrasse, the Märkisches Museum presents its collection of Circus, Variety and Cabaret material; open 10.00 to 18.00, closed Monday-Tuesday. *Admission*.

Turn right up Inselstrasse and left along Märkisches Ufer to the **Otto-Nagel-Haus** at Nos. 16-18 (exhibition of 'Proletarian, Revolutionary and Anti-Fascist Art') ☞; open 10.00 to 18.00, closed Friday-Saturday. *Admission*. Also nearby is the Ermelerhaus (No.10) with enjoyable cellar restaurant, closed Saturday-Sunday.

At next bridge turn right to **Fischerinsel**, where medieval fishermen landed their catches. At crossroads by spiky-roofed disco building, turn right along Mühlendamm, crossing bridge near lock and passing Nikolai Quarter on left. Continue over Molkenmarkt next to domed Stadthaus, former House of the Council of Ministers, and take next right along Parochialstrasse.

On right at next intersection is **Parochialkirche**, gaunt and blackened. Keep on beside churchyard towards front door of **Zur Letzten Instanz**, one of East Berlin's most popular old-world pubs.

Turn left along Waisenstrasse to find section of **Old City Wall** (*c.* 1250). Continue through gardens to shell of **Franciscan Abbey Church**.

Walk ends here. Nearest refreshments at Zur Letzten Instanz. Nearest Ⓤ Klosterstrasse; Buses 142, 257.

Märkisches Ufer

This walk passes through a section of East Berlin that many visitors never see. Although the district is no more than fifteen minutes on foot from the omnipresent Television Tower, it lies across the Spree and has a rather distant, transpontine relationship with the city centre – enough to remove it from the conventional tourist map (rather like Lambeth in London).

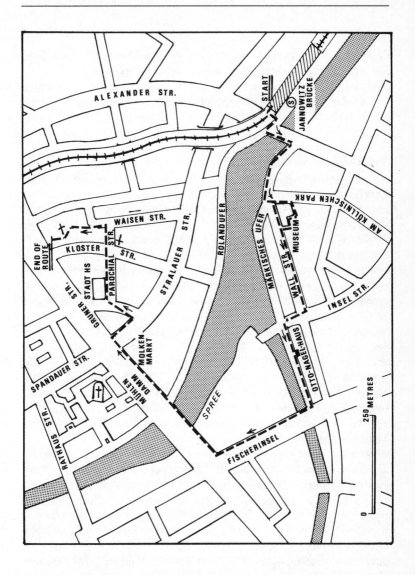

Chestnut trees line the bank of the Märkisches Ufer. To the right is one of the city's main boat stations, formerly run by the Weisse Flotte which since the *Wende* has been merged with, or submerged by, the

Stern und Kreisschiffahrt Company. Various boat trips leave from here, usually lasting around three hours or a full day.

Overlooking the river is the Marinehaus, a pleasant *Gaststätte* which has comfortable sofas beside the high bar stools, and fishy snacks on the menu.

Märkisches Museum

This is the parent museum of a group covering historic places in former East Berlin. Its own concern is with the pre- and early history of the city and the Mark Brandenburg up to 1815. Under its wing are several smaller museums and sites such as those visited in the Nikolai Quarter (*Walk 6*). In its scope the Märkisches Museum is the eastern equivalent of the Berlin Museum in Kreuzberg (*Walk 10*).

The Early History section in the basement opens with reconstructions of a hunter's hut from the Middle Stone Age (eighth to fourth century BC) and a Bronze Age house (1800-500 BC), and a display of pottery, tools and weapons. From the Early Middle Ages are coins, armour and pottery remains, and facsimiles of woodcuts from the first decades of printing. These form a trailer to a grand table model of the walled city, made in 1937 and showing Berlin around 1750. At the centre of the united townships of Berlin and Cölln are the great Schloss and the domed Catholic Cathedral of St Hedwig. Also prominent among the inner ring and narrow streets, protected by half-moon outworks, are the city's earliest spiritual buildings, the Nikolaikirche and the Marienkirche.

On the ground floor the Theatre History collection is wide-ranging and colourful, and upstairs are the Crafts rooms (much worthy but unexciting pewter, silver and pottery) and the galleries of Paintings and Graphics. Here, among the studied academic efforts, are some interesting views of the old city – the *Royal Schloss from the Lange Brücke* (Maximilian Roch, 1842); the *Gendarmenmarkt with French Cathedral* (Carl Traugott Fechhelm, 1780-90); the *Domkirche* seen in cleaner days (Carl Hasenpflug, 1825) and *View behind the Mühlendamm* (Johann Heinrich Hinze, 1852) showing the rafts where fishermen brought in their nets and the far shore decked with laundry boats. Artistically, the pride of the collection is probably Max Pechstein's *Portrait in Blue* (1919).

Seen from the gardens of Köllnischer Park the museum building displays a remarkable collection of architectural facets. All are by the same hand (Ludwig Hoffmann, 1901-7), and form an anthology of local Gothic and Renaissance brick building styles to be found elsewhere in the Mark of Brandenburg. Hoffmann's models included the Bishofsburg in Wittstock and the Katharinen Chapel in the town of Brandenburg. Among the monuments in the park are a 'bear-pit' populated with Berlin bears and a statue of Heinrich Zille, a popular cartoonist whose works are sometimes on show in the museum.

The park was laid out after the baroque fortifications of Bastion VII were cleared away. We continue along Wallstrasse – though *Wall* means 'dam' or 'dyke' and does not refer directly to the old city wall. In between the two entrances of U-Bahnhof Märkisches Museum, at Wallstrasse 76-9, is an extraordinary frontage decorated with columns of cherubs, grotesques, fish, birds and mammals. From July 1945 to April 1946 this was the seat of Wilhelm Pieck's Central Committee of the German Communist Party.

The western reach of the Spree at the southern tip of Fischerinsel (Fishermen's Island) is not quite Berlin's answer to Amsterdam – the bleak concrete wall and tower blocks on the far side preclude such thoughts – but on this bank are several fine baroque houses. At No. 10 is the Ermelerhaus (1808), moved here from Breite Strasse in the late 1960s; above the door is a frieze of craftsmen and merchants. Inside are two restaurants; upstairs is an opulent, rather stuffy French restaurant with eye-popping prices, and in the cellar is the much more jolly and reasonable Raab-Diele (recommended, but closed Saturday-Sunday).

Otto-Nagel-Haus

Close to the Ermelerhaus are two eighteenth-century houses which now form the Otto Nagel Museum, named after the naturalistic Berlin painter and less appetisingly subtitled the 'Collection of Proletarian, Revolutionary and Anti-Fascist Art'.

The subtitle makes me think of the long mural, dated 1952, inside the portico of the Haus der Ministerien in Leipziger Strasse, currently headquarters of the Treuhand and the biggest office block in Berlin. In the mural, cheery workers march with toothpaste grins, lay railway tracks and pull ingots from a furnace, pretty girls clap their hands and all is rosy beneath a banner which declares 'Long Live the German Democratic Republic'.

The Nagel Museum, misleadingly perhaps, deals not with the triumphs or otherwise of Socialist Reform but with the Depression Years. Nagel himself was a diligent recorder of urban desperation in the 1920s and '30s, as were most of his contemporaries featured on the museum's upper floor. He was born in 1894 and died in 1967. A self-portrait of 1936 reveals a thin-faced, gaunt cigar smoker with an unfortunately Hitlerian moustache. His gloomy street scenes reflect the downtrodden condition of the Berlin proletariat. In *Strasse am Wedding* (*c.* 1924), winter has drained the streets of colour. Dowdy anonymous figures shuffle between black trees and mounds of grimy snow. When in other pictures these cipher-humans are painted in close-up and given faces, as in *Park Bench in Wedding* (1927), the faces are grey-white like clowns' make-up, sad and drawn, the dull eyes seeing no future. When a worker is the subject, a man fortunate enough to have a job, he is exhausted and shrunken, halfway to the cemetery. The *Aniline Worker* (1928) is one of several examples.

Upstairs the palettes are brighter, though most of the paintings are stiff and unaccomplished, under the spell but lacking the magic of Ensor, Nolde, Dix and others of the day. There are semi-naive figures and landscapes by Magnus Zeller, and portraits of workers by Curt Querner – a heavily pregnant *Farm Worker in March Landscape* (1933), *Child Worker Doris* (1930) and *March Demonstration* (1933). In the large room the influence of Surrealism is widely apparent. From the time of the Second World War is a vivid bombed-over landscape by Franz Radziwill (*Where in This World*, 1940). Others to note are *Still Life with Masks* by Karl Völker and the dark grim figures of *Communist Party Meeting* by Hans Grundig (1932). Elsewhere are some downright untalented attempts at portraying mad people and revolutionaries, and a symbolic nightmare scene of trapped animals racing round a brick enclosure, which today may be seen as an apt prefiguration of life under the GDR.

It will be interesting to see if the Otto Nagel Museum survives, now that its one-time audience in East Berlin have so many things on their minds and are less likely than ever to say, 'I know, let's go down to the Nagel Museum and make ourselves even more miserable.'

Fischerinsel

At the next bridge, confront the gaunt high-rises which the Communists stamped across the foot of Fischerinsel. In the Middle Ages this was the fishermen's quarter in the growing township of Cölln. Today's inhabitants enjoy splendid views across the Lustgarten, but cannot be envied for having to live in those blocks (except by the people who live in worse blocks).

To the left are the ugly pointed roofs of, currently, the Exit Disco, in former times the Ahornblatt (Maple Leaf) Restaurant, a title which at least lent some *raison d'être* to the spiky architecture. In Mühlendamm, the view from the bridge looks down to the lock, where pleasure cruisers file in and rise slowly up to the level of the main River Spree beyond. Above the Nikolai Quarter from this angle is a striking cluster of towers and spires – the golden globes on the two spires of the Nikolaikirche, the square tower of the Rotes Rathaus and the extraordinary chimney of the Television Tower.

The old Dairy Market (Molkenmarkt) was once the centre of Cölln–Berlin; now it is reduced to a traffic junction. On the far side is the domed façade of the Stadthaus, anonymous and bleak, which formerly housed the GDR's Council of Ministers. Beside it, Parochialstrasse leads towards an outcrop of trees in the churchyard of the Parochialkirche. In outline the church remains a fine Italian baroque building, but close to it is black with soot and still punctured with bullet holes from the last war.

Thirsty walkers who keep straight ahead beside the churchyard will shortly find themselves on the front steps of Zur Letzten Instanz ('At the Last Chance'), one of Berlin's most popular old-world pubs. If you like the look of the place, and a table is free, grab it and scrap all other plans for the evening. Or reserve a table for another day.

To the left in Waisenstrasse is a section of old city wall, first built in about 1250. The wall was enlarged in the fourteenth century and strengthened some three hundred years later with bastions.

Franciscan Abbey Church

The original building was a simple stone church serving the monastery founded here in 1249. It was superseded by this red-brick basilica dating from the thirteenth and fourteenth centuries. In the 1570s the 'Grey Monastery' fell victim to the Reformation and was converted into a grammar school, and in the now vanished cloister buildings Thurneisser set up Berlin's first printing press. In 1945 an Anglo-American bomb raid destroyed the cloister and the adjoining church. In 1951 the ruins of the monastery were pulled down and the shell of the church was made safe, to stand as it does today: broad and long and empty, from the arch of the west porch and the naked mullions of the great window away to the distant apse. It is one of wartime Berlin's most melancholy remnants.

Walk 8

Old Jewish Quarter (Scheunenviertel)

Literally the 'barn quarter', a slum district with a long-established Jewish population – and a focal point for atrocities under the Hitler regime. Many streets of fine houses, some beautifully restored, others still in decay. See the Old Jewish Cemetery and the New Synagogue, and visit the Brecht House, where the playwright lived from 1953 until his death.
Allow 4-5 hours.
Best times Brecht House closed Sunday-Monday.

ROUTE

Begin at Ⓢ/Ⓤ Alexanderplatz; Buses 100, 142, 157, 257. Walk into the square and bear left to pedestrian underpass crossing Karl-Liebknecht-Strasse. Walk along Memhardstrasse and continue to Münzstrasse.

Turn right up Almstadtstrasse, where crumbling façades compete for attention with the newly restored. Turn left through Schendelgasse to Max-Beer-Strasse and keep on across Alte Schönhauser Strasse to Mulackstrasse. At end turn right in Kleine Rosenthaler Strasse to gate of old **Garrison Cemetery**, opened 1722.

At exit, turn left to Ⓤ Weinmeisterstrasse and continue along Rosenthalerstrasse. Take 1st right into **Sophienstrasse**, now a model street of restored houses and craft shops, containing also the arched entrance to the Craftsmen's Association Building (*Handwerkvereinshaus*).

At far end, turn left down Grosse Hamburger Strasse. On left, look in at churchyard of baroque **Sophienkirche**. Continue to the site of the first old people's home in the Jewish Quarter, destroyed by the Gestapo in 1943. Walk through to the **Old Jewish Cemetery**, also obliterated to make an assembly-point for Jews to be sent to concentration camps.

At foot of Grosse Hamburger Strasse, turn right along Oranienburger Strasse. On right see the great 'Moorish' domes of Knoblauch's **Neue Synagoge** (1859-66).

Towards end of road, look out on left for Tacheles art co-operative, in premises of undiluted squalor. Enter and wander round (at own risk).

At end **Oranienburger Strasse**, turn right and bear left at next junction along Chausseestrasse to the **Brecht-Haus** at No.125 (first house after cemeteries) ☞. Go through to courtyard at back. Guided tours of playwright's home (*Admission*) as follows:

Tuesday to Friday 10.00, 10.30, 11.00, 11.30

Thursday also at 17.00, 17.30, 18.00, 18.30

Saturday 09.30, 10.00, 10.30, 11.00, 11.30, 12.30, 13.00, 13.30

Note These are the official times; sometimes the guide overruns, throwing out the whole schedule.

At exit, turn right to **Dorotheenstadt Cemetery**, where Brecht, Hegel, Schinkel, Schadow and many other eminent people are buried.

Walk ends here. Nearest refreshments at Café 130 in Chausseestrasse, or return past Oranienburger Tor to 'Oscar Wilde' (Irish pub) in Friedrichstrasse. Nearest Ⓤ Oranienburger Tor; Bus 157, Trams 22, 24, 46, 70, 71.

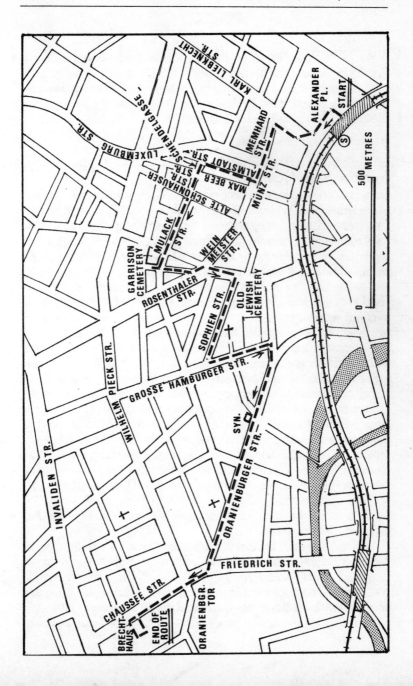

For a glimpse of East Berlin's theatreland, walk on down Friedrichstrasse. On left, the Friedrichstadt Palast variety theatre. To right, before bridge, see the Brecht Theatre, the Berliner Ensemble. Across Weidendammer Bridge is the Admiralspalast, housing the Metropol Theater and Distel Kabarett.

Into the Barn Quarter

Once clear of the totalitarian slabs enclosing Alexanderplatz, the character of the former slum begins to unfold. At this end it stands close to the elevated railway line and many of the houses are sooty and dilapidated. From mid-morning, push open the door of a corner bar (*Eckkneipe*) and most of the tables will be occupied by elderly locals, their lines to the real world already cast off as they drift into the daily stew.

How much longer the old ways can stagger on is a subject much exercised in these parts. In the new Berlin of fast-equalising rents, these hundred-year-old terraces are in a prime position and soon will be in great demand. They stand just around the corner from the ministry sector of Germany's next seat of government, and already the refurbishers and speculators are looking forward to handsome returns. Many locals look on with horror, and feel increasingly powerless.

Bright new shops are springing up in Münzstrasse, then in Almstadt-strasse the rotting façade of No. 5 presents the old face of the district – gargoyled and encrusted with plant reliefs which seem on the point of imitating nature and crashing to the pavement. Across the street is a long row of renovated houses, all with matching smart cream fronts and a uniform line of decorative heads above the first-floor windows. (One day soon, the authorities may also get round to fixing the pavements, which are in a terrible state of repair. Or perhaps not so soon. The sandy layer on which Berlin is built seems to make level pavement-laying an unenviable task.)

In Schendelgasse the pattern of decay resumes. At the corner house, scrawled on the shutter inside a broken window, someone has written, 'Projekt Kunst + Kneipe ('Art + Bar Project'). On the outside wall is a sprayed slogan familiar both here and in the neighbouring district of Prenzlauer Berg: 'Spekulanten Raus' ('Speculators Out').

A small, wildly overgrown park lies next to Alte Schönhauser Strasse (literally 'Old Beautiful House Street'). Across the tramlines, the house at No.31 is a model of post-war decay, or what happens naturally if you leave an old building untouched for fifty years. Behind the outer veneer of blackened stone and grimy red-brick facings is a once beautiful five-storey house. Five long windows stand evenly spaced on each floor. On the second storey are two side pairs with shallow arched mouldings; on the floor above, the windows were once all surmounted by gracious pediments but two have since fallen off completely, leaving a ragged scar across the brickwork.

Cross to Mulackstrasse. Here in the rows of run-down houses the remnants of finely detailed balconies cling to walls once ornate with plaster medallions and swags of leaves and fruit, all eroded now by time and neglect. Skips full of broken furniture stand in the gutters, a sign that new housing projects are on the way even if progress goes at a limping pace. In Mulackstrasse the graffiti of frustrated occupiers sound an unusually personal note:
WE ARE NOT ALL TOGETHER. WE ARE WITHOUT THE ONES WHO FELL, and WE WANT SOUND ROOFS AND DRY WALLS.

Garrison Cemetery

The entrance is in Kleine Rosenthaler Strasse, around the corner from Mulackstrasse: a modest doorway set in the wall. Many would never guess it was there at all, a cemetery opened in 1722 for the benefit of the Prussian Garrison which in the eighteenth century not only guarded Berlin but more or less occupied it too. When founded, the cemetery was larger and had two plots, one for officers and one for other ranks. The latter was given up for building land around 1900.

Most days the garden is all but empty in this last sanctuary of men who fought on horseback and slew each other with sabres and musket fire. In the spring sunshine a young mother in jeans basks face down on a strip of grass next to her baby's pram, snatching a few moments of peace from the daily grind in some nearby tenement. Children walk on top of the wall, not disturbing the calm within.

Near the entrance a noticeboard lists the most famous occupants of the graves, many of whom fought against Napoleon in the War of Liberation (1813-15). Adolph von Lützow, a brigade commander at Water-loo, lies behind an iron-railed enclosure on the Linienstrasse side of the garden. Facing the gate to Linienstrasse is the double-sided dark green tomb of General von Brauschitsch, Chief of the Gendarmerie and Commandant of Berlin. The tomb, with angels above, was designed by Karl Friedrich Schinkel, as was the nearby stone of General-Lieutenant von Holtzendorff, Officer of Artillery. A little way behind these two, near the wall by Kleine Rosenthaler Strasse, is the tomb of Friedrich, Baron de la Motte Fouqué, a distinguished member of an old Huguenot family. The Baron was a soldier-poet and wrote *Undine*, which inspired the opera by E.T.A Hoffmann and A. Lortzing.

Opposite the entrance gate, by the far wall, a black stone marks the grave of Sonja Horn. A Polish resistance fighter in the Second World War, she was captured in 1943 and sent to Ravensbrück. Thanks to Swedish mediation she was released in February 1945 and returned to Berlin, there to be killed by grenade splinters in the last days of the war.

Children and Fools

The vacant lot outside the cemetery is a landscape of expired cushions and rubbish bags, and pieces of defunct Trabant. A fractured pushchair, a rusted cooker, a torn sofa in drab green and grey. Next to this un-official dumping ground, on the side wall of a garishly coloured alternative house, four verses of poetry are daubed large in black paint. Few will ever see or take notice of their defiant proclamation. Here are two of them:

> Children and Fools need Freedom, love, Truth, the sun, light.
> Children and Fools laugh at Gold, despise the Power which man promises them.

As a political programme the message is unlikely to get far. Its presence in this battered neighbourhood is nonetheless apt. There is a large force of alternative-minded people living here, some of them locals and some refugees from Kreuzberg. An unpleasant and protracted battle lies ahead once the authorities decide to move in on them.

Sophienstrasse

This was one of the vaunted gems of the GDR's restoration pro-gramme. Rows of neat refurbished houses in pink, cream and beige stucco summon the atmosphere of Old Berlin. Great play was made of

Germany's pride in craftsmanship – probably too much so, for the street swarms with shops and workshops making and selling pottery, basketware, metalwork, woodwind instruments and jewellery. It all looks too clean and wholesome, and sits uncomfortably next to the decrepitude of the surrounding streets.

One building is of particular interest: the headquarters of the Association of Berlin Craftsmen (Handwerkvereinshaus). It was completed in 1904 after the Association had been in existence for sixty years, a pioneer in the field of workers' education. The original scheme, with reception halls and a library, was abandoned long ago but the double-arched frontage is a fine survivor from the Jugendstil period, with vertical tubes of red brick and green tile outlining the decorative framework.

At the end of the street a comfortably overgrown beer garden stands under the dark mass of the Sophienkirche, which is entered from Grosse Hamburger Strasse. The church was endowed in 1712 by Queen Sophie-Luise, and the upper tiers and spire of the baroque tower, added twenty years later, make an elegant landmark among the tenement rows of the quarter. Close to, however, the church is soot-blackened and wears a neglected look. The soot is partly explained by the presence, near the church wall, of a line of buckets filled with briquettes of brown coal, that great polluter of Berlin skies. The churchyard is a dusty patch of brown earth, dark-shadowed with overgrown trees. Under recent governments, Queen Sophie's church has done less well than the street also named after her.

Old Jewish Cemetery

In Grosse Hamburger Strasse, just before the Café RZ on the right, is an unusual monument to private lives suddenly terminated by war. A blank cavity marks the site of a house destroyed by Allied bombs. The walls of the houses next door are studded with plaques at every floor-level, each bearing a name, dates of occupation and profession. Among those remembered are:

1930-45	1934-45	1938-45
G. Jacobi	L. Miteau	M. Müller
Kaufmann	Verwalterin	Pensionärin
(shopkeeper)	(administrator)	(pensioner)

Across the road stands the Old Jewish Cemetery. Jews settled early in Berlin, concentrating in this quarter from the seventeenth century. Along with the Huguenots and other persecuted groups, they benefited from the Great Elector's liberal, if self-interested, policy of welcoming select minorities to the city. The cemetery dates from 1672, and between then and 1827 some 12,000 Jews were buried in this ground. In 1943 the Gestapo destroyed the cemetery, wrecking tombstones and digging up bodies.

Nearby stood the first old people's home of the Jewish community. The site is marked by a stone bearing the Cross of David. The inscription explains that in 1942 the Gestapo turned the place into a collection point for Jewish citizens. Fifty-five thousand Berlin Jews, from 'suckling to old man', were transported to the concentration camps of Auschwitz and Theresienstadt and bestially murdered. The message concludes:

NEVER FORGET THAT RESISTING WAR IS THE
SAFEGUARD OF PEACE

Now the site is empty, a bare garden decorated with the standing figures of Will Lammert's monument – a group of emaciated and helpless Jews, herded together to await their fate. The cemetery too is empty, save for a few broken gravestones with Hebrew inscriptions, a memorial plaque to Berlin's oldest burial ground and a headstone for Moses Mendelssohn, the Jewish philosopher and writer (1729-86). This is a recent addition, erected after the war.

New Synagogue

In 1778 Moses Mendelssohn founded Berlin's first Jewish school at No. 27 Grosse Hamburger Strasse. A portrait relief on the wall of the building commemorates his achievement. Until the Nazi regime began its policy of systematic persecution, this district was the centre of Jewish life and culture. Jews made up some five per cent of Berlin's population and worshipped at several nearby synagogues. Today the only working synagogue in East Berlin is in Prenzlauer Berg.

The glittering domes of Eduard Knoblauch's Neue Synagoge were completed in 1866. They were visible from afar and gave Jewish life a nourishing substance, reinforcing the immigrants' sense of identity.

Kristallnacht – 9 November 1938, when the Nazis unleashed a night of terror and destruction against Jewish businesses and synagogues – left this building partly wrecked by fire, its windows shattered. A bomb raid in 1943 brought virtual destruction, and only in 1988 was the decision taken to rebuild. In 1966, when the synagogue was still in ruins, a plaque was put up to record the hundredth anniversary of its completion, and to announce that:

> *The front of this house of God shall for all time be a place of warning and remembrance*
> NEVER FORGET

The Moorish style of the Neue Synagoge is both striking and of great architectural interest. It reflects a contemporary vogue for exotic motifs – Indian, Egyptian and Moorish among others – which found adherents throughout Europe, from the Modernists and their precursors in Barcelona to the designers of temples and palatial warehouses in mercantile Glasgow.

Oranienburger Strasse

On the corner of Tucholskystrasse stands another gigantic building, also with Moorish overtones – the Postal Transport Office (*Postfuhramt*), built in 1875-81. It replaced an earlier *Postillonhaus*, and when operating at full strength had stabling in the courtyard for two hundred horses, arranged on two storeys. The building is now let out to various offices.

A little way to the right in Tucholskystrasse, another aspect of Jewish culture is upheld at Beth Café (No. 40), bringing kosher food to the district of Stadtmitte. The café is open from 10.00, closed Friday-Saturday.

Near the end of Oranienburger Strasse, on the left, is the amazing Tacheles art co-operative. Here they seem to worship chaos and urban wreckage. Samples of work in progress spill out onto the road, barely distinguishable from the raw materials from which they were plundered. A sculpture of smashed-in furniture leans groggily against a chunk of painted masonry, and the ultimate in defunct Trabis lies skewed across the pavement, wrapped in its own shower of broken glass. Feel free to enter the building and prowl around, but watch out for caved-in floorboards. There are regular art events, and rock concerts until dawn (see *Tip* or *Zitty* for details).

The Trabi is already part of German folklore and soon will become officially extinct, outlawed by new emission controls which its sulphurous working parts cannot cope with. In the meantime it crops up in all kinds of jokes and reminiscences.

By night this raw neighbourhood is a whores' parade. Chief trading method is known as *Autostrich*, which involves flagging down kerb-crawlers and climbing aboard to honour the contract in some quiet side-road. Some of the girls were interviewed for a television programme. 'Yes,' said one, 'since the *Wende*, business has been looking up. I don't have to keep getting into Trabis all the time.'

At the junction with Friedrichstrasse, trams swerve sharply round the corner, bells jangling. Still in service on these routes are a number of venerable Hungarian trams fitted with heavy manually operated doors. To enter or leave, passengers must heave on a large chrome handle; these always remind me of post-war refrigerators.

At No.124 Friedrichstrasse, across from the U-Bahn exit, is the Bärenschänke (Bear Tavern). This was a well-known foreigners' bar in pre-war times. Here members of the *Rote Kapelle* (Red Chapel), a large Communist resistance group, recruited foreign forced-labour workers to carry out secret assignments. When the group was exposed in 1942 the Gestapo arrested a hundred and eighteen people, of whom fifty-five were executed.

Brecht Haus

The reputation of the radical writer Bertolt Brecht (1898-1956) rests on such challenging plays as *The Threepenny Opera, Mother Courage, The Life of Galileo* and *The Caucasian Chalk Circle*. In Berlin he is re-vered almost as much for his work at the Berliner Ensemble, the theatre company which he founded in 1949 with his wife Helene Weigel. They lived in exile in the United States from 1933 to 1948 and moved into this house in 1953.

The tour of the house is usually brief but thorough, always in the company of a knowledgeable guide. Around the visitor goes, from room to room, and at the end the entrance door is once more unlocked . . . and goodbyes are said. No souvenirs or junk handouts; the visitor gets only what can be seen or heard. As a style of presentation, it will never catch on.

The author's rooms are much as they were in his lifetime, austerely furnished in concordance with his Calvinist upbringing. In the Library are many collected works of German, English and other writers, a range that includes Shakespeare and Smollett as well as Lessing, Schiller and Kleist. On the walls are a Chinese scroll and a figure of Confucius, and a row of Japanese Noh masks.

On to a large workroom. There are armchairs in threadbare cloth and brown leather, oddly like in a club room, and around the walls are a series of tables where Brecht piled up the papers of the various projects he kept on the go at the same time. On each is a pewter plate for the cigars he was rarely seen without – photographs show his monkish face, rubicund, gazing out, and a hand always fastened round a cigar. From the windows is a view of the Dorotheenstadt Cemetery where he and Helene Weigel are buried. A friend of mine, whose father was a stage designer in East Berlin in the post-war years, recalled meeting Brecht in this room. The playwright gestured through the window at the cemetery. 'One day I'll be lying in there', he said, cheerfully enough; and not long after, he was.

The bedroom is small and precisely ordered. Bed, apparently, was viewed as an unproductive place, a non-working zone to be passed through without undue delays. For decoration there is a Chagall drawing and a Chinese picture of *The Doubter*, in harmony with Brecht's belief that creative art should have no neat beginnings or conclusions. Downstairs is the more brightly furnished apartment of Helene Weigel (1900-71), an eminent actress who married Brecht in 1928. At the Berliner Ensemble she performed many roles, and was specially praised for her Mother Courage; she also directed plays and managed the theatre. In this house she liked to be by herself sometimes, keeping at a distance from the often overpowering figure of her husband, a voracious talker credited with saying that in company he preferred to eat fast – that way, he could control the talking while others were still busy clearing their plates.

Dorotheenstadt Cemetery

Many great figures in Berlin and German life are buried in this cemetery. In the main avenue, near the chapel, a map (*Lageplan*) fixed to a tree indicates their resting-places. Among them are (using the map's reference numbers):

2. In the first row, the Brecht-Weigel tomb. A simple rock slab set in an angle of red-brick wall, inscribed with the names of the playwright and his actress wife.

4. Nearby, Heinrich Mann, author (1871-1950), a bust on a crudely carved plinth, and a memorial stone to his wife Nelly.

11. Georg Wilhelm Friedrich Hegel (1770-1831), one of Germany's most influential philosophers.

12. Johann Gottlieb Fichte (1762-1814), classical German philosopher and first Rector of the Humboldt University.

23. John Heartfield, a photographer associated with the Dadaists. A simple stone with a tall spiky 'H'.

24. Arnold Zweig, author (1887-1968), a simple rock carved with the signatures of Zweig and his wife Beatrice (1892-1971).

34. Johann-Gottfried Schadow, architect (1764-1850), a sculpted figure on a plinth, set behind railings.

35. August Borsig, industrialist, a bust in a miniature temple. (Borsig Haus stands opposite the Brecht Haus in Chausseestrasse.)

38. Karl Friedrich Schinkel (1781-1841), Berlin's finest architect, a gilded portrait head in profile.

49. A mass grave of Resistance fighters, murdered by the SS on the night of 22 April 1945. Among those buried here, beneath a stark black metal cross, are Professor Albrecht Haushofer and Klaus Bonhoeffer.

Walk 9

Schöneberg and Viktoriapark

The district where novelist Christopher Isherwood lived from 1929 to 1933. See Nollendorfplatz and Winterfeldtplatz, good for café life and the twice-weekly market. From the Colonnades at Kleistpark, take a bus to Tempelhof and the Airlift Memorial, and bask on the slopes of Viktoriapark.

Allow 3-4 hours.

Best times Wednesday and Saturday morning, for the market in Winterfeldtplatz.

ROUTE

Begin at Ⓤ Nollendorfplatz; Buses 106, 119. At exit turn left towards Metropol Theater and cross to Maassenstrasse. Take 1st right in Nollendorfstrasse to find house at No. 17 where Isherwood lived (the lair of Fräulein Schroeder).

Return to Maassenstrasse and walk down to **Winterfeldtplatz**. Twice-weekly market on Wednesday and Saturday, 08.00 to 13.00. Walk through to Catholic Church of St Matthias and turn left along Pallasstrasse. At block of flats spanning road, see rare surviving *flak tower* from Second World War.

Continue to Potsdamer Strasse and turn right to Kleistpark and its **Colonnades**. Beyond stands the imposing **Kammgericht**, where the organisers of the 1944 July Bomb Plot were sentenced. Follow Potsdamer Strasse to Ⓤ Kleistpark.

Diversion To visit **Rathaus Schöneberg** (scene of President Kennedy's Cold War speech), take Bus 148/248 along Hauptstrasse to corner of Dominicusstrasse and walk N to John-F-Kennedy-Platz and the Rathaus. To rejoin walk, take Bus 104 to Platz der Luftbrücke.

From Ⓤ Kleistpark take U-Bahn to Mehringdamm (U7), change to U6 and get off at Platz der Luftbrücke. In garden in square, see **Airlift Memorial (Luftbrückendenkmal)**.

Facing away from monument, bear left ahead into Dudenstrasse. Walk down past shops towards outcrop of trees and take steps on right into **Viktoriapark**. At top of first rise, turn right to top of the **Kreuzberg**, and Schinkel's green pinnacled monument to Prussian soldiers in the War of Liberation against Napoleon.

Wind down through park beside waterfall. Walk ends here. Nearest refreshments in park at Golgotha Café. Nearest Ⓤ Mehringdamm; Buses 119, 247.

Nollendorfplatz

From the dingy station entrance, walk through to the main part of the square, facing the newly cleaned-up caryatids and ornate relief above the doorway of the Metropol Theater. In Art Deco days this was the Theater am Nollendorfplatz. Now it doubles as a concert venue (the Metropol) and club (the Loft), the latter promoting itself with the impossible boast that 'None of Our Bands Suck'.

On a wall of the U-Bahn station, an inverted triangle in pink-brown

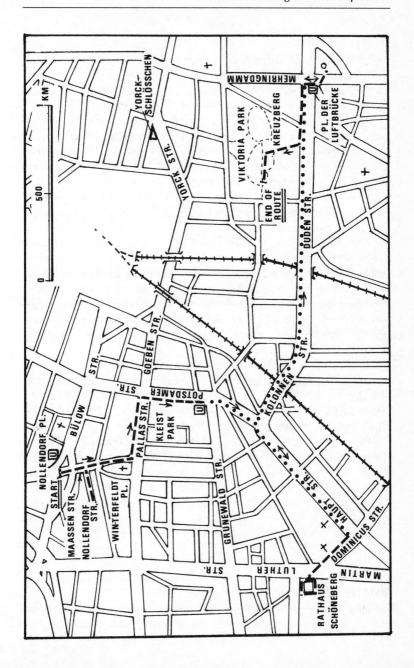

granite records the sacrifice of homosexuals murdered by the Nazis. The triangle repeats the shape of the identity patches worn by prisoners at concentration camps such as Sachsenhausen (see *Walk 17*); pink was the colour allotted to male homosexuals.

It was a consistent part of Hitler's purification programme to extract and remove homosexual culture from German life. Around Nollendorfplatz, gay men and women had flourished openly in the Twenties and Thirties, attracting people from all social levels, including a large foreign contingent. In the cafés, bars and clubs the exotics gathered, and ordinary folk came to sit and stare. Christopher Isherwood's ironic vignette of goings-on at the Salomé club pinpoints the false atmosphere:

'. . . A few stage lesbians and some young men with plucked eyebrows lounged at the bar, uttering occasional raucous guffaws and treble hoots – supposed, apparently, to represent the laughter of the damned. The whole premises are painted gold and inferno-red – crimson plush inches thick, and vast gilded mirrors. It was pretty full. The audience consisted chiefly of respectable middle-aged tradesmen and their families, exclaiming in good-humoured amazement: "Do they really?" and "Well, I never".'

Then came the Nazi clamp-down, the reckoning. Foreign homosexuals, suddenly fearful for their lives, found themselves in an even more dangerous plight than they had known in the countries they had escaped from. German nationals had few places, if any, to turn to. The Gestapo compiled their lists, and the round-ups began.

Maassenstrasse links Nollendorfplatz to Winterfeldtplatz. Halfway down is Nollendorfstrasse, where at No.17 a plaque marks the house where Christopher Isherwood lived from March 1929 to January-February 1933. Homage is paid to his famous novels *Mr Norris Changes Trains* (first published in 1935) and *Goodbye to Berlin* (1939, quoted above), and to the fact that they inspired the musical *Cabaret* which then took on a life of its own. As any Berliner will tell you, 'Money makes ze voorld go round . . .'

Winterfeldtplatz

In the post-war years Isherwood became for many a symbol of the intellectual who preferred exile in Berlin to hushing up his homosexuality in Britain, where to be gay was generally thought a disgusting condition, meriting social and professional banishment – though not attracting the death penalty.

Gay culture in today's Berlin recognises few limits, and this quarter has again become the principal settling-ground, reflected in its street life and nocturnal calendar. The atmosphere is not stridently gay, in public that is; rather it demonstrates a peaceful tolerance to all forms of emotional partnership. At the corner facing Winterfeldtplatz, the patrons of Café Sidney are united in their taste for quiet gossip around the bowls of *Milchkaffee* and decorous salads.

To the left are more cafés in Winterfeldtstrasse, including the Belmundo and the Labyrinth which offers French, English, Egyptian and Turkish breakfasts. Breakfast is a staple of life here. The full version – with eggs, yoghurt, cereal, toast, fruit, coffee, etc. – may be served up to four o'clock in the afternoon. This is the period of the day when Berlin's night people surface once more. On Friday and Saturday nights they are joined by thousands of ordinary working people. Bedtime at three in the morning becomes the norm for those two nights; then on Sunday the workers prepare for their usual dawn start on Monday. How the body copes with this routine, no one can tell me. It seems it just does, like some well-trained dog which always knows when an outing is on the way, and arranges its sleeping hours around it.

On Wednesday and Saturday mornings the awnings of market stalls spread across the great concrete rectangle of Winterfeldtplatz. Vans selling hot food pump a perpetual reek of fried onions over the trading lanes. Here they sell eggs, vegetables, brooches, bread rolls, wispy scarves, flowers, cheese, children's socks, woolly slippers and much besides.

Supreme Court (Kammgericht)

Turn east along Pallasstrasse, perhaps under the booming noonday bells of St Matthias, the Catholic church in Winterfeldtplatz. In Eissholzstrasse stands the pedimented rear façade of the old Kammgericht building, once the Prussian Supreme Court. Keep on towards the bleak and looming apartment block which bridges the road. To its right is an extraordinary apparition: the remains of a massive Nazi flak tower which has withstood all post-war efforts to demolish it. The flat-topped tower seems at first to have pierced a vast square hole in the apartment block which had to be built around and over it, creating the impression of two buildings locked in combat for the same piece of ground, like concrete dinosaurs.

On the wall of the flak tower, a grim mural by Sigurd Wendland shows how Potsdamer Strasse looked in 1945, shattered far beyond mere repair. Across the road, a line of Turkish shops marks an extension of the Turkish colony in Kreuzberg (see *Walk 10*).

In Potsdamer Strasse, the eastern entrance to Kleistpark has a neoclassical double arcade topped with pairs of soot-blackened cherubs and a sprinkling of new replacements. Carl von Gontard designed these *Kolonnaden* in about 1770, and until 1910 they occupied a site in Königsstrasse, near Alexanderplatz, then were moved here when the park was redesigned. In earlier times it had been a botanical garden.

Dominating the grounds of Kleistpark is the Kammgericht building. In the Nazi years the court served as a department of the People's Court, the Volksgerichtshof, whose main building was close to the Esplanade Hotel in Potsdamer Platz. In 1944 the organisers of the July Bomb Plot were brought to Kleistpark to be tried and sentenced; many were later executed at Plötzensee Prison (see *Walk 16*).

Rathaus Schöneberg

Schöneberg is a large district of mainly suburban character. It stretches from Tiergarten down to Steglitz, and its Hauptstrasse – once the high street of the medieval village of 'Sconenberghe' – slants away from the corner of Kleistpark, by the U-Bahn station.

The residential streets and squares of Schöneberg are quietly orthodox and self-contained, each little neighbourhood with its own row of food shops, florist, hair salons and, of course, *Kneipen*, where a hush may break out on the entry of a stranger. Not an unfriendly hush, as these go, but a palpable pause in the inhabitants' routine of gossip sharing and froth watching.

Into these unexciting backwaters it is not necessary to go at all, though one reason may be to visit the town hall – the Rathaus Schöneberg – which until the *Wende* was the seat of West Berlin's ruling Mayor (*Bürgermeister*) and the *Senat* or city government. The building itself is hardly worth the trip, an undistinguished fortress of civic power, four-square with a steep roof and frontal tower, built in 1911-14. In the Second World War the tower lost its cupola, and the present pared-off look is not an improvement.

The Town Hall acquired international fame when President Kennedy came to address the people of West Berlin on 26 June 1963. Here, too, on the night of 22 November that year, Berliners gathered as news of his assassination reached them. Kennedy was rightly seen as the effective voice of democracy in the early miserable years of the Wall, when those in the Western enclave grappled with their renewed insecurity, and the East under Khrushchev threatened to squeeze them into extinction.

Airlift Memorial (Luftbrückendenkmal)

At the edge of Tempelhof Airport stands the great three-pronged curve of concrete which commemorates the Berlin Airlift. It represents the beginning of a gigantic bridge, and a similar monument in Frankfurt-am-Main marks its other end. The three prongs stand for the three air corridors which joined Berlin to the West.

In 1948 the Russians cut off power supplies to West Berlin and blocked road and rail links out of the city. The Allied response was to mount a massive airlift, beginning on 26 June 1948, which flew in food and fuel at a rate of up to 8,000 tons per day. Once every two minutes or less, an aid plane landed at Tempelhof, until on 12 May 1949 the Russians caved in and the siege was lifted.

Around the foot of the shallow plinth are the names of Allied servicemen lost in this great venture: forty-one were British, thirty-one American and five German. In a city of so many caustic views, the monument was bound to hatch a nickname. Soon it was widely known as the *Hungerkrallen* ('Hunger Claws') scratching at the sky for food. It was a modest enough joke given the hardships of that time, when living standards crashed to the precarious levels of the post-war months.

Viktoriapark

The Kreuzberg, the Mountain of the Cross, is a natural outcrop rare in this flat city where most so-called *Berge* are composed of grassed-over heaps of wartime rubble. The 'mountain' rises to 66m (217ft) and vines once grew on its southern slopes. Today the alcoholic connection is sustained by the wreaths of steam rising from the Schultheiss Brewery. This essential of Berlin life was founded 150 years ago when a local chemist, August Heinrich Prell, decided to give up selling pills and go into beer production.

At the mountain's peak, assailable by steps, is a green cast-iron monument to Prussian victories in the War of Liberation (1813-15). This was the final episode in the struggle against Napoleon. It began after the *Grande Armée*'s retreat from Moscow and culminated in the Emperor's flight from the field of Waterloo, known in Germany as the Battle of La Belle Alliance. The monument was designed by Karl Friedrich Schinkel in neo-Gothic style and was completed in 1821. Beneath its steepling pinnacles, warrior angels stand in a series of niches, and plaques record the decisive battles of the war. The cross on top of the monument is the source of the name Kreuzberg.

In summer months the park-keeper switches on the waterfall – a dramatic tumble of water inspired by the Zackenfels in the Riesengebirge, the Giants' Mountain range. Turn down the winding path beside the waterfall and enjoy the pleasures of the park. If the weather is fine, the Golgotha Café (on the way to the Cross) offers a resting-point for the foot-weary. The entrance is tucked away near the Turkish football ground. On a Sunday afternoon in season, the roar of the fans will guide you to it.

Another possibility is the Yorckschlösschen, a jazz pub where trad-mainstream bands play on Sunday afternoon from 14.00 (see map for location).

Walk 10

Kreuzberg

A walk into District 36. Begin at the entertaining Berlin Museum, then visit the 'real' Kreuzberg at Kottbusser Tor and in surrounding streets. Continue by overhead U-Bahn to Schlesisches Tor, and cross the Spree to the East Side Gallery, a long stretch of the Berlin Wall, preserved and painted.

Allow 4-5 hours.

Best times Not Monday, when Berlin Museum closed.

ROUTE

Begin at Ⓤ Kochstrasse; Bus 129. From island exit of U-Bahn station, cross to E side of Friedrichstrasse and walk S. Take 1st left in Besselstrasse, past wholesale flower market, and 2nd right in Markgrafenstrasse. At intersection with Lindenstrasse, bear right towards ochre and stone front of **Berlin Museum** 👁; open 10.00 to 22.00; Weissbierstube (old Berlin pub) open 11.00 to 18.00, closes 16.00 on Saturday-Sunday; whole museum closed Monday. *Admission.*

At exit, turn right to bus stop outside Employment Office and catch Bus 141 along Oranienstrasse to Oranienplatz.

From the square, bear right down Dresdner Strasse and under buildings at end to market-bazaar at **Kottbusser Tor**. Continue up Adalbertstrasse, turn right along Oranienstrasse (the 'high street' of Kreuzberg) and next left up Mariannenstrasse to **Mariannenplatz**, dominated by former **Bethanien Hospital**.

Leave square on E side along Muskauer Strasse and take 2nd left in Pücklerstrasse to the 19C **Markthalle**. Walk through market to Eisenbahnstrasse where old-fashioned restaurant – Wirtshaus Mewes. Turn right down Eisenbahnstrasse to Lausitzer Platz and Skalitzer Strasse. Here either turn right and take U-Bahn from Görlitzer Bahnhof to **Schlesisches Tor** (one stop) or turn left and walk there (1km) along Skalitzer Strasse.

From Schlesisches Tor station, walk ahead through Bevernstrasse to River Spree at Gröbenufer. Look across to preserved stretch of Berlin Wall. For frontal view (of **East Side Gallery**) cross by the road bridge next to Oberbaumbrücke and turn left along Mühlenstrasse. Walk ends here. See a section of Wall and return to Schlesisches Tor or walk to end and turn up to Hauptbahnhof.

Berlin Museum

The approach from the blocks of Friedrichstrasse is uneventful, brightened on working days by the flower boxes and ornamental trees in the grounds of the wholesale flower market which occupies much of Besselstrasse. The district lies close to the old Nazi power centre and much of it was flattened in the Second World War. The replacement buildings are rarely more than efficient spaces for living and working.

The Berlin Museum traces the history of the city – in the post-war

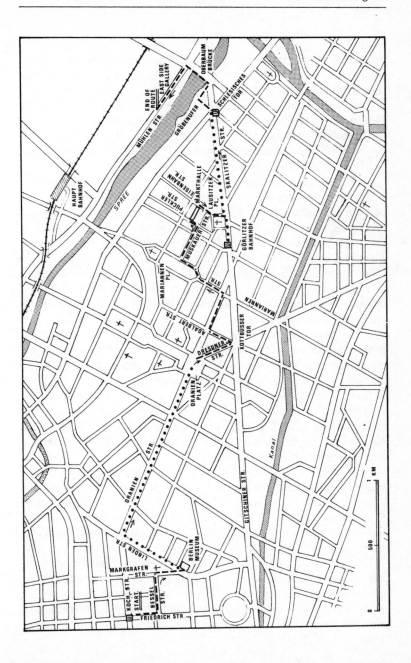

years from the West Berlin angle – and possesses a large collection of paintings. It is also the holding point for most of the city's Jewish collections.

The baroque lines of the original Kollegienhaus were designed by Philipp Gerlach in 1734, and the building then served many generations of city administrators. After severe damage in the last war it was restored in 1962, and in 1969 opened as West Berlin's equivalent of the Märkisches Museum (see *Walk 7*).

From the entrance hall, turn left to the standing exhibition of portraits and stately furniture from the seventeenth and eighteenth centuries. To the left is a map room with early plans of Berlin. The centrepiece is a fine model in pale wood of Berlin-Cölln in 1690, showing the ring of gates and fortifications, the medieval Schloss, the Franciscan Cloister Church and the spires of the early parish churches.

To the right of the entrance hall, the paintings section opens with some fairly stodgy views spiced by brighter genre pictures on the upper landing. Among these are satirical pieces aimed at Prussian militarism and an evocative winter street scene by Adolph Menzel (1862).

In the large gallery upstairs are cityscapes from the Biedermeier years, approximately between 1815 and 1860. An 1840 picture of the old Rathaus, by Wilhelm Brücke, is close in spirit to the style of the English artist Thomas Shotter Boys. Angled in one corner of the room is Eduard Gärtner's two-panelled *Panorama* of Berlin seen from the roof of the Friedrichswerdershe Kirche; a more ambitious version is currently in the Schinkel Pavillon at Charlottenburg (see *Walk 14*). Nearby is a bright view by Johann Ludwig Schultz of new houses overlooking the Tiergarten.

The rapid march of industrialisation is captured in Carl Eduard Biermann's picture of the iron foundry and machine factory founded by August Borsig in Chausseestrasse. The lower half of the scene is filled with sunlight and rich colours, for English viewers reminiscent of Hunt and Millais, and the upper half is blackened with smoke from the Borsig chimneys.

By the turn of the century, painters were hard pressed to keep up with Berlin's dynamic expansion. Steam power, motor traffic and the gouging out of tunnels for the U-Bahn were just some of the new themes which presented themselves. Lesser Ury is represented by two dark pictures of railway stations, Ernst Ludwig Kirchner by lemon-green trams crossing at Nollendorfplatz (1912) and Lyonel Feininger by *Gasometer in Berlin-Schöneberg*. Topographical views proliferate, and the café society of the Twenties is chronicled in posters, models and printed ephemera.

The persecution of the Jews is summarised, as is the chaos of the city laid flat in 1945. For want of space, these sections are lamentably sparse. As yet, Berlin has no museum which fully comes to terms with the Hitler era.

The Cold War years, and West Berlin's life as a walled-off island, provoked many images. From 1974 is Karl Horst Hödicke's compelling picture of the sky above a back courtyard (*Hinterhof*) in Schöneberg, shimmering in the bronze glare from a hovering UFO. From 1977 is Rainer Fetting's *First Wall Picture*, a simple yet urgently felt painting of a purple wall hacking through the middle of a city street.

On the ground floor is a small Jewish section – a token presence while the city argues over the funding of a full-scale Jewish Museum. Plans exist to build a major extension at this museum, but the estimated costs are quoted at US $68 million, enough to fuel a long-running debate over cultural priorities which to date is unresolved.

From the hallway, take a step back in time through the brick-vaulted Porcelain Gallery, lined with cabinets representing some of Berlin's best porcelain makers: Chinese vases and figurines by Gerhard Wohlbeer, stout faïence and pewter beer mugs by Cornelius Funcke, plates by Wilhelm Caspar Wegely and the Royal Porcelain Manufacturers.

By now a growing waft of *sauerkraut* may have introduced itself. Follow it to the museum's most curious and delightful exhibit – the Weissbierstube, a minutely detailed reconstruction of a Berlin bar-room at the turn of the century. Arguably it is the most frequented room in the building – or do people just stay there longer? The dark sludge-green walls teem with paintings, cartoons, lithographs and photographs of café scenes, craftsmen at work and ordinary Berliners pursuing their usual proclivities. The buffet drips with bulbous flower arrangements which overhang the stacked slices of cold meats and sausage, fat cheeses, salad dishes and what you will. The beer comes in tall jugs, meticulously drawn from the barrel.

And into the heart of Kreuzberg

Bus 141 stops outside the shabby rusticated front of the Employment Office, then turns into Oranienstrasse and whines past the Government Printing Office to Moritzplatz. The next square, Oranienplatz, is a suitable point to begin exploring the controversial quarter of East Kreuzberg.

District 36 has a vastly overheated reputation, thanks mainly to the world's magazine and travel writers. In the last ten years they have swarmed here to pick among the refuse and write crisp weekendy pieces about the great alternative culture which they have discovered. Their prose is garnished with colour pics of Turkish food shops, and grainy black-and-whites of ancient hippies and trendy moochers draped in paramilitary scarves. Kreuzberg, they will tell you, throbs to the beat of the New Radical West.

The sad reality is that East Kreuzberg is at best patchy, at worst a dump. If its streets were its industrial index, its chief product would be dog shit. If its cafés were the index of its spiritual temperature, they would register big on the drug and hangover scale, and nil otherwise. Here are some samples of the embattled writings on the wall:

> FORWARDS ON THE PATH STEERED BY MAO-TSE-TUNG
> YANKEE GO HOME
> DEATH TO WEST GERMAN IMPERIALISM
> ORDER IS NOT EVERYTHING
> DON'T WORK WITHOUT THINKING ABOUT IT

What saves East Kreuzberg from sinking under the weight of its own self-pity is the never-say-die nucleus of art galleries, small theatres and good cinemas which have set up here and somehow make a living. No less important have been the efforts of the Turkish community to found what for them is virtually a town in exile.

The Turkish inflow began in the 1960s when West Germany welcomed *Gastarbeiter* (guest workers) from poorer countries, largely to fill the dirty jobs which ordinary Germans no longer wished to take on. Now the Turkish population is more widely integrated in the city – though all but excluded from wealthy districts such as Zehlendorf where the stock of subsidised housing is kept unreasonably low. Partly because of this selective resistance to foreigners in other parts of Berlin (and exotic foreigners in particular), Kreuzberg remains the focus of Turkish life in the city, and in fact sustains the largest concentration of

Turks outside Istanbul.

Oranienplatz is relatively spruce, the gardens neatly laid out and fringed by a mixture of new buildings and mansion apartments from the nineteenth century. From the square, Oranienstrasse runs in either direction across the district, a scruffy shopping street with a plentiful choice of cafés, though most are dismal. A highlight is the Café Unart, a small theatre at No.163 where the savage and sometimes brilliant Charla Drops is a regular performer. Her act is a sequence of mime and dance sketches, in which she is accompanied by her very funny assistant, the ageless and sublimely po-faced Frau Dochnoch (to name just one of her many roles). For an evening of Kreuzberg at its best, book seats by phone and eat before the show at Max & Moritz, an old Berlin restaurant a couple of doors away.

In search of Kreuzbergian squalor, bear right down Dresdner Strasse past the Türk Discount, the herbalist, the tribal junkware store and the Babylon Cinema which regularly shows films in English. At the end, go through a sordid passage beneath a tenement block and arrive at Kottbusser Tor. This is the district's chief meeting-point, a claustrophobic piazza framed on one side by shops and flats plastered with Marxist slogans, and on the other by the girders and superstructure of the overhead U-Bahn. The square is a home of sorts for people who look as if they got off the train and stayed. Down-and-outs drink and beg their days away, unemployed drifters cluster next to the fruit and trinket stalls, and vast piles of scraped-up rubbish stand on the pavement.

The May Day demonstration is a regular feast of mayhem in Kreuzberg. In advance of the day, police distribute leaflets warning householders to look after their property and park their cars at a safe distance. From noon on 1 May, crowds gather to demonstrate in Oranienplatz and along Kottbusser Damm, a police helicopter squats overhead and everybody waits for the first brick to be thrown. Someone obliges with a rock through a shop window, and the afternoon deteriorates into ritual violence. Rioters set fire to cars and lob Molotov cocktails at the ranks of helmeted police. A local variant of this weapon is a beer can filled with glass shards and a firework. Freelance looters plunder the shops of their fancy. Around 16.30 the official 'Revolutionary 1 May Demo' is declared closed, and the rioting peters out. In an average year the police arrest two hundred, half that number of police officers are injured and the damage bill is colossal.

To be fair to Kreuzberg, it is not the only district prone to violent gatherings. Prenzlauer Berg, formerly in the East zone, also has its riots on May Day, though on a smaller scale. Meanwhile, demonstrators in search of more realistic aims such as better pay and job security confine their May Day activities to a peaceful meeting in the Lustgarten. Here up to 15,000 gather in front of the Altes Museum to hear speeches by trade union leaders.

Mariannenplatz

The other charms of Kreuzberg are thin on the ground. The Route (above) describes a further loop through District 36. Alternatively, catch the U-Bahn from Kottbusser Tor and go straight to Schlesisches Tor.

The large open space of Mariannenplatz was laid out as a garden in 1853 by Peter Joseph Lenné. Its much-trampled centre is a traditional site for street parties and other celebrations. On the west side stands the Bethanien. This forbidding yellow-brick monster was founded as a hospital in the 1840s, which helps to explain its austere lines broken only by the pointed turrets at the main entrance. In the 1960s the Bethanien survived threats of demolition and now operates as a cultural centre with studios, a print workshop and exhibition rooms.

Until recently the Church of St Thomas on the north side stood directly beneath the Berlin Wall. A sturdy example of nineteenth-century Historicism, it was designed in 1864 by F. Adler, a pupil of Schinkel. On the south side stands a strangely flippant monument to the *Fallen of the Berlin Fire Brigade* (D. Wolff and G. Jendritzko, 1960). Two firemen of the red-nosed school of comedy fire jets of water at each other under the directions of a third fireman.

Continue to the Markthalle, a small but honest and colourful covered market. Shops display enticing snacks of cheese, fruit and vegetables; there is a Greek store renowned for its olives, and the cake and bread shop is a specially succulent oasis after the drabness of the surrounding streets.

Schlesisches Tor

This was the first U-Bahn line in Berlin. It opened in 1902 between

Warschauer Strasse, across the river, and what is now Ernst-Reuter-Platz beyond the Zoo. The overhead route along Skalitzer Strasse cleaves a path between two apparently quite separate cultures. On the north side is the now familiar patchwork of desolate blocks and one-eyed shops, and end walls ablaze with violent daubs and messages; on the other side is conservative Kreuzberg, manifested in a range of restored houses, where middle-class habits may quietly thrive behind tall elegant windows.

Schlesisches Tor (the 'Silesian Gate') is currently the terminus of Line U-1, which was severed at the river when the Wall went up. The station stands on a curve, and passengers descend to the street through a brick-built pavilion with pleasant Jugendstil detailing; the local *Imbiss* shelters beneath a small onion dome next to the ticket hall.

Walk ahead to the gardens beside the River Spree. Until 1989 this embankment was the effective boundary between East and West. The GDR claimed not only the far bank, where the Wall is still intact, but also the river as well. Patrol boats cruised the waters and escapers trying to swim across were shot on sight.

The stretch of wall is now preserved as the East Side Gallery. To reach it, take the footbridge beside the once-fine red-brick castellations and arcade of the Oberbaumbrücke. Two round stumps in the centre are the sorry remains of a pair of sturdy neo-Gothic towers with pointed roofs. In 1992, the line at railway level was still blocked by a steel fence, grooved harshly into the ornate brickwork.

East Side Gallery

Turn along Mühlenstrasse to the East Side Gallery, 'the largest open air gallery in the world'. For a kilometre or so, the panels of the Berlin Wall were turned over to individual artists. Here are some of the best-known images provoked by the Wall, and since relayed round the world via postcard and T-shirt: the Trabi crashing through the Wall (*Test the Best*, by Birgit Kinder); Brezhnev and Ulbricht in violent embrace (*My God, Help Me to Survive This Deadly Love*, by Dmitri Vrubel); the exploding barbed wire of *Berlyn*, by Gerhard Lahr. The site is now officially protected, though not by any fence to keep the souvenir hunters at bay, nor by any screen to fend off traffic fumes from Mühlenstrasse. But then, as history has shown, nothing in Berlin lasts for long.

Walk 11

Prenzlauer Berg

The war-battered district to the north of 'Alex', re-emerging with new shops, restored streets and the beginnings of a night life. Explore Schönhauser Allee, the main street. Visit elegant (if overdone) Husemannstrasse and its strange museums, and the café-bars of Kollwitzplatz.

Allow 4-5 hours.

Best times Not Sunday-Monday.

ROUTE

Begin at ⑤/Ⓤ Schönhauser Allee; Trams 22, 46, 49. At exit, cross to E side of street and walk S beside elevated U-Bahn tracks. Turn left in Stargarder Strasse to **Gethsemane Church**, an important centre of protest and refuge in the last days before the Wall came down.

Return to Schönhauser Allee and follow across Eberswalder Strasse junction. At Sredzkistrasse, turn left past old Schultheiss Brewery to **Husemannstrasse**. Turn right to **Museum of Working-Class Life in Berlin around 1900 (Museum Berliner Arbeiterleben um 1900)** ☜; open 10.00 to 18.00, Friday closes 15.00, closed Sunday-Monday. *Admission*.

Next door is the **Museum of Hairdressing (Friseur Museum)**; open Tuesday-Wednesday 10.00 to 12.00, 13.00 to 17.00, Monday and Thursday on request, closed Friday and Sunday. *Admission*.

Continue to **Kollwitzplatz**. On corner, elegant bar-restaurant Restauration 1900. In gardens, monument to artist Käthe Kollwitz; on E side, by Knaackstrasse, a copy of her *Mutter* sculpture.

Turn left in Knaackstrasse. To left in courtyard of No.53 Rykestrasse is East Berlin's only functioning synagogue. Cross to **Water Tower (Wasserturm)** and brick monument to German 'resistance fighters' killed by SA troops in 1933.

Walk round square and return to Kollwitzplatz. Walk ends here. Nearest refreshments in square. Nearest Ⓤ Senefelderplatz or Eberswalder Strasse; see main text for further suggested route back to city centre.

Schönhauser Allee

This is High Street, Prenzlauer Berg. For new retailers wanting to make their mark in difficult times – whether with a computer centre, a fashion shop or hardware store – this must be a nerve-racking place to start up. The street is sliced in two by the superstructure of the elevated U-Bahn, with the result that would-be customers can never really see more than half the shops at any one time.

Try the east side. A straggle of neighbourhood shops and cafés leads to Stargarder Strasse and the Gethsemane Kirche. In the last months of 1989 the church was the effective headquarters of the New Forum group of dissenters. On 7 October, as police in East Berlin beat up demonstrators who had failed to celebrate the GDR's fortieth birthday

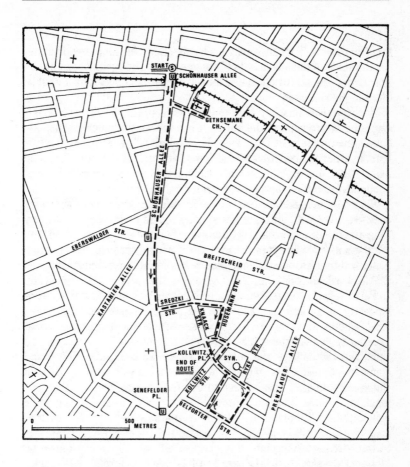

in the expected spirit, people flocked here for protection and were barricaded in for many hours, until the police waiting outside were called off.

In the immediate neighbourhood of the church are many majestic late nineteenth-century apartment buildings. Sooty and crumbling now, victims of half a century of neglect, their time will eventually come again. Once restored, they will look magnificent. That, in short, is the story of Prenzlauer Berg since 1945. It is tragic that so little was done to repair the bullet marks of the last war or to shore up tottering façades – not only for the buildings themselves but, more importantly, for the spirit of the inhabitants. Two generations lost, sacrificed by the policies of the all-caring state, as the German Democratic Republic liked to project itself.

Perhaps two consoling factors emerge from the débris of the past. One: the future can only be better, even though not much will happen tomorrow or the next day. Two: here on its hill, Prenzlauer Berg at least escaped the bulldozers which churned through Friedrichshain and Mitte, and the architects who refilled those neighbourhoods with rectilinear ghettoes designed for compliant worker ants.

Back to Schönhauser Allee. To either side the bright shops and cafés seem to blaze with an extra garishness beside their failed and empty neighbours – the Konsum co-operatives and the enterprises launched after the *Wende* which never took off or were swept away by rocketing rents and the devious plans of greedy landlords and speculators.

All the while, trains bang through above the middle of the street, up to Pankow and down to Alex. On the bisected roadway, trams squeeze narrowly by parked cars and the ever present trucks and diggers of roadmenders and cable-layers. If noise were a true indicator of urban prosperity, Schönhauser Allee would be rich indeed. But perhaps, this time, the foundations of a better life really are being dug, drilled and clamped into place. Down on the west side of the street, the cabins of the weekly market reach west to the football stadium. At the next junction, by Eberswalder Strasse Station, trams pause at the traffic lights, then roll thunderously forward in a bewildering criss-cross of directions, all bells jangling. Until recently, the U-Bahn station and one of the streets issuing into this six-pointed crossing were known as Dimitroffstrasse. Now the deeds of Georgi Dimitroff, a Bulgarian Communist who did rather well against the Nazis but then became a dictatorial prime minister in his own country after the war, have been tidied beneath oblivion's carpet.

Husemannstrasse

At the corner of Sredzkistrasse is the Franz Club, one of East Berlin's better jazz and blues clubs – open 21.00 until late. It occupies part of an old Schultheiss brewery, built *c.* 1890 on quasi-Byzantine lines and now mostly in the hands of a discount warehouse.

We are moving into restoration territory – to see some of the lucky few streets selected by the GDR to pump up tourism in places not within a stone's throw of Unter den Linden. On the left is an attractive revitalised terrace in Hagenauerstrasse – and currently the *Bauwagen* of the construction teams are parked across the road, while the process is repeated on the facing houses. At the next crossing is Husemann-strasse, the southern half of which is one of the showplaces of East Berlin.

Reactions vary to these selective renovation schemes. While generally accepted as a great and necessary improvement, yielding much-needed new housing in a blighted district, there is much behind the concept that is not so admirable.

Firstly, why was so little done, and so late? It is not difficult to find an answer. Since 1989 it has become clear that by Western standards the GDR was an appallingly backward and deficient country. Renewal of old housing stock, as opposed to shooting up new prefabricated blocks, was a thorny problem which evidently received a too low priority.

But then, when a street was eventually chosen for renovation, what actually was done? In Husemannstrasse the tweeness of the decorative schemes provides a useful clue. Like the boutiques and workshops of Sophienstrasse (see *Walk 8*) the decorations here border on the camp – at street-level a sudden eruption of Jugendstil lettering and glass panels, and on the frontage of an upmarket cobbler's a neat set of pictures of ladies' shoes and bootees, as worn *c*. 1900. As nostalgic dabs and flourishes they are all very pretty, but the suspicion persists that they are inappropriate in a district still reeling under mass deprivation. Less appealing still is the thought that this is precisely what the GDR planners proposed – to distract and buy off the populace with a tarted-up rendition of a past that, it could safely be assumed, few would now remember.

Such misgivings multiply when confronted with the next show building, the Museum of Working-Class Life in Berlin around 1900. The centrepiece is a reconstructed tenement flat. The rooms appear to be faithfully researched and furnished – as they should be, for the museum is a department of the Märkisches Museum. Here is the cramped kitchen, hung with tiers of washing; there is the living room which doubled as a bedroom and was also where the wife and mother worked at her sewing table, running up clothes for the family. Sanitary facilities are notably absent, and yet it all seems so warm, neat and cosy. There lies the trap. For *some* tenements, relatively high up in the building and with a frontage on the street, there could be light and air in those high-ceilinged rooms. The majority, though, were dark and depressing, stuck away in damp and rotting back courtyards (*Hinterhöfe*) where the light of day hardly penetrated at all. In every tenement, light or dark, the difficulties were compounded by dreadful overcrowding, a high incidence of disease and every concomitant form of social hardship.

The museum plays down these negative aspects, relying perhaps on the public's natural optimism when out for the day, and certainly on its proven appetite for nostalgia and fantasy. Thus, like Disneyworld, history becomes entertainment – with a useful dimension of added propaganda. Get them wittering on about how it was in Great-Grandma's day, so the thinking must have run, and they will forget to wonder why, a hundred years later, living standards in Prenzlauer Berg remain so squalid.

Next door, campness reaches an out-and-out climax at the Friseur Museum, devoted to the history of hairdressing. Enough, surely, of the content can be glimpsed through the windows. For professionals, or the obsessed (barnettophiles?), there are guided tours.

Kollwitzplatz

Continue to the triangular gardens of Kollwitzplatz, named after the artist Käthe Kollwitz (1861-1945) who spent much of her life in Prenzlauer Berg. On the corner of Husemannstrasse is Restauration 1900, an elegant local hangout, open evenings only, its bar front decorated with old metal advertising signs. In the morning, before eleven o'clock, little stirs in this square, though breakfast and coffee are on hand at the shabby-trendy Café Westphal on the east side, which has tables outside and in the afternoon and evening is packed with young locals.

And as for the breakfasts – what breakfasts they serve here! One morning, sheltering behind an orange juice and trying not to stare, I watched as three young Germans, two men and a woman, began their first meal of the day (I assumed it was their first). It was a sunny morning in late September, around 10.45. They started with *Milchkaffee* or orange juice. Then a plate of crisp rolls arrived, with jam or cheese and salad, and plates of muesli mixed with yoghurt. They enjoyed these with an agreeable lack of urgency, and then two were ready to receive boiled eggs while the other shaped up to an omelette. After this, out came the waitress with a large dish of peach halves topped with banana slices. This appeared to be the final blow of, for me anyway, a mesmerising *Frühstück*! Proof too, if proof were needed, that Prenzlauer Berg is an up and coming area, with a waxing population of young executives and not exactly starving students to counterbalance the squatters and others who are so obviously pushed for cash.

In the centre of the gardens, by the children's playground, is a monumental seated figure of Käthe Kollwitz, who from some angles looks unfortunately like a wise old gorilla. At the foot of the square, close to the junction with Knaackstrasse, is a copy of one of her *Mother* sculptures. A mother crouches forwards and holds her young children close, to protect them from some fearful unseen danger. The sculpture stands on the site of the artist's own house, which was destroyed in the war. (The best place to see her drawings and sculpture is at the Käthe-Kollwitz Museum in Fasanenstrasse, described in *Walk 1*.)

Two other buildings are worth looking for in the neighbourhood. In Rykestrasse, at No.53, is East Berlin's only functioning synagogue. Its high red-brick front stands at the back of the courtyard, invisible except to the knowing eye. To the front was once a Jewish school, which survived Nazi repression longer than most before it too was shut down in 1942.

In the gardens flanking Knaackstrasse is the great circular Water Tower (*Wasserturm*). This famous landmark has been converted into desirable apartments with curving exterior walls. In 1933 it was used by SA (Storm-trooper) investigators, who tortured and killed their victims in the basement. A brick monument, on the corner of Kolmarerstrasse, pays tribute to those who died.

This introduction to Prenzlauer Berg covers the central part of a large and sprawling district. To see a little more, follow Knaackstrasse back to the junction by U-Bahnhof Eberswalder Strasse and catch a 46 tram south to Friedrichstrasse Station. The route runs past more neglected housing in Kastanien Allee, then winds downhill past the blackened Zionskirche, another place of refuge for dissenters in 1989. The more one sees of Prenzlauer Berg, the more one appreciates the scale of the housing problem in East Berlin, and how such deprivation creeps, like damp on a wall, into every fibre of daily life.

Walk 12 🏃

Museum Island

Museuminsel – the island treasure-house of East Berlin. Follow this walk to establish where everything is; to avoid cultural indigestion, perhaps visit selectively and return later. Chief attractions: Bode Museum, Pergamon Museum, Nationalgalerie, Altes Museum and Berlin Cathedral.
Allow   5-6 hours.
Best times   Not Monday-Tuesday.

ROUTE

Begin at Ⓢ / Ⓤ Friedrichstrasse; Buses 147, 157, Trams 22, 46, 70, 71. At exit in Friedrichstrasse, turn N past ornate Admiralspalast (Metropol Theater) and continue to river bridge. Turn right along Am Weidendamm towards dome of **Bode Museum**. Cross bridge to museum entrance ☻; open 10.00 to 18.00, closed Monday-Tuesday. *Admission*. Mixture of collections: Sculpture, Egyptian, Early Christian/Byzantine, Picture Gallery, Coins, Pre- and Early History.

At exit, turn left after bridge, go under railway and turn left over next bridge to **Pergamon Museum** ☻; open 10.00 to 18.00. *Admission*. Monday-Tuesday, only downstairs architectural rooms open, i.e. not Far Eastern, Small Classical Antiquities, Islamic and Ethnology collections. Chief attractions, on view all week: Pergamon Altar, Ishtar Gate and Processional Way.

Refreshment break Head for Café Am Zeughaus, entrance beside river walk occupied on Sunday by small crafts market (*Kunstmarkt*).

Walk down, or back up again after break, to Bodestrasse and follow to **Nationalgalerie** ☻; open 10.00 to 18.00, closed Monday-Tuesday. *Admission*. 19-20C paintings and sculpture.

Turn S to Lustgarten and front of Schinkel's **Altes Museum** ☻; open for special exhibitions 10.00 to 18.00, closed Monday-Tuesday. *Admission*.

On E side of Lustgarten, visit **Berlin Cathedral (Berliner Dom)** ☻; open 10.00 to 17.00, Sunday closes 20.00. *Admission*. See renovations in shell of bombed rotunda. Around corner in Karl-Liebknecht-Strasse is restored Baptism and Marriage Chapel.

Walk ends here. Nearest refreshments across Schlossbrücke (*Marx-Engels-Brücke*) at Cafe Am Palast in Palast Hotel. Nearest Ⓢ Hackescher Markt (*Marx-Engels-Platz*); Buses 100, 157.

Museum Island

'The State Museums of Berlin were founded at the beginning of the nineteenth century in a period of renewed strengthening of the bourgeois-democratic movement and the flare-up of revolutionary struggles. In the inaugural year of the Museum Am Lustgarten (1830), which today bears the name Altes Museum, the July Revolution in France

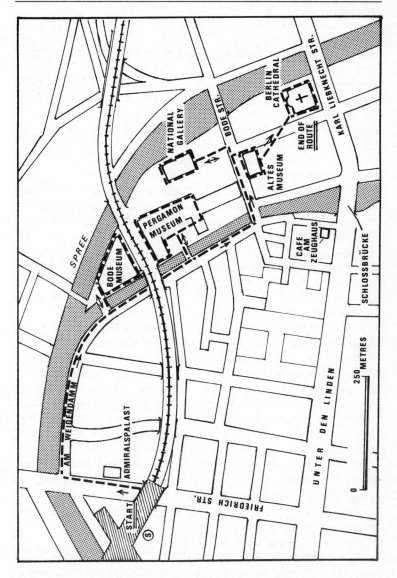

removed Bourbon dominion for ever. In Belgium an independent
state grew out of a bourgeois revolution. In 1830-1 the Polish
War of Independence was once more suppressed. In Italy,

Switzerland and some small states in Germany there were bourgeois movements and uprisings.'
(Introduction to *Treasures of World Culture*, published by The State Museums of Berlin – Capital of the GDR, 1988 edition.)

The official GDR handbook-guide to the collections of Museum Island, from which these opening lines are quoted, makes creaky reading now, not least in its later outbursts of praise to the Soviet Union for saving Berlin's artistic heritage after the Second World War. Yet even its most tortured grapplings with two hundred years of European history cannot conceal all the facts. The handbook, by the way, is still available in museum bookstalls – at a knockdown price – and is worth getting for the colour pictures alone.

Museum Island was a hugely important cultural enterprise. It came about in response to a general public awakening throughout Europe, a realisation that the time had come for national artistic treasures to be made available to the people and not remain tucked away in royal archives and castle galleries.

The Altes Museum (Old Museum) was the first of five major museum buildings erected at the northern end of Kölln (Spree Island) between 1825 and 1830. Its first collections were of Antiquities and Paintings. Most of the Antiquities were brought here from the Antikentempel at Sanssouci Park, Potsdam. The Paintings consisted of more than 1,200 works, of which 677 came from the Solly Collection. Other collections were held for the time being at Schloss Monbijou, a royal summer residence to the north of Museum Island (obliterated in the Second World War).

Almost before it had opened the Altes Museum was too small for the weight of artistic treasures pressing for admission. The next solution was to build the Neues Museum (New Museum) directly behind it. This opened in 1859 and housed the Egyptian and Prehistoric Collections and the Engravings *Kabinett*.

The political and military successes of Prussia in the mid-nineteenth century created a wave of nationalistic self-confidence and led to the founding of a third museum. The Nationalgalerie opened after German unification in 1876, a Corinthian temple dedicated to trumpeting the glorious rise of Prussia. History pictures, portraits of generals and the nobility, battle scenes and studious landscapes were the stuff of this 'patriotic art store', which has suffered ever since from the banality of its founding programme.

Still more museum space was needed. Seized by the prevailing neo-Renaissance mood of his capital, Kaiser Wilhelm II authorised the building of museum number four, the Kaiser-Friedrich, which opened in 1904 and is now known as the Bode Museum after its founding spirit, Dr Wilhelm von Bode, who organised a mixed display in the new premises, a blend of art, furniture, sculpture, tapestries and precious objects. Finally, the questing spirit of Germany's nineteenth-century archaeologists was rewarded by the building of the Pergamon Museum. After long delays it opened in 1930, its centrepiece the west side of the great altar taken (looted) from its original site in Turkey.

The Second World War brought havoc to Museum Island. In 1939 all the museums were closed and most of their contents taken for safe keeping to bank vaults, cellars and warehouses, and to fortified bunkers under Zoo Station and at Friedrichshain. Other works were sent away from Berlin and buried in deep mines. On 3 February 1945 Museum Island was virtually destroyed by bombs. Reconstruction was slow and difficult but now all the museums, with the exception of the Neues Museum, are again alive and functioning. After 1945, however, they no longer possessed that part of their heritage which finished the war in the zones of the Western Allies. Many of those works were taken, first of all, to Wiesbaden and Celle and later returned to new museums in the Western sector of divided Berlin. Since the *Wende*, moves have been launched to reunite some of the severed collections, though this promises to be another long-drawn-out process.

The notes below list the principal holdings of each of the Museum Island buildings, and indicate plans to move collections to other sites in the reunited city.

Bode Museum

This walk approaches from the north, along the scruffy riverside road of Am Weidendamm, a section of the Eastern centre which the planners have yet to deal with. Around the curve of the river, the flattened dome of the Bode Museum commands the prow of Museum Island. Look along the narrow arm of the Spree towards the Pergamon Museum and the railway bridge where elevated S-Bahn trains slice between the two buildings.

The Bode Museum now acts as a holding-point for collections which may eventually be reunited elsewhere with their Western 'double'. The current arrangement of its multiple parts is as follows:

Ground floor Sculpture Collection, Early Christian and Byzantine Collection, Egyptian Museum and Papyrus Collection.

First floor Picture Gallery, Coin Cabinet, Museum of Pre- and Early History, Children's Gallery.

Staff cutbacks mean that some parts of the museum are not always open.

The **Sculpture Collection**, although it was the largest in the former GDR, suffers from being mainly confined to one room and a corridor and is dwarfed by its Western double in Dahlem. The two may be brought together at Dahlem after 1996. The Bode collection ranges from the twelfth century to the eighteenth; its strengths are in Late Gothic German works and Italian pieces from the High Renaissance.

The **Egyptian Museum** currently competes for attention with its Western half at Charlottenburg. At the Bode, despite reedy piped music in the background, there is much to enjoy: grave carvings, statues and large stone fragments, painted sarcophagi and gilded mummies. The Papyrus Collection is renowned, with some 30,000 texts.

In the **Early Christian and Byzantine** rooms the emphasis is on later medieval pieces, brought in to illustrate artistic continuity over the centuries. Dusty and rather dull, but includes a good Coptic section and the prized mosaic from the apse of San Michele in Ravenna (*c.*AD 545).

From the downstairs galleries an unworthy orange carpet winds up the grand staircase beneath the coffered dome. Set in niches around the landing are Prussian kings, princes and generals in Roman and contemporary dress. Of the warriors the best known are the cavalry generals von Ziethen (1699-1786) and von Seidlitz (1721-70).

The **Picture Gallery** is a poor relation to the Dahlem collection, and should be reunited with it in new premises at the Kulturforum after 1996. Highlights include works by Cranach the Elder, Poussin and Gainsborough. Look in at the small Miniatures Room which has paintings by Hans Bol, Cranach and Jan Brueghel the Elder.

It is also worth visiting the Children's Room (*Kindergalerie*) to see what is going on. A small theatre occupies the vestibule, and one day in the room beyond I found the walls covered with Rembrandt engravings, an overspill from a much bigger show at the Altes Museum.

Pergamon Museum

Walk along Am Kupfergraben to the bridge facing the massive recessed front of the Pergamon Museum. The entrance hall is a recent addition (1982) to the neo-classical design of A. Messel which was later modified by L. Hoffmann's Babylonian temple front (1909-30). Collect a map in the foyer (copies available in English). The building is divided between the following collections:

Ground floor and basement Classical Antiquities, Western Asiatic Antiquities, Museum of Ethnology.

First floor (wings) Small Classical Antiquities, Far Eastern Collection, Islamic Museum.

The Great Hall contains the crowning piece of the **Classical Antiquities Collection**, and of the whole museum: the Hellenistic Pergamon Altar, excavated in 1878-86 from its site in Turkey by Carl Humann and conveyed piece by piece to Berlin. The original altar was almost square in shape, measuring 36m × 34m (118ft by 112ft). Exhibited here is the west front, cut by a massive central staircase leading up to the arcade which flanked the inner altar court. Around the base of the building was a massive frieze depicting the struggle of gods and giants. The friezes from the other three sides of the building are displayed on the inner walls of the room. The violent animation of the figures is striking; even though much is missing, the eye travels easily from one image to the next.

Pergamon was built on the site of what is now the modern city of Bergama. It was raised in tribute to Zeus and Athena after a succession of military victories under Kings Attalos I and Eumenes II. To one side of the altar is F. Thiersch's 1882 tableau of the whole Acropolis.

Facing the altar, turn right to find another heavyweight: the Market Gate from Miletus, Turkey, a two-storey columned portal built AD 120 and recovered in 1903-5 by the archaeologists Theodor Wiegand and Hubert Knackfuss. On the floor of the hall is the Orpheus Mosaic, discovered in the dining room of a private house in Miletus and also dating from the second century AD.

Continue to the **Western Asiatic** section. Its most celebrated exhibit is the reconstructed Ishtar Gate from Babylon, built 604-562 BC in the time of Nebuchadnezzar II and dedicated to the gods Adad and Marduk. Towering walls of deep blue and ochre glazed brick are layered with reliefs of bulls and dragons. A scale model shows the enormous size of the original; the portal on view was merely part of the interior of a colossal gatehouse.

Similarly, the original of the nearby Processional Way was more than 20m (64ft) wide and some 250m (820ft) long. Follow its path, patrolled by lions between a double frieze of daisies, to the end hall.

Here is the Inner Gate of the Citadel of Sam'al in northern Syria (10th-8th century BC). The entrance is flanked by snarling lions and the dominant statues are a brooding figure of Hada, the god of the weather, and a giant beaky bird which squats on a nearby pillar.

In the basement is a **Museum of Ethnology** exhibiting traditional dress over the last century and the story of the museum from 1889.

From the Processional Way stairs lead up to the **Islamic Museum** on the first floor. In many ways this is a double of the collection in Dahlem, though stronger in its stone reliefs and tablets. The high point is the great bastioned façade of the Mshatta Palace (eight century) from present-day Jordan, presented to Germany in 1903. Exhibited here is a 45m (148ft) section of the principal front, the whole of which measured 144m (472ft). The walls are alive with triangular stone panels which enclose delicately worked motifs of leaves and fruit and forest animals.

Upstairs in the other wing is the **Far Eastern Collection**, containing archaeological discoveries, art and crafts from Japan and China dating from the Neolithic period to the twentieth century. After the Second World War the collection was almost entirely rebuilt with comradely gifts from the Government of China which sent ceramics, porcelain, jade, lacquerware and enamel. Also on view are modern silk pictures and woodcuts from China and Vietnam.

The Far Eastern exhibits occupy one long set of rooms. Intervening doors give access, bewilderingly, to the overflow collection of **Small Classical Antiquities**. To see these, it is best to go back to the stairway and work through again. Highlights are: Roman portrait sculptures, Attic black-figured vases and small, intricately detailed Boeotian terracotta figures of gods and idols.

Nationalgalerie

After a break – the Café Am Zeughaus is the nearest watering hole – return past the war-battered end of the Neues Museum to the first of Berlin's National Galleries. The other, Mies van der Rohe's black building in the Kulturforum, is usually known as the Neue Nationalgalerie, though confusions can occur.

This museum was designed by Schinkel's pupil Friedrich August Stüler and completed by Johann Heinrich Strack in 1876. Set over a two-storey lower section and entered from a sturdy double staircase, it is a splendid, much underrated building – a glowing deep red temple to the fine arts. In the gardens beside it stands an even more neglected arcade which, if it were restored, would be the finest river walk in Berlin.

The quality of the art within is disappointingly tedious, thanks to the restrictive Prussia-first policy which guarded its foundation. Although later gifts and acquisitions have improved the museum's scope, the walls of the nineteenth-century section make a sombre parade of portraits, landscapes, flower paintings and academic sculpture. In the surrounding torpor it is a relief indeed to find the occasional brighter piece by, for example, Menzel, Blechen and Liebermann.

Later the monotony is broken by a clutch of mostly French works: Cézanne's *Mill on the Couleuvre at Pontoise* (*c.*1881); a wonderfully rich *Landscape* (*c.*1915) by Maurice Vlaminck; Raoul Dufy's *Harbour* (1908); Maillol's portrait sculpture of *Auguste Renoir* (1919); Rodin's *The Thinker* (*c.*1862) and a pair of Degas dancers.

In the twentieth-century German rooms upstairs there is more to enjoy: look for Otto Dix, *Marianne Vogelsang* (1931); Lyonel Feininger, *Dämmerdorf* (1909), *Still Life with Brushes* (1915) and *Teltow II* (1918); Karl Schmidt-Rottluff, *Grünes Mädchen* (1914-15) and other works striking in their use of colour; Ernst Ludwig Kirchner, *Rhine Bridge at Cologne* (1914); portraits and views by Oskar Kokoschka; Gotthardt Kuehl, *Das Blaue Zimmer* (*c.* 1902) and Lesser Ury's *Nollendorfplatz* (1925).

Altes Museum

The symmetrical grandeur of Karl Friedrich Schinkel's museum is best seen from across the Lustgarten. The two-storey portico is extraordinarily wide – 87m (285ft) across. Its Ionic columns, eighteen in all, stride across the full width of the Great Elector's Pleasure Garden in an evenly spaced progress, their continuity reinforced by a line of eagles above the entablature. To the front of the grand staircase is a vast granite bowl formed from a single natural piece of rock and measuring 7m (23ft) across; to either side are the colossal equestrian statues of *Fighting Amazons* by August Kiss (1842) and *The Lion Fighter* (1861) by Albert Wolff.

Inside, the impressive coffered rotunda is banked with images of angels, signs of the zodiac and rosettes, and rises to a glazed summit. Around the perimeter of the hall, set between columns, are statues of gods, each one helpfully labelled – as of course they should be, but in many such buildings are not.

The Altes Museum is the third oldest in Germany, after the Fridericianum in Kassel and the Glyptothek in Munich. In 1830, when it was completed, it gave the people of Berlin a marvellous architectural showplace in which to contemplate and enjoy a relatively new world – the visions and reflections of art. Until then, few outside court circles had regular access to such a concentration of painting and sculpture.

The museum is now reserved for special exhibitions, usually of the touring international blockbuster variety. The change of use demonstrates, among other things, how greatly public tastes and requirements have advanced since museums first began.

Berliner Dom

It is hard to feel much enthusiasm for this bulbous usurper. In 1891, by Imperial command, it took the place of a widely admired baroque cathedral designed in 1747 by Johann Boumann and later remodelled by Karl Friedrich Schinkel. There can be little doubt which was the better building, but in the eyes of Kaiser Wilhelm II that was not the point. Berlin appeared to lack a sufficiently grand Protestant cathedral, suitable for state services in the Prussian manner. To this end the architects Julius Carl and Otto Raschdorff plundered the pomposities of the Italian High Renaissance and produced a building of acceptable height (113m/371ft) and capacity (up to four thousand could be bidden here).

In May 1944 the Cathedral was hit by fire bombs. Before firemen could arrive the upper dome and lantern crashed inwards to the pavement at the crossing. The loss has yet to be made good. Restoration was delayed until 1975, though from 1980 worshippers have been able to use the Baptism and Marriage Chapel which is entered from the side facing Karl-Liebknecht-Strasse.

In the meantime the restoration of the main church is an exhibition in its own right, and well worth a visit. From the gallery the visitor confronts an extraordinary spectacle. To a background din of relentless hammering and the whine of stonecutters the still shattered Cathedral stands revealed. The floor is a gutted grid of cross-beams and brick underpillars. The inner dome is shrouded horizontally with a giant striped sheet which luckily does not wholly mask the gilt relief work above, already completed, and the further tiers of scaffolding which climb up to the lantern. Ahead, carved figures above the altar stand wrapped in plastic sheeting, and the untreated pulpit is layered in thick plaster dust.

Progress on the exterior is more advanced. The west entrance on the Lustgarten is still partly blocked with crude metal fencing, but most of the upper part is finished, albeit to GDR standards. This is particularly apparent from the S-Bahn, where the view from the carriage window looks directly across to the new lantern – a cheap brassy addition that Kaiser Wilhelm would surely not have tolerated.

Walk 13 ✒

Kulturforum

Berlin's newest and growing centre for art and music. See the Bauhaus Archiv, Museum of German Resistance, Neue Nationalgalerie and Kunstgewerbemuseum (Applied Art).
Allow   5-6 hours.
Best times   Not Monday. Resistance Museum closes at 13.00 Saturday-Sunday and holidays.

ROUTE

Begin at Ⓤ Wittenbergplatz; Buses 119, 129, 142, 146, 185. Take Bus 129 to Lützowplatz and walk up to Landwehrkanal. Cross Hercules Bridge and bear right to entrance of **Bauhaus Archiv** 👁; open 10.00 to 17.00, Friday closes 20.00, closed Tuesday. *Admission*.

From *Archiv*, turn left along canal footpath to road at Reichspietschufer. At corner by Shellhaus, turn left along Stauffenbergstrasse to Nos. 13-14: **Museum of German Resistance (Gedenkstätte Deutscher Widerstand)** 👁; open 09.00 to 18.00, closes 13.00 Saturday-Sunday and holidays. Enter courtyard, turn left to south wing and go up to 2nd floor.

Return to canal road (Reichspietschufer) and turn left to next bridge. On left is Mies van der Rohe's black, flat-roofed **Neue Nationalgalerie** 👁; open 09.00 to 17.00, Saturday-Sunday opens 10.00, closed Monday and some public holidays. *Admission*.

At exit, turn left and left down steps to **Church of St Matthew (Matthäikirche)** 👁; open 11.00 to 17.00, closed Monday. Cross square in front of church to **Museum of Applied Art (Kunstgewerbemuseum)** 👁; open 09.00 to 17.00. Saturday-Sunday opens 10.00, closed Monday. *Admission*.

Facing the gold-plated lumps of the concert halls, aim for the upswept corner of the Philharmonie building and keep on to the entrance of the **Musical Instruments Museum (Musikinstrumenten-Museum)** 👁; open 09.00 to 17.00, Saturday-Sunday opens 10.00, closed Monday. *Admission*.

Go out to Tiergartenstrasse, turn right to Entlastungsstrasse which joins up with Potsdamer Strasse. Opposite is **State Library (Staatsbibliothek)**. Walk ends outside Neue Nationalgalerie. Nearest refreshments across canal in Schöneberger Ufer. Nearest Ⓤ Kurfürstenstrasse; Buses 129, 341.

From Wittenbergplatz

This is the easiest approach from central West Berlin. The 129 bus stop is the one on the corner of KaDeWe, facing Wittenbergplatz. In the central piazza, outside the cruciform pavilion of the U-Bahn station (1911-13), stands an oddly matter-of-fact signboard. It looks like the type used to announce destinations, which in fact it does, though these are no ordinary destinations. The wording reads:

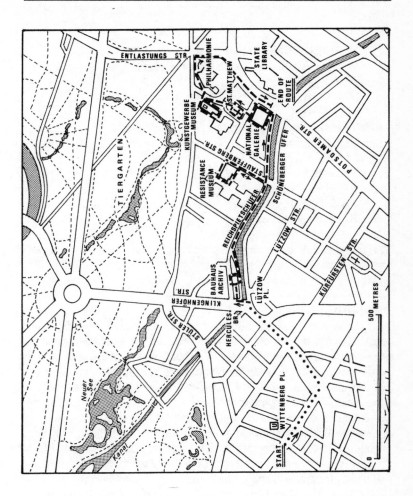

PLACES OF TERROR
WHICH WE SHOULD NEVER FORGET
AUSCHWITZ
STUTTHOF
MAIDANEK
TREBLINKA
THERESIENSTADT
BUCHENWALD
DACHAU
SACHSENHAUSEN
RAVENSBRÜCK
BERGEN-BELSEN

It is an apt pathfinder for anyone preparing to visit the Museum of German Resistance.

Bauhaus Archiv

At Lützowufer cross the Landwehrkanal by the Herkulesbrücke and walk towards the graceful curving walls of the Bauhaus Archiv or *Museum für Gestaltung* (Design). The building was designed in 1964 by Walter Gropius, co-founder of the Bauhaus Movement, and adapted to its present site in 1976 by Alexander Cvijanovic (it was originally to have been built on sloping ground at Darmstadt). Alas, its white walls have proved an irresistible target for graffiti sprayers.

Follow the steep walkway down to the entrance, past Max Bill's slender twelve-coloured mast. The Bauhaus School began life in Weimar in 1919, moved to Dessau in 1926 and later Berlin where it was banned by the Nazis in 1933. The archive traces the development of the Bauhaus style and exhibits many of the plans and completed works which raised the school to the fore in European and world design.

The section on the Weimar years (1919-25) records the period when Gropius recruited artist-teachers such as Lyonel Feininger, Paul Klee and Oskar Schlemmer, Wassily Kandinsky and Laszlo Moholy Nagy. Despite the growing recognition of the school, and its successful partnership with industrial concerns, it was closed down after six years by the conservative authorities of Thuringia.

The school relocated to Dessau and carried on its pioneering work under the successive leadership of Walter Gropius, Hannes Mayer and Mies van der Rohe. Famous individual pieces from this era are on view: Marcel Breuer's leather armchair (1925-6) and upright dining chairs (1928) – only their chrome is now less than brilliant; at the press of a button, activate Moholy Nagy's elegant *Licht-Raum-Modulator* (1922-30, reconstructed 1970), an assembly of metal grids, glass, plexiglass and wood which turns on a platform. Elsewhere look for plans and models of Bauhaus buildings: Gropius's Arbeitsamt, Dessau (1928-9) which features an uptilted roof presented in transparent sections to show the room layout beneath, and Mies van der Rohe's German Pavilion for the International Exhibition of 1929 in Barcelona, which has recently been restored on its exhibition site.

At the end of the circuit are a projection room and a neat and restful black and white cafeteria with a useful snacks menu.

Canal Walk

From the museum take to the canalside footpath which runs in front of a 'Greek' mansion, the Villa Von der Heydt (1862). Across the Landwehrkanal rise the daringly angled façades of the Grand Hotel Esplanade (1988), its drive-in discreetly masked by an inward-facing water-wall or cascade. Moored on the canal, the hotel's gigantic white pleasure boat is often to be seen, and uniformed chefs and waiters hurrying across the road with food trolleys and piles of white tablecloths and all the other apparatus of luxury which underpins a five-star twilight cruise.

Berliners are seldom slow to tell visitors that their city has more bridges than Venice. This reach of the Landwehrkanal is a particularly good place to announce the fact. Confronted with such evidence, the newcomer is less likely to reflect that Berlin is, well, rather bigger than Venice.

At Nos.72-76 Reichspietschufer is the old Navy Office, a gigantic office block erected in 1911-14 when Germany was in the final phase of a battleship-building drive with which Kaiser Wilhelm II and his naval chief Admiral Tirpitz hoped to overcome Britain's naval supremacy. Under the Third Reich the building became the headquarters of the Wehrmacht (Armed Forces, incorporating Army and Navy); today it serves in part as an AIDS centre.

Next in the architectural parade is the Shellhaus. Dingy now, with flaking walls and rusted window frames, its curving staggered tiers won international attention when it was completed in 1931. The best view of the Shellhaus is from the far side of the canal, from where the fluid drama of the terracing is most pronounced. Present occupants are Bewag, the Berlin Electricity Board.

Museum of German Resistance (Gedenkstätte Deutscher Widerstand)

Turn along beside the Shellhaus in Stauffenbergstrasse. In the Second World War this was Bendlerstrasse, and at Nos. 13-14 was the Bendler-block, an extension of the Wehrmacht office. In its rooms and corridors the chief plotters organised the July 1944 bomb attempt on Hitler's life (Operation Valkyrie). When it failed, the ringleaders were executed in the courtyard on the same night, the 20th July. General Beck pre-empted the firing squad by committing suicide; those who did not were Colonel Count von Stauffenberg, General Olbricht, Colonel Ritter Mertz von Quirnheim and Lieutenant-Colonel von Haeften.

In the courtyard is Richard Scheibe's 1953 monument to the re-sisters. A naked male figure faces a black strip on the ground which represents the firing stand. From 1968 the building housed a Memorial Exhibition, and in 1989 this was expanded to the present Museum of German Resistance which occupies the second floor on the south side of the courtyard (left from the entrance). Twenty-six rooms trace the growth of dissent in Germany as the National Socialists acquired more and more power, at first through workers' movements, Christian bodies and individuals, then through organised cells such as the White Rose in Munich and the Red Chapel Group in Berlin (the Harnack/Schulze-Boysen Organisation). Opposition to Hitler spread through the ranks of the military, culminating in the group which formed around von Stauffenberg, Chief of Staff at the Armed Forces Office. It was he who triggered and placed the bomb, concealed in a briefcase, beneath the conference table at the Wolf's Lair in Rastenburg. Minutes before the explosion, another officer at the conference shifted the suitcase to the far side of a heavy table leg, which unwittingly saved the Führer's life – he was seated only six feet away. Had the attempt succeeded, the plot-ters had complete plans to take over the country, plead for peace

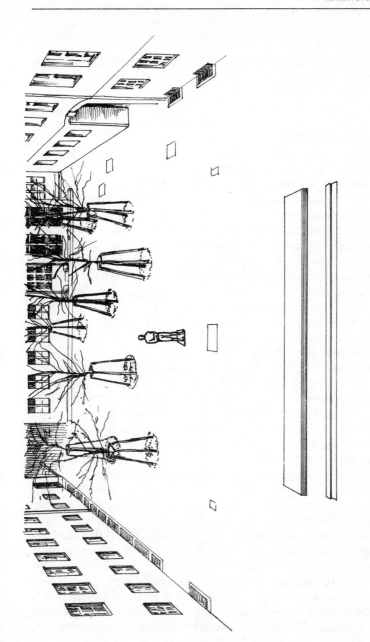

Victim before the firing stand – memorial in courtyard of Resistance Museum

and set up a new government headed by Carl Friedrich Goerdeler as Chancellor. He with many other conspirators was later executed at Plötzensee Prison (see *Walk 16*).

Neue Nationalgalerie

If the black superstructure of Mies van der Rohe's modern art gallery (1965-8) has been imitated by a million other canopied slabs, most of them serving as weather shelters for petrol pumps and their customers, this could be claimed a tribute to the flexibility of Mies's design. Perhaps its subtlety also, for despite appearances it really is only a superstructure, enclosing an entrance hall and adjoining space used for showing huge works like the Rauschenbergs and the Lichtensteins. The main part of the museum is downstairs in a set of largely windowless rooms equal in area to the black hangar and its surrounding sculpture terrace. The interior is very much the thing here, the building itself given no opportunity to interpose visual distractions.

The museum is the principal venue in Berlin for big shows of twentieth-century art such as the splendid Otto Dix retrospective of 1991-2 which marked the hundredth anniversary of the artist's birth. The standing collection, 'From Menzel to Picasso', occupies about half the downstairs space and consists of works from the Nationalgalerie on Museuminsel which ended the Second World War in Western hands, having previously been sent westward for safe keeping.

The collection begins in the first half of the nineteenth century with portraits and views by Adolph von Menzel and his contemporaries. Menzel was an acute observer of the conceits and follies of polite society, as well as the graver shortcomings of Prussian militarism. In *The Ball Supper* the guests try like anything to behave correctly but the demands of dealing with a buffet supper in their best outfits are nearly too much for some. An officer in silver epaulettes bends to fork up a chunk of meat while hanging on to a gilded plate with his other hand and clamping his goblet to it with a thumb. We have all had to do that at some time in our lives, but we did not also have to remember to keep our knees jammed together to hold our dress hat in place.

On the facing wall are a Delacroix nude, a shadowy Constable (*Higham Village on the River Stour*), then his *Admiral's House in Hampstead*; Daumier's *Don Quixote and Sancho Panza*: Courbet's *Cliffs at*

Etretat. Arnold Böcklin is well represented: a famous *Self Portrait with Death the Fiddler* (1872) and *Death Island* (1883) in which the funeral boat nears the steep rocks of the island burial ground.

The adjoining sections are mostly dull: academic renditions of a monastery, a lobster, a pair of hanging partridges, and so on. Then, after the soulful temptress of Franz von Stuck's *Sin* (*c.*1894) – a favourite with all compilers of Symbolist picture books – turn the corner into a new world of colour and light. This is the back gallery, facing a sunny sunken courtyard. Here too, light and warmth pour from a row of Impressionist views – Monet's fields dotted with poppies, parasols and women in summer dresses, and Renoir's charming *Afternoon with the Children at Wargemont* (1884).

Social earnestness resumes with works by Kokoschka and Max Beckmann's death-bed picture *Kleine Sterbeszene* (1906) hung next to his much later Expressionist paintings *Birth* (1937) and the nightmarish *Death* (1938). Two excellent scenes by George Grosz complete this section: *Grey Day* (1921) and *Pillars of Society* (1926) populated by drunks and old soldier wrecks. On to an eclectic grouping, a picture or two each by Léger, Braque, Gris, one of Robert Delaunay's *Eiffel Towers*, a case of collages and constructs by Arp and Schwitters, and other works by Magritte, Miró and Dubuffet. At the end Max Ernst's statue of *Capricorn* takes the eye, dominated by a bull-headed master of ceremonies gripping a staff and his mermaid escort who stares glumly down as though the fish piercing her skull has brought on a head-ache.

That seems to be all, but no, the cunning layout of the partitions has so far concealed a trove of Klees, among them the delightful *Departure of the Ships* (1927), their route indicated by a large arrow, and one of his cuboid townscapes in dreamy pale lemon and various blues, *Architecture* (1923).

Thread back past the Böcklins and Menzels to the main hall. If no food or drink has been sighted since the Bauhaus Archiv, try the comfortable, often crowded Café Buchhandlung next to the bookshop.

On the ground floor are large abstract paintings by such modern masters as Robert Rauschenberg, Morris Louis and Roy Lichtenstein and sculptures of variable quality. Best of these, or so I think, is Naum Gabo's spherical *Thema* (1970-1), a four-sided construct of wires fixed to a great wheeling outer saucer of stainless steel. So tactile is the cradle of wires, it merits a special 'Do not touch' plate screwed to the floor beside it.

Take a tour round the terrace, a sculpture park in its own right which would be even more enjoyable if the museum were not so cool about labelling its works. I can reveal that there is a *Herkules* by Matschinsky-Denninghoff in the north-west corner, but the author of the aluminium wind panels must remain a secret. Other sculptors may be more identifiable.

Kulturforum

From the terrace of the Neue Nationalgalerie, look north. We are standing on the fringe of the Kulturforum, a sprawl of museums and concert halls and a state library planned in the 1950s and '60s to connect with the Eastern half of the city when better times arrived.

It is easy to be unkind about the wasteland that greets your eyes: a 'Golden Car Park' is it? Shouldn't that building have a fried egg on top of it? And so on. Anodised gold cladding is certainly the key material which binds together these chaotic blockhouses – the paired Philharmonie and Chamber Music Hall and the State Library, and the utterly nondescript Museum of Applied Art. In the middle an appalling acreage is given up to car parking. The massed roofs of all those BMWs, Opels and Mercedes will never be an adequate exchange for the lawns and fountains which could be here.

A further upheaval is scheduled here for 1996, when the Picture Gallery at present at Dahlem is due to arrive. At one time there was a plan to build no fewer than five museums of European art at the Kulturforum, but political changes and shrunken budgets have reduced this prospect. Just as well, really. Who could bear slogging round them all in one day? People do, of course, it is one of the more demented aspects of tourism which I try to combat in my *Slow Walks* books. No museum need be visited simply on the grounds that it is *there*. In Berlin, however, museums tend to exist in massive huddles, with six to a dozen collections between them. In the end the visitor must decide for himself or herself when the time has come to pack it in for the day and look for something more soothing, like cakes and ice cream. All the same, I wish the city authorities could find it in themselves to be a little less hell-bent on *trying to please*.

Matthäikirche

If strength persists, and I freely admit this walk has been heavy on culture despite the warnings implicit in its title, there is one more worthwhile museum – the Applied Arts collection. On the way, walk down to
Friedrich August Stüler's Matthew Church (1844-6). It is a striking
Italianate building but isolated and too often lacking a blue sky and a
warm sun to burnish its striped brickwork. Its compartments are perhaps too regular – the box-like nave and side aisles, the apses and
tower. The interior has a very different character, coolly refurbished
with rows of chairs and pews painted pale grey, an angular slatted roof
and a three-pointed organ case in the gallery. Above the altar a large
Crucifixion hangs from chains invisibly anchored behind the curve of the
central apse. The walls may be adorned with a temporary exhibition of
pictures, and against the second column of the east aisle is a *Head of
Christ* by Gerhard Marcks.

Museum of Applied Art (Kunstgewerbemuseum)

Of all the museums in the Kulturforum the Applied Arts is the biggest
visual disaster, bereft of all external character like a jumble of building
blocks which a child has assembled to make a fortress and then partly
knocked over. Visitors are not slow to complain, comparing it un-
favourably with Dahlem and generally griping about the lack of landscaping and walkways between the *Kultur* buildings.

Inside, the collection is housed neatly but confusingly on four main
floors. The entrance level (*Zugangsgeschoss*) is the second from the
top. To follow the exhibits chronologically you have to go first down one
floor, then back up two and finally down three. From top to bottom the
order is:

**Upstairs (Obergeschoss) – Renaissance, Baroque, Jugendstil
and Art Deco**

Groupings in the low-ceilinged, grey carpeted sections are by type, retaining a necessary control over the profusion of glass, silver, porcelain, stoneware, pewter, ivory and rhinoceros horn, and wonderful
cabinets with decorated drawers and lids. In 'Baroque-Rococo
Fayence' are vivid green-coated huntsmen, their liver and white
hounds and lumbering, snarling boars at bay. The early Meissen figures
and larger pieces cast a rare spell: courtly couples and harlequinades,
an elephant candelabra, bacchantes and musicians. The inlaid

mirror chamber from Schloss Wiesentheid is a wonder. Move shortly to 'Jugendstil' and smoky plantiform glass by Emile Gallé and the Daum Brothers. Glittering Art Deco dresses from Paris, jewel boxes and enamelled vases complete the exhibits on this floor.

Entrance Floor (Zugangsgeschoss) – Information Galleries, Cafeteria and Shop

Ground Floor (Erdgeschoss) – Middle Ages to Renaissance

The first room, celebrating the medieval goldsmith, offers the Enger/ Herford Treasure, the Guelph (German *Welf*) Treasure and ecclesiastical and secular pieces. Among the museum's greatest prizes are the *Domed Reliquary* (Guelph, *c*.1175) and the *Reliquary Cross* (Enger/Herford, *c*.1100). Another marvel is the gold *Heinrich Cross* from the Abbey Treasure in Basel, inlaid with precious stones, crystal and a carved ivory head.

On to Renaissance tapestries, majolica and glass, then metalwork including the silver *Mary and Child* (*c*.1500) partly gilded and decorated with pearls and semi-precious stones; wheel-lock muskets and a hand bombard with elaborate inlays from stock to muzzle; jewel boxes and cups and the silver *Universal Bowl* with zodiacal figures.

Lower Ground Floor (Untergeschoss) – Modern Crafts and Design

In 1920 Marcel Breuer optimistically wrote, of chairs: 'From year to year it is getting better and better. You end up sitting on an elastic column of air.' He must have sat on something not visible here, if anywhere. These rooms demonstrate the modern chair as it really is – with repeated injunctions not to sit on any of them, which, given Breuer's quotation displayed at the entrance, is the first thing you might think of doing. Then at last, in a side gallery, comes an offer to try out a few. The next question is, all right, but would I want one of these in my house? The sight of them, in rows, reminiscent of the waiting room of a progressive dentist, followed by the experience of them, angular if not downright spiky, nowhere for your head or arms, may at least help to explain why chiropractors do so well these days.

Other showcases attempt to interest us in modern pottery. Much more fun is the round-up of twentieth-century product design: clocks, lighters, typewriters, telephones, kettles and hairdryers, from which the Twenties emerges as the triumphant pioneering decade.

At the end of the visit, a longish walk through the copiously detailed

Information Galleries leads to a very smart and comfortable cafeteria serving hot and cold lunches, snacks and drinks. Probably the best museum café in Berlin.

Concert Halls and Musical Instruments Museum

Out to the unlovely car park. This walk is all but done, and now indeed may be the time to quit as nothing else in the neighbourhood is as engaging as what has gone before. Proof of this is soon established by the view across the gold-plated carapaces of the Philharmonie, West Berlin's most prestigious concert hall. This was the first of two music buildings to arise at the Kulturforum, in 1960-3. Now it is attached to the Chamber Music Hall/Kammermusiksaal (1984-7), the bigger lump next to it, rather like a cement mixer done up as a wedding present. The architect Hans Scharoun was largely responsible for both projects.

If there are one or two reasonable viewpoints from which to look at the Philharmonie, the other building defeats every effort to like it. Apparently, however, this is all quite immaterial. Both halls were planned from the inside out. The first priority to absorb the architects was the central platform for the orchestra, and then they concentrated on seating the audience in tiers around the platform. Then they walled in what they were left with and coated the exterior with perforated gold plates. The acoustics are excellent, and audiences appreciate their good view and comfortable surroundings. This must all be borne in mind. Merely standing on the street outside and criticising the look of these concert halls will certainly get you nowhere in Berlin architectural circles.

As for getting into a concert, that may be even more frustrating. Berliners have a way of scooping up the seat allocations several months in advance, and little will be left by the week beforehand. It is always worth a try, though, especially for the smaller concerts.

The Musical Instruments Museum inhabits a low Brutal block to one side of the Philharmonie. Enthusiasts will find plenty to enjoy among the harpsichords, harmoniums, pianos and organs interspersed with wind and string instruments in showcases, harps on stands and various instruments for producing oompah music. In the gallery is a Folklore Room for concerts, and a saxophone family all in a row. Touching the exhibits is strictly out of order, but there are plenty of opportunities for listening on earphones to, say, Gerhard Kastner playing cembalo (harpsichord) in Pasquini's *Partita sopra l'Aria della Follia d'Espagna*. Up the stairwell from the Sim Café floats the jolly sound of fairground or beer garden music supplied by a 1920 Orchestron, a frantic mechanical combination of drums, pianola, cymbals, glockenspiel, saxophone and much besides. The museum is really for specialists, though good too for children if they can be induced to keep their fingers off all those tempting keys and strings.

On the way back to the bus stop outside the Neue Nationalgalerie, or onward down Potsdamer Strasse to the U-Bahn station, pass the Staatsbibliothek or State Library, last of 'the Golden Symphony', designed by Scharoun and Edgar Wisniewski and completed in 1978. Visitors to Berlin may freely benefit from the comfortable reading room next to the front hall, stocked with foreign newspapers and armchairs placed thoughtfully to face outwards for views of the Neue Nationalgalerie and the Matthew Church.

Walk 14 🦅

Charlottenburg: Palace and Museums

A baroque palace with massive lateral extensions, a vast park, a Belvedere, a dark Mausoleum and Schinkel's version of a Neapolitan villa. Add to these a clutch of good museums in the palace and neighbouring buildings across the main road.

Allow   All day. (Many visitors will want to spend more than a day at the Charlottenburg complex, which luckily is just a quick train or bus ride from Kurfürstendamm.)

Best times   Not Monday for Palace. Not Friday for Egyptian Museum and Collection of Antiquities in Schloss-strasse.

ROUTE
Begin at Ⓤ Richard-Wagner-Platz and take Bus 145 to front of Palace, or arrive directly by Buses 109, 145, 204.

Schloss Charlottenburg
Cross courtyard past statue of Great Elector Friedrich Wilhelm to front of **Palace** ☞; open 09.00 to 17.00, Saturday-Sunday opens 10.00, closed Monday and some public holidays. Guided tours only of royal apartments. Check time of next departure in front hall. *Admission; best value is a combined ticket* (Sammelkarte) *covering all palace buildings (except special exhibitions in Orangerie) and valid for one year.*

From central block, bear left through door to New or Knobelsdorff wing containing, upstairs, Rococo Golden Gallery and White Hall, and on ground floor the **Romantic Gallery (Galerie der Romantik)** ☞; opening hours as above. Paintings by Caspar David Friedrich, Schinkel, Blechin, Gärtner *et al*.

Refreshment break Facing W wing, on Spandauer Damm side, is Kleine Orangerie café-restaurant; pricey but convenient.

In W wing see **Great Orangery (Grosse Orangerie)**; open for occasional exhibitions (*separate Admission*).

In end block of W wing (Langhans building) is **Museum of Pre- and Early History (Museum Für Vor- und Frühgeschichte)**; opening times as above.

Palace Grounds
Walk out past Knobelsdorff wing to grounds. Ahead is **Schinkelpavillon** ☞; opening times as above. Drawings and paintings by Schinkel and contemporaries, similar in spirit to Romantic Gallery.

Continue in gardens beside River Spree to far end grounds and **Belvedere** ☞; opening times as above. Good collection of Berlin porcelain.

Wander across grounds to W side to find **Mausoleum** ☞, the royal burial shrine; summer opening times as above, closed November to March.

Return to front of Schloss, having probably done enough for one day. Good refreshments across Spandauer Damm at Eosander café-restaurant, with conservatory front and summer terrace. Nearest transport, same as for arrival.

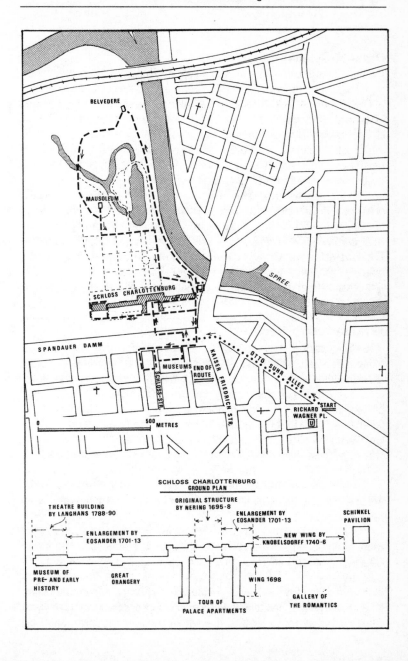

BELVEDERE

MAUSOLEUM

SCHLOSS CHARLOTTENBURG

SPREE

SPANDAUER DAMM

SCHLOSS-STR.

MUSEUMS END OF ROUTE

KAISER FRIEDRICH STR.

OTTO SUHR ALLEE

RICHARD WAGNER PL.

START

0   500 METRES

SCHLOSS CHARLOTTENBURG
GROUND PLAN

ORIGINAL STRUCTURE
BY NERING 1695-8

THEATRE BUILDING
BY LANGHANS 1788-90

ENLARGEMENT BY
EOSANDER 1701-13

SCHINKEL
PAVILION

ENLARGEMENT BY
EOSANDER 1701-13

NEW WING BY
KNOBELSDORFF 1740-6

MUSEUM OF
PRE- AND EARLY
HISTORY

GREAT
ORANGERY

WING 1698

TOUR OF
PALACE APARTMENTS

GALLERY OF
THE ROMANTICS

Other Museums
Perhaps another day, try museums facing front of Palace in Schloss-strasse, beginning with domed former barracks at head of street.

On E side at No.70 is the **Egyptian Museum (Ägyptisches Museum)** ☜; open 09.00 to 17.00, Saturday-Sunday opens 10.00, closed Friday. Home of famous bust of Queen Nefertiti.

Across road at No.1 is **Collection of Antiquities (Antikensammlung)** ☜; open as Egyptian Museum. Noted for Attic vases, jewellery and Hildesheim Silver Find.

At No.1a is **Bröhan Museum** ☜; open 10.00 to 18.00, Thursday open until 20.00, closed Monday. *Admission*. Best collection in Berlin of *Jugendstil* (Art Nouveau) furniture, glass, porcelain and pottery.

Also in Schloss-strasse, at No.69, is museum of local history, the **Heimatmuseum Charlottenburg**; open 10.00 to 17.00, Sunday opens 11.00, closed Monday, Saturday.

Return to Spandauer Damm. Refreshments and transport, as above.

Schloss Charlottenburg

The Palace is one of those grand buildings it would be best to approach along a two-mile driveway. The huge breadth of the orangery wings, their modest height in relation to the central tower and its heavy bull's-eyed French cupola, the creamy warmth of the stucco – all deserve to be absorbed slowly by the oncoming eye. And so they once were, for when the Palace first took shape in the end of the seventeenth century, Charlottenburg was still in its infancy and quite separate from Berlin, whose nearest gateway stood on the far side of the Tiergarten.

Here in 1695, close to the village of Lützow, the Elector Friedrich III authorised the building of a new town and a summer residence for his second wife Sophie Charlotte. Even after he had crowned himself King of Königsberg (Prussia) in 1701 and launched the first phase of en-largement at the Palace, a cousin of Sophie Charlotte was making no more than an astute prediction when she said, 'Because Berlin and Charlottenburg are so close together, they might one day become just one city.'

Today only a few metres separate the Palace front from the traffic-laden boulevard of Spandauer Damm; the approach across the cobbled courtyard is all too brief and the whole of Charlottenburg has been

Charlottenburg Palace

swallowed by the metropolis. Immediately ahead is a famous interloper. Andreas Schlüter's powerful equestrian statue of the Great Elector Friedrich Wilhelm (1640-88) was first erected in 1703 on the Lange Brücke near the Berliner Schloss. Then in 1943, as the Allied bombardment intensified, it was loaded onto a Spree barge, ready to be shipped to safety. The barge broke its moorings and wandered off on a strange journey, eventually coming to rest half-sunk in the Tegeler Hafen. In 1949 the statue was finally recovered and cleaned, and installed in this courtyard three years later.

The core building at the centre of the Palace was a fairly modest pavilion designed by Johann Arnold Nering, the Elector's Chief Director of Buildings. In 1701, when the Elector became King and needed a more prestigious building, he brought in the Swedish architect Johann Friedrich Eosander who had worked in France for the court of Louis XIV. The cupola and West Orangery wing were designed and built in the next twelve years.

Palace Apartments

Sophie Charlotte was an intellectual queen, a friend of artists and philosophers. She wanted her palace to become a desirable meeting-place for cultured guests who enjoyed music, art and abstract discussion. The style of the royal apartments reflects her taste for lavish but controlled ornamentation, for beauty without the self-aggrandisement that some Prussian monarchs found irresistible. Alas, much of the Palace was burnt down in 1943 and most of what we see is the result of painstaking restoration rather than original work, but the effect is convincing and the replacement furniture, pictures and porcelain were acquired with great discernment.

From the entrance hall the conducted tour of the ground-floor rooms (for which gigantic slippers must be worn) leads to a large model of the Palace and then to the First Wood-panelled Room and the Queen's Bedchamber, its walls covered with alternating long mirrors and green damask panels. Then we reach the Green Antechamber hung with eight wall carpets depicting the story of Amor (Cupid) and Psyche, and the Oval Hall which projects beyond the garden front. Next are the Gobelins Rooms, each hung with tapestries from a series of 'Watteau Scenes'. On to the Reception Room, its vaulted ceiling set with stucco figures representing the Arts and Sciences, then the pilastered Red Braid Room decorated with red damask and gold braid appliqué. Continue to the Study and Bedchamber of Friedrich I, his adjoining Marble Bath and the magnificent Porcelain Chamber. Return from here past a Bedroom with a ceiling painting of *Night and her Children*, a Dressing Room and the Writing Chamber of Sophie Charlotte. The ornate Chapel is nearby, but open only for concerts in summer.

Knobelsdorff Wing

The New Wing on the east side was the creation of Frederick the Great (1740-86). After the austere reign of his father Frederick William I – whose main contribution to Charlottenburg apart from general upkeep was to stock the pond with carp and see the herb garden and Orangery were well tended – the new king showed immediate enthusiasm for the Palace. In the first weeks of his reign he commissioned Georg von Knobelsdorff to design a matching wing to Eosander's western extension, though without a second orangery. The New Wing was to be a royal residence; its grandest room, the Golden Gallery on the upper floor, was completed in 1746.

Go upstairs and turn right to find a series of small rooms richly decorated with gilt and silver, finely restored after the blitz of 1943. Here is Frederick the Great's cedarwood Library from Sanssouci (*c.*1768) and the bedroom of Queen Luise, wife of Frederick William III. Although the quality of the paintings is mediocre, the courtly portraits of the prolific Antoine Pesne (1683-1757) are at least consistently adequate.

To the left of the stairs are the White Hall, which occupies the central pavilion of the wing, and the Golden Gallery. Pesne's original ceiling for the White Hall proved impossible to copy after the room was damaged by fire in the war (there being no other evidence of the original colours) and we must put up with a 'contemporary paraphrase' created in 1972-3. In the Golden Gallery the green stucco marble of the walls has been magnificently restored and no surface left untouched by the rococo gilder's art: candelabra as twisted tree branches, door panels and mirrors brimming with cherubs, helmets, amorous courtiers, fruit, flowers and violins. Beyond in the Concert Room hangs Watteau's

Trade Sign for the Art Dealer Gersaint (1720) and in the Gris de Lin chamber his *Embarcation to Cythera*.

Gallery of the Romantics

This enjoyable small museum was installed at the Palace in 1986 and focuses on painters of the German Romantic Movement. To the right of the hall are the looming landscapes of Caspar David Friedrich (1744-1840), heavy with imposed spiritual qualities: figures glimpsed through overbearing mist and cloud, isolated in some place at the edge of the world, at a crucifix on the Riesengebirge or silently watching the moon. Nature alone evokes the mood in *Cloister among Oak Trees* (1809-10) and *Oak in the Snow* (1829).

Paintings by Karl Friedrich Schinkel (1781-1841) celebrate his enthusiasm for Gothic cities and cathedrals, and there is an 1824 self-portrait of the artist in Naples. For Carl Blechen (1798-1840) the romantic impulse is here represented in a gravestone, a ruined cloister, a *Mountainous Landscape with Monk* and a *Mountain Gorge in Winter* (both 1825). He exalts the power of nature in waterfalls, and depicts a darkly Romantic sky over Sanssouci. Beside the passion of these works his Italian scenes look saccharine, over-idealised.

To the left of the hall are sentimental landscapes by Weidmüller and more interesting topographical pictures by Eduard Gärtner – *Unter den Linden* (1853), the red *Bauakademie* (1868) and *Parochialstrasse* (1831). Look also for Johann Erdmann Hummel's *Granite Basin in the Lustgarten* (1831).

Orangery and Langhans Building

Close to the New Wing is the Schinkel Pavilion, and the next logical move is in this direction, followed by a turn round the park. However, at some stage refreshment is inevitable and may be taken most efficiently at the café in the western quadrangle. From here one may like to take a look at the Orangery. Now reserved for special exhibitions, it was the centrepiece of Eosander's enlargement, completed in 1713. At the far end stands the Langhans Building. This was designed by Carl Gotthard Langhans in 1788 as a theatre for Frederick William II, who reigned from 1786 to 1797 and helped to establish the spirit of the Enlightenment *(Aufklärung)* in Berlin.

The Langhans Building now houses the **Museum of Pre- and Early History (Museum für Vor- and Frühgeschichte)**. Its most regular visitors are parties of German schoolchildren, brought here for the well displayed overview of early civilisation in Europe and the Near East. Of special interest are the rooms devoted to early German cultures (first to fourth centuries AD), the Migration Period which followed the invasion of the Huns, and the growth of Slav settlements in the seventh to twelfth centuries. Many examples are taken from the excavations at the *Burgwall* in Berlin-Spandau. The period ends with the conquest of lands east of the Elbe by German feudal nobles (robber barons is a closer description) and the establishment under the Askanian dynasty of towns such as Berlin, Brandenburg and Spandau.

Schinkel Pavilion

This charming symmetrical pavilion was designed by Karl Friedrich Schinkel and carried out by his eminent pupil Albert Dietrich Schadow in 1824-5. Its function was to trigger echoes of Italy in the mind of Frederick William III (reigned 1797-1840), who wanted a Mediterranean summer residence where he could live with his morganatic wife Augusta, Countess of Liegnitz. Burnt down in 1943, it was restored in 1957-70.

Many of the exhibits are a sympathetic continuation of the Romantic Gallery: state porcelain, engravings, landscapes by Schinkel and topographical views by Blechen, Gärtner and others. These include two wings of Gärtner's 1834 *Panorama* of central Berlin, seen from the roof of Schinkel's Friedrichswerdersche Church – each half a triptych bent into facing corners of a small upstairs gallery. In an adjoining room, the same artist's triptych of *Moscow* (1839) is presented flat on one wall.

The Park: Belvedere and Mausoleum

From the Schinkel Pavilion stroll out into the park and follow the riverside path along the eastern perimeter. At the top end of the grounds is the Belvedere, designed in 1788 by Langhans as a teahouse. Three-tiered and topped by cherubs holding a gilded flower basket, it now serves as a **Museum of Berlin Porcelain**. Romantic and Biedermeier pieces are shown on all three levels, joined by a spiralling staircase: a profusion of dinner and coffee services, decorated with gods and goddesses, 'clothed cherubs', poets and statesmen, and a very plastic bust of Frederick the Great by F.E. Meier (1778).

Close to the Belvedere is the white *11 March* obelisk, designed by the Yugoslav artist Braco Dimitrijevic in 1979 and placed here as a focal point in line with the north-south Carp Pond and the central block of the Palace.

Wander westward through the wilder 'English' part of the grounds, arriving eventually at the Mausoleum, a Doric temple designed by Schinkel in memory of Queen Luise, who died in 1810. She was a popular queen and remains something of a folk-heroine to this day, largely thanks to her handling of the peace negotiations with Napoleon.* Her tomb and memorial sculpture, by Christian Daniel Rauch, is by far the finest of the four figures lying in the main chamber. Berliners lay flowers at her feet and can be heard to mutter to each other, 'She was too good for him, poor woman,' – gesturing sideways at the tomb of her husband – as though she had died only a few months ago. The other principal tombs are of Emperor William I and his wife Queen Augusta.

Return to the Palace front via the Bogenbrücke, where 'clothed cherubs' in coloured stone cavort on pedestals by the water. A visit to Charlottenburg is essentially a Romantic day, a journey round the playground of Queen Sophie Charlotte for whom it was built. Across the formal French gardens on the balustrade of the garden front, twenty large modern figures, erected in 1978, re-create the spirit of the past – leaping playfully, each brandishing an instrument to extol the Arts and Sciences: a harp, a trumpet, an abacus, a pair of dividers. Much of the early life of the Palace was lived in these gardens. At the Elector's birthday celebration of 1700, a particularly famous occasion, the Elector and Sophie Charlotte joined the masked company dressed as a sailor and a doctor's wife. The philosopher Leibniz was allotted the part of an astrologer, which he carried out by retiring to a distance and observing the fireworks and the dancing through a telescope.

---

* This task had been too much for her husband, Frederick William III, described to me by an amateur historian as '*ein Schwächling und ein Pisser*' (a weakling and a drunk).

Museums in Schloss-strasse

A first visit to Charlottenburg could well end here, or across the road on the terrace of the Eosander café-restaurant which faces the Knobelsdorff Wing of the Palace on the far side of Spandauer Damm.

Three further attractions stand close by, two of them housed in the domed mansions at the head of Schloss-strasse. These were designed by Friedrich August Stüler in 1852-9 to enhance the approach to the Palace. At first they served an unlikely role as barracks for the Royal Bodyguard, but after the Second World War they were converted into museums to accommodate artistic treasures which had fallen into Western hands. As such, they were a rather makeshift counterpart to their Eastern cousins on Museum Island. Now the city is united, a new solution is needed to circumvent the doubling-up process which has given Berlin two Egyptian Museums, two Islamic, two of Classical Antiquities, etc.

Chief highlight of the **Egyptian Museum**, in the eastern *Stülerbau*, is the limestone bust of Queen Nefertiti (*c*.1340 BC). In Cold War days her graceful profile and swan neck became an icon of West Berlin culture. Although the collection is relatively small, there is much to enjoy in the form of mummy masks, painted sarcophagi, votive objects and the reconstructed Palace Gate of Kalabasha (*c*.20 BC), a monumental entrance standing 8m (26ft) high in Nubian sandstone.

Across the road, beyond the Iron Cross in the pavement and the militaristic statue of Prince Albrecht of Prussia (1809-72), is the **Collection of Antiquities**. Here are tiny votive bronzes of the ninth to seventh centuries BC, from Crete and Greece, and Attic vases depicting athletes, gods and heroes, with enough erotic scenes to satisfy the groups of students who range these galleries. On the lower ground floor is a good jewellery section with three rooms of ancient gold ornaments and the Hildesheim Silver Find of Roman table silver from the first century AD, and jewellery and coins from Rome and the Early Christian era.

More unusual is the private Jugendstil (Art Nouveau) collection housed in the **Bröhan Museum** at 1a Schloss-strasse. The museum covers Jugendstil and Art Deco paintings, furniture, ceramics, silver and glass from 1890 to 1939. Though well displayed in spacious rooms, many of the paintings are bland and much of the furniture now seems uninspired, somehow stuck on a cultural bridge waiting for the Bauhaus to happen. Recommended pieces: paintings by Hans Baluschek; café-society heads in the shape of bacchantes from the Wiener Werkstätte; animals and candleholders from the Majoliker-Manufaktur Karlsruhe; porcelain musicians by Robj and bronze figures by Jean Lambert-Rucki. On the top floor is Josef Hoffmann's elaborate chair, a *Sitting Machine* of 1905, and a fine silver display in the galleried Treasury (*Schatzkammer*).

Walk 15 🦅

Dahlem

The great museum complex in a quiet south-western suburb.
The building houses a brilliant collection of European paintings
from c.1300 to 1800, and many other small museums of
Eastern art as well as a large ethnographic collection. Selective
viewing is called for. Continue with a stroll through the
terraces and hothouses of the nearby Botanical Gardens.
Allow All day.
Best times Not Monday.

ROUTE

Begin at Ⓤ Dahlem-Dorf; Buses 110, 180. From station exit, turn right along Iltisstrasse. At end, a choice of routes:

A. Turn left in Lansstrasse to new main entrance of **Museum building** ☞. Best access from here to **Museums of Indian Art**, **Islamic and Far Eastern Art** and **Ethnography**.

B. To see the paintings of the excellent **Gemäldegalerie** in chronological order, turn right in Lansstrasse and walk round block to old main entrance in Arnimallee. Early Italian Masters (1300–1600) are in rooms to left of entrance hall.

Note This order of things should hold good until about 1996, when the Gemäldegalerie is due to move to new premises in the Kulturforum.

Dahlem Museums open 09.00 to 17.00, Saturday-Sunday open 10.00, closed Monday and some bank holidays. *Admission*.

From whichever museum exit, turn right along Lansstrasse or left along Arnimallee to Königin-Luise-Strasse, then right downhill to front of **Botanical Gardens (Botanischer Garten)** ☞. Museum open 10.00 to 17.00, closed Monday. Gardens open 09.00 and close as follows: January-February 16.00, March 17.00, April 19.00, May-August 20.00, September 19.00, October 17.00, November-December 16.00. *Admission (at gate or in museum building)*.

Walk through, visiting hothouses, and leave at exit on far side of Unter den Eichen. Cross to Begonienplatz and keep on to Hortensienstrasse. Turn left to Ⓢ Botanischer Garten. Walk ends here.

This line, S1, runs through Anhalter Bahnhof and terminates at Oranienburg. For an interesting final excursion, get off at Anhalter Bahnhof. From station, cross square to Anhalter Strasse and look for café-restaurant sign at foot of tall block on right. Here take glass lift which climbs outside of building to 16th-floor **Berlin Fenster** for outstanding views over city. From here, nearest Ⓤ Kochstrasse; Bus 129.

Which Museum?

To keep it simple, Dahlem is not one museum but several (six principal collections and two minor, the Junior Museum and the Museum for the Blind). The building has two main entrances and it is a good idea to choose in advance which collections to aim for. Once inside, it is awfully

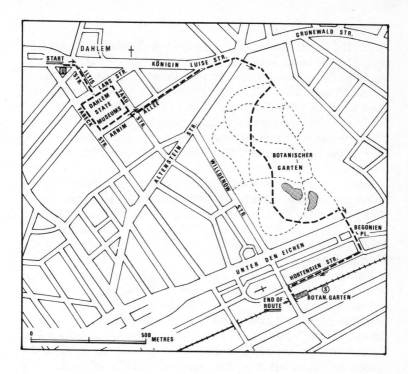

easy to get lost. The various sections are bewilderingly interleaved on the two main floors; something or other is always being shifted, and key thoroughfares blocked off for rebuilding. Sometimes you wonder if you will ever escape from the stony gaze of Mexican gods, or whichever deities command that corner of the labyrinth in which you find yourself going round in circles.

Below, and in the Route section, are suggested paths for two virtually separate tours. The museums' guide/*Wegweiser* plan, available at the entrance, may be helpful too, but is certainly not easy to follow.

Picture Gallery (Gemäldegalerie)
From the entrance hall on Arnimallee, turn left to a wonderful collection of **Early Italian Masters** (1300-1600). A range of altarpieces leads to

Room 114 and the luminous conceptions of Fra Angelico, part of a retable by Masaccio, Fra Lippo Lippi's *Mary Venerating the Child*, and works by Veneziano, Piero della Francesca, Pollaiuolo and Piero di Cosimo. There is a small Botticelli room – *Mary with the Child and Singing Angels* (*c.*1477), *Profile Portrait of a young girl* (*c.*1480), *St Sebastian* (1474) and a version of his famous *Venus Rising* figure in the Uffizi, Florence. In a facing side room is Giovanni Bellini's *Body of Christ supported by two Faithful Angels* (*c.*1480) and his *Mary and Child*.

The collection continues with Raphael's Madonnas, including the pale *Madonna Colonna* (*c.*1508) and the early tondo, the darker more forceful *Madonna Terranuova* (*c.*1505). The Venetian room nearby has a warm *Self Portrait* by Titian (1550-62), his *Venus with the Organ Player* (*c.*1550-52) and Tintoretto's *Portrait of Giovanni Mocenigo* (shortly before 1580).

That, anyway, is the disposition of the Early Italian works at the time of writing. Eventually, the entire Paintings Collection will move to a new site in the Kulturforum and its gallery space here will be occupied by the Sculpture Collection. It is also possible that the 'Dahlem' pictures will be joined by other masterworks currently housed in former East Berlin – those at the Bode Museum are one example. In any event the Dahlem Picture Gallery is very short of space and only able to show half its collection of 1,500 works at any one time. In the long term, a move to larger premises is inevitable. Latest reports indicate it will happen in about 1996.

German and Netherlandish Rooms

In the meantime the present groupings of this marvellous assembly are likely to remain valid for the next three years. The next rooms to visit, to the right of the entrance hall, contain the German and Netherlandish sections. Here is a *Pietà* by Hans Baldung Grien (*c.*1517) and his fascinating *Pyramus and Thisbe* (*c.*1530). Magical pictures and allegories by Albrecht Altdorfer share a gallery (138) with portraits by Albrecht Dürer. At the far end are brilliant small portraits by Jan van Eyck of *Giovanni Arnolfini* (he of the marriage picture in the National Gallery, London), *Baudouin de Lannoy* (*c.*1430) and the delicate and intensely detailed *Madonna in the Church*.

Continue to Rogier van der Weyden's acutely perceived triptychs –

the *John the Baptist Altar, Middleburg (Bladelin) Altar* and *Mary (Miraflores) Altar*. There are works too by Hans Memling and Dieric Bouts. In Room 145 are Lucas van Leyden and Brueghel the Elder, and round the corner is Brueghel's famous *Netherlandish Proverbs* (1559), illustrating more than a hundred proverbs in episodes testifying to man's insanity and sinfulness in a godless world. Each room in this section could be an hour-long feast for those with the appetite. Nearby are the restrained Hieronymus Bosch of *John the Baptist on Patmos*, Joachim Patenier's *Rest on the Flight into Egypt* (1520), the *Lament of Mary Magdalene* (*c*. 1525) by Quinten Massys, and the meditating *John the Baptist in the Desert* by Geertgen Tot Sint Jans, beside the monumental crypt scenes of Hugo van der Goes.

Baroque Masters
Return to the entrance hall and go upstairs to find the Flemish and Dutch Baroque Masters, and further rooms representing the baroque and rococo periods in France, Italy and Spain. Here, in Room 240, are Rubens, Jordaens and Van Dyck. Tucked behind them (243) are works by Pieter Saenredam (*The Ambulatory at St Bavo in Haarlem*, 1635) and genre pictures by Jan Steen, Gerard Terborch and Pieter de Hooch, and Vermeer's *Pearl Necklace* (*c*.1664). Keep on to Room 238 for a splendid collection of Frans Hals portraits. Then, in 236-5, relatively sidelined but still one and a half rooms when you reach them, are the Rembrandts. They include a portrait of his wife *Saskia* (1643), a *Self Portrait* (1634), *Old Man in a Fur-lined Coat* (1645), *Man in a Golden Helmet* (*c*.1650-55) and the *Rape of Proserpina* (*c*.1630).

Return to the end and turn left for works by El Greco and Velásquez, followed by the rooms of Caravaggio, Poussin and Claude Lorrain. In the end room is a fine assembly of Canaletto's Venetian landscapes, including the unfamiliar *Vigil of Sta Marta* which with the *Vigil of San Pietro* constitute the artist's only nocturnal pieces.

Cranach and Holbein
Back on the ground floor the final wing of the *Gemäldegalerie* has a magnificent Cranach room. Here is one of Lucas the Elder's famous *Lucretias* (1533), the sword to her bosom, a pair of *Venus and Amors* (*c*.1530 and *c*.1537), and *Adam and Eve* in the Garden with stag and lion (1531) and the extraordinary *Spring of Youth* (1546), in which old and

decrepit women are carried out of a barren landscape to the magic pool, there to be rejuvenated as beautiful maidens who dance off to a changing tent and join the men in dancing, dining and amorous dalliance. The men, it seems, need no ritual bath to restore their beauty but draw it without effort from the company of the young women.

In Room 133 are many portraits of Hans Holbein the Younger – *Count Anton the Good of Lothringen* (1543) and the *Merchant Georg Gisze* (1532) surrounded in his counting-house by scales, weights and coinage. In the last two rooms, the eighteenth century in France, England and Italy is represented by a broad mix of paintings. The resolutely middling Antoine Pesne, a near-monopolist at the Palace of Charlottenburg, is not surprisingly here too, with better work by Nicholas Lancret – an undated *fête champêtre* entitled *The Italian Meal* – and François Boucher's *Resting Venus with Eros* (*c*.1742). A group of Watteaus is dominated by *The Dance* (*c*.1719) in which the charming girl protagonist is outlined against a sky of pallid blue.

Room 131 is an English room with pictures by Reynolds, Sir Thomas Lawrence and Gainsborough – his calm portrait of *Joshua Grigby* (1760-5) and a more fluid group of the ruby-lipped *Marsham Children* (1787). Room 130 is much occupied by Panini's topographical views, and there is an interesting self-portrait by Angelika Kauffmann in the role of a *Bacchantin* (1785).

From here, turn briefly through the Sculpture Gallery to reach the front hall at the Lansstrasse entrance. Downstairs is a very adequate cafeteria, and on the way the bookshop sells a large range of postcards, slides, posters and books.

Museums of Indian, Islamic and Far Eastern Art; Museum of Ethnography

The three art museums might more properly be called departments, each devoted to a part of the oriental tradition. The scale is small, the collections displayed in no more than eight rooms or so, but of a rich-ness and variety that should more than satisfy the casual visitor.

The **Indian Museum** is on the ground floor, and incorporates works from Nepal and Tibet and a South-East Asian collection of casts from the temple reliefs at Angkor Wat: a double row of vibrant and bloodthirsty battle scenes between gods and demons. The main part of the exhibition focuses on figures, busts and reliefs of Indian deities. The stone reliefs grow ever more complex; the bronzes are shown in a long narrow room beside silk wall hangings of a simple beauty, the largest the *Great Temple Picture* from Nathadvara, Rajasthan. Look also for a striking wooden *House Temple* (Gujarat, eighteenth century); portal panels; and eighteenth-century book illustrations – brilliantly coloured pictures offering a feast of court scenes, royal portraits, banquets, courtship and a polo match.

Upstairs in the **Islamic Museum** the decorative tone is set by the fine collection of carpets from Turkey and Iran which hang from the walls and ceiling. All Islamic countries are represented, including Moorish pieces from medieval Spain and Venice. The range includes ceramics and glassware, jewellery and metal vessels, and illuminated texts from the Koran.

The strength of the nearby **Far Eastern Collection** lies in its paintings, which survived the Second World War when much of the early collection, housed in the Martin-Gropius-Bau, was destroyed. Among the greatest treasures are *River Landscape*, a hanging scroll attributed to Tang Di (fourteenth century) and a hand scroll by Fan Qi called *Landscape on the Yangtse River* (seventeenth century). To guard against light damage, paintings and prints are rotated every three months.

The **Museum of Ethnography** poses more of a challenge, being spread around the building in a variety of rooms specialising in American Archaeology (2 on museum's plan-guide); Oceania (3); Africa (7); Southern Asia (11) and East Asia (14, on the small top floor). Most popular of all is the hall of the Oceania/South Seas Collection, which has a number of large-scale exhibits. They include rigged sailing ships with long raked masts as well as outrigger canoes and other more modest folk-boats; also the fronts of reconstructed communal houses from New Guinea and a men's long house from the Palau islands.

Botanical Gardens

From the museums building it is a short walk past the faculty buildings of the Free University to Königin-Luise-Strasse, then the way is agreeably downhill to the front of the Botanical Gardens. The Botanical

Museum in the adjoining building is old-fashioned in layout and design, and is best left to experts and enthusiasts. Much better value are the gardens themselves.

Walk up past the deciduous and beech woods to the bulbous fronts of the Glasshouses (*Schaugewächshäuser*), as steamily satisfying as any of their kind. Coats may be left at the *Garderobe*. Follow the circuit (*Rundgang*) signs to the right. Haus G is particularly impressive, where the bromeliads grow in a jungle of thick-leaved lusciousness. Move on through Tropical and Subtropical Ferns. Turn up steps by a *Monstera deliciosa* to find that the *Kigelia africana* is known in these parts as the Liver-Sausage Tree (*Leberwurstbaum*).

The Orchid Room is a delight, and in the tall Palm House are banana leaves of stupendous length, puffy with fine ribs. Nearby, parents point out the coffee and chocolate trees to their children – *Coffea arabica* and *Theobroma cacao* – and all marvel at the furry, whitish marrow-sized pods of the *Benincasa hispida* pumpkin.

From the Glasshouses walk down the terracing and cross towards the exit on Unter den Eichen. Next to the gate is a café with a large garden. The walk to the S-Bahn station is thoroughly botanical. 'Under the Oaks' faces onto Begonia Square. Continue past the intersection with Geranium Street and Tulip Street and keep on via Carnation Street to Hydrangea Street. Turn along here past Lily Street and at Gentian Street emerge by the station which has a fine ticket hall in Egyptian Jugendstil (by Erdmann and Spendler, 1908) and a florist's fragrant shop.

Skyscraper Views

The S1 line runs into the city centre, stopping at Anhalter Bahnhof, once a grand terminus before it was destroyed in the Second World War. Only a fragment of the old statued yellow-brick portal has survived. The surrounding square looks at first glance to be in the middle of nowhere, though in reality the Martin-Gropius building and Potsdamer Platz are just round the corner.

Near the foot of Anhalter Strasse seek out the sign to the Berlin Fenster café-restaurant. From inside the front door, take the glass lift which scales the building to some of the best close-up views of central Berlin. From a table by the panoramic windows look down to the Gropius building and the low white shed of the Topographie des Terrors and the viewing platforms in the gardens. These face a stretch of surviving Wall, the old Goering Air Ministry building and the gaunt House of Ministries. Look over these to find, from west to east, the saucer roof of the Kongresshalle, the Reichstag and top of the Brandenburg Gate, then across to the gilt-medallioned domes of the French and German Churches and the Berliner Dom.

Even though we are on the West side of the Wall, the cuisine and service at the Berliner Fenster sometimes have all the charm of an Eastern bloc café during a food shortage. But the views . . . the views are matchless.

Walk 16

Plötzensee Prison

A visit to the execution chamber at Plötzensee Prison, where some 2,500 men and women were put to death under the Nazi regime. Walk on through the neighbouring *Kleingarten* colonies – the Berliners' own patch of countryside in the city. **Allow** 3 hours.
Best times Any day with dry weather.

ROUTE

Begin at Ⓢ Tiergarten. Take Bus 123 north through the Hansa Viertel and Moabit to Saatwinkler Damm and get off at first stop after Ring Road (announced in bus as 'Gedenkstätte Plötzensee').

Cross road and follow narrow Hüttigpfad to **Memorial** entrance ◉ ; open 08.00/08.30 to 16.00/18.00 according to time of year (08.00 to 18.00 March to September). Cross courtyard past memorial wall to execution chamber and documentary room.

At exit, turn left beside small houses of garden colonies. At large colony map, go ahead along Meterweg. Take 1st left into Krümmerweg. Take 2nd left along Kurzer Weg and 2nd left into Riedemannweg.

At end, walk to bus stop and catch Bus 123 either back to city or onwards past Volkspark Jungfernheide to Siemensstadt (a complete suburb set up for employees of Siemens, the engineering and computer manufacturers). From Ⓤ Siemensdamm, return to city centre.

North from Tiergarten

From beneath the S-Bahn bridge to Bahnhof Tiergarten, Bus 123 turns up to the Hansa Quarter, a model estate on the north-west fringe of the park. After the Second World War the quarter lay in ruins. Its revival began in 1953, and in 1957 the district became the focus of Berlin's International Building Exhibition. Distinguished architects from four-teen countries and a team of garden designers contributed to the new mixed estate of tall blocks and low apartment houses set at a variety of angles in a green environment and provided with churches, a shopping centre, cinema, library and kindergarten. In the Cold War years the Hansa Viertel was West Berlin's response to the totalitarian architec-ture with which the Communists had swamped the old streets of Friedrichshain.

The bus continues across the Spree to Alt-Moabit, an old working-class neighbourhood with cobbled side-roads and some blocks sadly run-down. Overall, though, and particularly in comparison with East Berlin, the shops are busy, there are few graffiti and the general mood, if less than prosperous, suggests that bourgeois aspirations have long held the upper hand.

Up by the Ring Road (Stadtring), the Westhafenkanal, the wholesale Berliner Grossmarkt and the Moabit goods yard leave a thick scar

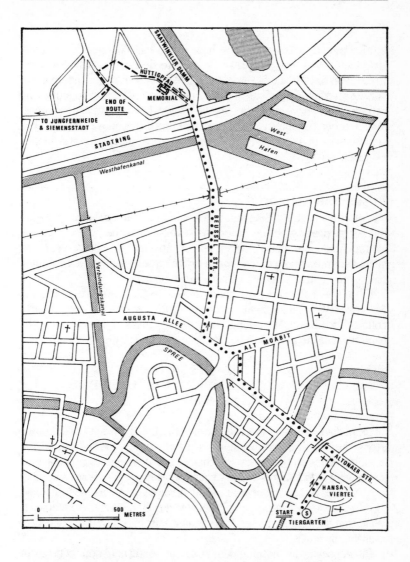

across the map, marking the edge of human habitation in the inner city. From the first bus stop in Saatwinkler Damm, cross the thundering truckway beside the canal and enter the secluded confines of Hüttig-pfad, which leads to the memorial gate.

The way is narrow and the high brick wall on one side is aptly forbidding. Now the old prison is used to detain juvenile offenders. From 1933 to 1945 it was the last destination of hundreds condemned to judicial murder. Conscious of this, it needs no poetic leap to feel a kind of hovering menace. Imagine, fifty years ago, being brought down here, under the wall, seeing the tall brick chimneys rising above, the kind you seldom see in cities except outside prisons, hospitals and lunatic asylums.

Prison and Memorial

Under Hitler's rule, Plötzensee Prison had all the qualifications for a modern bedlam, with the gruesome reversal that the jailers were the lunatics, the sane their reluctant guests, an appalling twelve-year succession of men and women whose brave dissent had failed a common test – they had been caught by the Gestapo.

From the gate the path opens into a large courtyard facing the Memorial Wall. To the right, a stone urn with a bronze lid contains earth collected from concentration camps in Germany. On the wall, wreaths hang from stone inserts. The simple inscription reads:

TO THE VICTIMS
OF THE HITLER DICTATORSHIP
IN THE YEARS 1933 – 1945

Immediately behind the Memorial Wall stands a brick building, one storey high with barred windows and two shallow arched entrances. The first leads to the execution chamber, the second to an exhibition room where documents try to explain what happened here. The material is displayed on wallboards and supplemented by a useful free booklet: *Plötzensee Memorial*, published by the Gedenkstätte Deutscher Widerstand (Memorial Sites of German Resistance), Berlin; copies are available in English.

Plötzensee was nothing less than an extermination centre for enemies of the state. Most of these perceived enemies were German. After the court had pronounced sentence, prisoners were brought here, then eventually moved to the cells of a 'death house'. When their time came they were led to the execution chamber. This grim room is today much as it was then, apart from a guillotine which was removed at the end of the war. Across the chamber runs a heavy metal beam to which eight iron hooks were fixed; five are still in place. A black curtain divided the room in half. Each prisoner was brought through in turn and marched behind the curtain. The executioners placed a noose around his neck, then hoisted his body up and looped the other end of the rope over one of the hooks. When the prisoner was released, his body dropped and death in most cases followed quickly.

Before bringing in the next victim, the executioners pulled small side curtains across to conceal bodies already hanging from the hooks. Working in batches of eight, they killed off the condemned with a factory-like precision. One night in 1943, they dispatched 186 people in this room.

These final acts of terror began in 1933, as soon as Hitler became German Chancellor. In the years that followed, the civil courts passed more than 14,000 death sentences, the military courts upward of

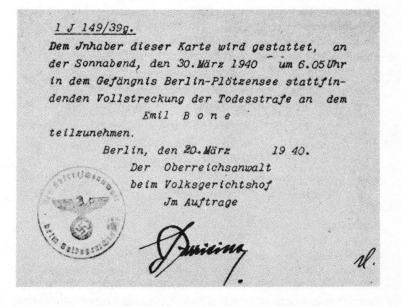

Ticket to watch an execution, 1940

40,000. The victims were Communists, Social Democrats, Christians and others who in some way, however small, had indicated their disagreement with the National Socialists and their police state. Some belonged to organised factions, others distributed leaflets without any formal attachment. Most famous of the dissenters were the organisers of the July Bomb Plot of 1944. The active ringleaders, including Count von Stauffenberg, were shot in the courtyard of the Bendler Block, Tiergarten; hundreds more were rounded up for trial and of these eighty-nine were put to death at Plötzensee. Some, on Hitler's specific orders, were executed by the slow and much crueller method of garrotting. Hitler also commanded cameramen to film the executions, for viewing later, such was his rage at the conspiracy and all who had some involvement in it.

In 1954, on the tenth anniversary of the July Bomb Plot, Federal President Heuss paid tribute to the courage of all the resisters. Those taking part in the plot had showed their determination to 'rescue the state from this murderous, evil regime and, if possible, save the Fatherland from utter destruction . . . The shame into which we Germans were forced by Hitler was washed from the sullied name of Germany by their blood. The legacy remains a living force; our obligations have not yet been fulfilled.'

One day in 1992, while returning from Plötzensee in the U-Bahn, I took more than usual notice of two stickers on the carriage window. One said:

NO MORE WAR
NO MORE FASCISM

The other raised an even more pressing cry: 'NEO-NAZIS STOP!' Weeks later the extreme right-wing Republican vote took another bound forward in the regional *(Bundesländer)* elections. New waves of economic refugees from Eastern Europe and asylum-seekers from the Third World were beating at the gates of prosperous Germany, and the new slogans of the right carried uncomfortable echoes of the past. 'Germany for the Germans' was the main official message, but clearly it cloaked a multifarious growth of hatred towards foreign immigrants. Now this hatred is directed towards Slavs, Arabs, Africans and others who are seen – yet again – as racially unacceptable. It could easily include Jews as well. There is little reason to suppose that the friends of the swastika have altered their views.

Down Lime Blossom Way

Apart from the Memorial Wall and the execution block there is little to see at Plötzensee Prison, but after the little that you *do* see it is a relief to leave the place. Calming, then, to turn and amble through one of the 'small garden' colonies which border Hüttigpfad. Each cluster of dwellings has its own suitably saccharine title – Lime Blossom Colony, Good Hope, Alpine Rose, Fountain of Youth – redolent of that other Germany where stout pink-faced pensioners slumber in the shade of a vine.

The *Kleingarten* tradition is strong throughout Germany, where so many families live in apartment houses and yearn for a piece of green space they can escape to at the weekend. To judge from the television aerials and plumes of smoke rising from the chimneys in winter, many of these summerhouses are warm and cosy enough to be inhabited all through the year. The designs are modest and rarely rise beyond the garage-as-bungalow concept, and most are evidently self-built. Each garden is an individual haven of fruit trees, ponds with gnomes and windmills, tiny lawns and vegetable beds, all tightly packed together. Cars are limited to a few broader arteries, and most of the paths are sandy tracks for cyclists and pedestrians, like those we traverse on the way to the bus stop.

Here the route divides. Return by Bus 123 to the city centre or travel onwards to take a look at the admittedly grim estate of Siemensstadt. It lies on the far side of Volkspark Jungfernheide – a concrete encampment founded for the workers of Siemens AG, the engineering giant. One trip there is usually enough.

Walk 17

Sachsenhausen Concentration Camp

Pass through the grey streets of Oranienburg to the preserved
site of Sachsenhausen 'Protective Custody Camp', set up in
1936. Between then and 1945, more than 100,000 prisoners
were beaten, starved and left to die, or were executed.
Allow 6 hours.
Best times Not Monday.

ROUTE

Begin at ⑤ Oranienburg, north of Berlin. Direct trains run on cross-city S-Bahn lines from Potsdam-Wannsee and Berlin-Schönefeld; about one hour from central Berlin.

At station exit, facing Post Office, turn right on August-Bebel-Strasse. At crossroads with Oranienburg's main street, Strasse des Friedens, turn right under railway bridge. Keep on beside cobbled roadway for about 600m, then turn left into Strasse der Einheit. Follow for 400m, then at plaque to Death March (*Todesmarsch*) turn right along Strasse der Nationen to entrance gates.

The camp's official title is **Sachsenhausen National Warning and Memorial Site (Sachsenhausen Nationale Mahn- und Gedenkstätte)**l; open April to September 08.00 to 18.00, October to March 09.00 to 16.30, closed Monday. At kiosk by entrance gate see start times for cinema. About 50m into grounds, a shop sells guide plans and other publications (former available in English; recommended).

The account below follows a route from Tower A to Roll-Call Square, Museum, Monument, Station Z, Pathology Department and Jewish Barracks.

Return to exit and follow road back to station. Refreshment possibilities at *Imbiss* stands near camp or in town at Café Lena, corner Strasse des Friedens facing road to station.

In the Train

The S-Bahn train rolls placidly out to the northern fringe of Berlin, past marshalling yards and factories. The profile of the city grows lower, the older blocks of flats no more than four storeys high at Pankow-Heinersdorf. Then long colonies of *Kleingärten* – summerhouses with gardens and tiny orchards – flank the railway track.

The landscape of the Brandenburg Plain is relentlessly flat, not an appreciable mound to break the view. On the platform at Berlin-Blankenburg, where travellers to Oranienburg may need to change trains, the prospect is like standing in the middle of a giant plate (the world), the rim of which never seems to be more than the nearest clump of birch trees away, reachable within five minutes in a reliable Trabi.

The interval between stations opens out. In early spring the land is a brown scrub of dried-out grasses and marsh plants, and here and there

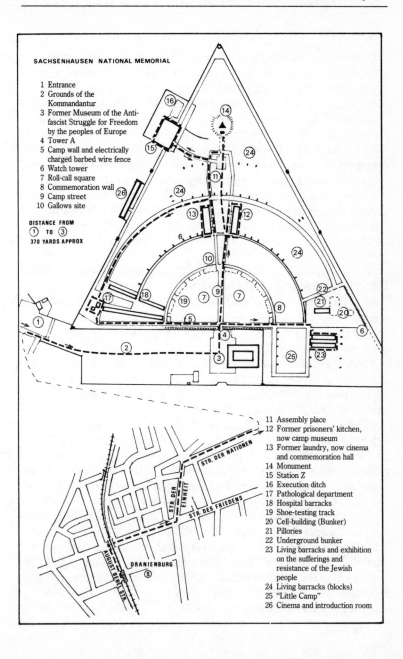

SACHSENHAUSEN NATIONAL MEMORIAL

1 Entrance
2 Grounds of the Kommandantur
3 Former Museum of the Antifascist Struggle for Freedom by the peoples of Europe
4 Tower A
5 Camp wall and electrically charged barbed wire fence
6 Watch tower
7 Roll-call square
8 Commemoration wall
9 Camp street
10 Gallows site

DISTANCE FROM ① TO ③ 370 YARDS APPROX

11 Assembly place
12 Former prisoners' kitchen, now camp museum
13 Former laundry, now cinema and commemoration hall
14 Monument
15 Station Z
16 Execution ditch
17 Pathological department
18 Hospital barracks
19 Shoe-testing track
20 Cell-building (Bunker)
21 Pillories
22 Underground bunker
23 Living barracks and exhibition on the sufferings and resistance of the Jewish people
24 Living barracks (blocks)
25 "Little Camp"
26 Cinema and introduction room

beside some pond an exposed beach of yellow sand, the soft substratum with which all living things here must come to terms. The stationmaster at Schönfliess, two platforms and a bridge in the middle of a field, blinks through a cloud of flying grit as the train draws out. In his dark blue uniform and red cap he seems an alien figure, marking time in the empty brown land.

After Bergfelde (though no *Berg* was sighted) comes a stretch of woodland, thick stands of silver birch and pine beside the line, running along to Hohen Neuendorf. From Borgsdorf the mixed woods continue to Lehnitz, which has a scattering of houses with tall gingerbread roofs. Then the train winds in through the decrepit industrial outgrowth of Oranienburg.

Oranienburg to Sachsenhausen

This small town dozing at the head of the S-Bahn line might be left to terminal peace were it not the site of an infamous concentration camp, one that can rank with any in the range of atrocities committed there under the Third Reich.

From the station it takes fifteen to twenty minutes to walk to the camp, which is located in the suburb of Sachsenhausen. The way is signposted with a logo suggesting a crematorium chimney and the words 'SACHSENHAUSEN – NATIONALE MAHN- UND GEDENK-STÄTTE' (SACHSENHAUSEN NATIONAL WARNING AND MEMORIAL SITE). Town traffic – juggernauts, trucks loaded with brown coal, vans, cars and motorbikes – bumps along the cobbled road of the Street of Peace (Strasse des Friedens). At the corner of Strasse der Nationen is a memorial to the Death Marches ordered at the end of the war. In April 1945, as the Russians advanced through eastern Germany, prisoners from Sachsenhausen and other camps were force-marched across Brandenburg towards the Baltic (Ostsee). The aim was to put the prisoners on board ships and sink them in deep water. The marches followed Himmler's directive of 14 April 1945: 'No prisoner is to fall into enemy hands alive.' Six thousand of the marchers lost their lives before Soviet tanks caught up with the toiling columns and liberated the prisoners.

Concentration Camp

After the Information Centre near the gate a notice explains that now Germany is 'united in freedom and peace', it is possible to remember also those who 'sacrificed their freedom, health and lives under the Soviet occupying power and the injustices of the GDR'. These revisions were being worked on at the time of writing. To what extent the promised 'reorganisation of the memorial site' turns out to be a convenient rewriting of history remains to be seen.

The long tree-lined avenue from the entrance continues, unvaried and mournful. A thought takes hold: something dreadful is waiting at the end. Apprehension grows, as it might for someone attending a first funeral.

Something dreadful *is* waiting, but all that immediately awaits is an empty hall. Up to the *Wende* this was the Museum of the Antifascist Struggle for Freedom of the Peoples of Europe. The building stands on the site of former SS garages. A notice explains that the museum is being reorganised following the 'free and sovereign decision of the peoples of East and South-Eastern Europe to redetermine their political and social position'. When it reopens, no doubt with a shiny new title, the museum will house special exhibitions relating to the post-1945 period. From August 1945, under Soviet control, the camp was redesignated 'Speziallage Nr 7 Sachsenhausen', one of a number of camps where prisoners were held for internment or after they had been tried and sentenced. Special Camp No.7 operated until 1950. It will be interesting to see how its role is accounted for.

Tower 'A' and Roll-Call Square

The camp proper begins at Tower 'A', the former main entrance. The iron gate bears the motto, chilling in context: 'ARBEIT MACHT FREI' (WORK MAKES FREE). The tower block contained the offices of the camp's administrators and the switchboard controlling the electric perimeter fence. It stands at the base of the camp's triangular layout, the sides of which were guarded by eighteen control towers. To the right is a preserved stretch of barbed-wire fence and two small signs planted in the perimeter track. One shows a skull and crossbones and the other warns:

NEUTRAL ZONE
Anyone seen here will be shot
immediately without warning.

Ahead is Roll-Call Square (*Appellplatz*). Prisoners assembled here three times a day to be counted, and had to stand for hours in all weathers when collective punishments were ordered. Around the edge of the square runs the shoe-testing track, where the camp command tried out the durability of substitute materials on an assortment of street surfaces, from rolled gravel to rough cinders. For the prisoners this meant a forced march of some 40km (25 miles); weighted sacks added to their misery. At the top of the square a stone marks the site of the camp gallows. All prisoners were called out to witness public executions.

Camp Museum

Beyond the gallows the prisoners' huts stretched away in a series of arcs towards the apex of the camp grounds. The wooden barrack houses are gone, each site marked by a numbered slab of granite about the size of a sarcophagus. One of the surviving buildings (Point 12 on the official plan) was the prisoners' kitchen. It now serves as the camp museum.

Inside, a map shows the alarming total of camps and their distribution in Germany: more than 2,000 in all, including the subsidiary feeder camps located around the principal establishments. They were built originally as so-called Protective Custody Camps (*Schutzhaftlager*). Their inmates were political prisoners, rounded up and held there until they died of physical deprivation. Later the camps were retitled Concentration Camps (*Konzentrationslager*).

Sachsenhausen camp was built in 1936 with war in mind. The evil and duplicity of National Socialist policies by then took many forms. In those same months, while Hitler presided at the Berlin Olympics, five hundred prisoners (*Häftlinge*) were transported here from Esterwegen, Lichtenburg and Sachsenburg. By the outbreak of war in September 1939, 60,000 were imprisoned here and in outlying camps around Berlin and to the north towards Ravensbrück which had its own network.

Sachsenhausen was the closest major camp to Hitler's capital, and here the Government set up a training school for camp commanders and other officials. Nearby was the office of the Concentration Camp Inspectorate, later known as SS Official Group D responsible for administering all such camps in Germany and occupied territories.

Who was sent to Sachsenhausen? Most of the prisoners came from Germany, Poland and the USSR, and many were Jews. They were grouped by offence and wore triangular patches which labelled them variously as political prisoners, criminals, anti-social elements, homosexuals, the workshy and other categories including several for various kinds of Jew. For every man or woman, regardless of origin, there was always a label to fit. Out of more than 220,000 prisoners brought to Sachsenhausen from at least twenty European countries, more than 100,000 died or were put to death there.

In the museum the displays follow a well-laid-out sequence of documents, information boards and reconstructions, grouped by theme. A section on accommodation shows the three- and four-tiered bunks in which the cold and hungry prisoners slept on straw mattresses. The work section shows the forgery workshop, principally manned by Jews who were later killed to keep their work secret. Here, it is claimed, some £132 million sterling was forged in £10 and £20 notes, of which 'a part' went into circulation. Probably this part was very small; German attempts to forge British currency generally failed to make the hoped-for penetration. This would have been small consolation to the workforce.

Prisoners were made to work for up to fourteen hours a day. Those who became sick faced almost certain death. Nazi doctors used patients in the camp hospital to carry out experiments with chemical prototypes: new gases, the effects of various poisons, heart drugs and remedies for typhus, blood-poisoning and other illnesses.

Punishments were no less gruesome. They ranged from extra duty on the shoe-testing track, or building new cells, to being strapped to a whipping block for fifteen to a hundred lashes; to being hung by the wrists with an iron chain fixed to upright posts; to being deprived of food for days, or being sent to the black pit of the underground *Erdbunker*.

The camp authorities applied their large and helpless work-force to many profitable ventures. In April 1942 Himmler's deputy, SS-Obergruppenführer Pohl, described the changing position as the war grew more burdensome. Merely keeping undesirables prisoner in order to subdue them was no longer enough: 'The main emphasis has been shifted to the economic side. The mobilisation of all prisoners as manpower, firstly for the tasks of war (increasing armaments) . . . is being pushed more and more into the foreground.'

The SS concluded lucrative deals with arms, chemical and other manufacturers. They hired out their 'livestock' of prisoners and in return received huge fees (up to 50 million Reichsmarks a month) for virtually no outlay except in lives exhausted. What financial costs they did incur were coldly set against the receipts from such firms as Heinkel, IG Farben, Krupp, Siemens and Daimler-Benz. The costs per prisoner were worked out thus:

Daily average wage	6,00 Reichsmarks (RM)
less food	0,60 RM
less wear and tear on clothing	0,10 RM
	5,30 RM

at an average lifespan of
9 months = 270 days × 5,30 RM =   1,431 RM

There were further profits to be made from the dead prisoner. These were described as 'proceeds from the rational utilisation of corpses' and were added to the balance sheet:

gold teeth	
clothing	
valuables	
money	
less cost of cremation	2,00 RM
average net gain	200 RM
Total gain after 9 months	1,631 RM

Station 'Z'

From the museum, walk up to the camp monument, the 'crematorium chimney' of the camp logo, carved with eighteen inverted triangles to represent the eighteen categories of prisoner. The pillar commemorates all soldiers and civilians who lost their lives at Sachsenhausen and lists twenty countries of origin from *Albanien* (Albania) to *Ungarn* (Hungary).

Cross the bleak compound. Trees now grow here, and grass and clover, and the groans and screams of prisoners have long yielded to silence. What took place here is not so distant in time. Many can remember some personal fragment of those years.

To understand the horror of Station 'Z', and the slaying method practised there with factory timing, it is best to look first at the model in front of this strange roofed-over assemblage of ruined buildings. Station 'Z' was an extermination centre. It was used, against all international laws, to dispatch Soviet prisoners of war as fast and cheaply as possible. About 18,000 Soviet solders were killed off here, though exact records were not kept. Later in the war, prisoners from the Eastern Front were sent directly to places such as Station 'Z', and their names were no longer entered in the camp records.

A prisoner entered the building thinking he was about to receive a medical examination. He went through a door to the Undressing Room, then into the Doctor's Examination Room. Then he was taken through another door and made to stand against a wall facing an eye chart. Behind him was an aperture, in some camps concealed by a height chart. Behind the aperture an SS soldier waited in the next room. The prisoner was shot in the neck, then dragged into the Corpse Hall, later to be pulled off the stack of bodies and carted through to the ovens of the crematorium.

The stone floors of the killing rooms are much cracked and do not show the inward slope which was part of the standard design of SS Execution Chambers, although the drain at the centre, for prisoners' blood, is still to be seen. Another standard fixture of these rooms was a hosepipe fixed to the wall, used to wash away stains before the next prisoner was brought through.

From Station 'Z' a sloping path leads down to a sandbagged shooting stand. Thousands were killed here by SS bullets or by a gruesome mechanical gallows. The prisoner's neck was passed through one of a row of four nooses suspended from iron hooks; his feet were forced into boxes secured to the ground, and clamped in. When the executioner pulled his lever, the prisoner's body was ripped apart.

Pathology Department

Walk down beside the western perimeter. The camp cinema (26 on plan) was being renovated at the time of writing. Either here or in the former camp laundry (13, facing the museum) films are shown at various times during the day. Planned timings are not always kept to, though usually someone turns up to switch on the projector.

At the south-western edge of the camp is the Pathology Department. Its cellars and examination rooms were an important part of the camp's economic programme. Bodies were stored for dissection and the skulls, skeletons and preserved organs sold to universities and medical institutes. Other skeletons and body samples went for further study to branches of the SS Institute for Racial Research.

The main upstairs room has two examination tables, kept as surgically clean today as they were in operational times. Around the walls are cabinets of instruments used for cutting up limbs and removing gold from teeth; the gold was sent to the Reichsbank. Tattooed prisoners were a subject of unusual interest. Camp doctors removed tattooed skin from the bodies and had the pieces converted into lampshades and covers for handbags and ornamental boxes.

Jewish Barracks

The list is long of civilian groups which the Nazis deemed alien and planned to eradicate. But the group which suffered most was the Jewish population of German-occupied Europe. On the far side of the camp (23) the barrack blocks are a memorial to Jewish suffering.

From September 1939, when a group of some 900 Jews and Polish citizens were transported to the camp and imprisoned in these blocks, the toll of Jewish lives grew and multiplied. Where members of other races might only be imprisoned if they were captured while on active service for the Allies, Jews were condemned in their own homes. Their crime was merely being Jewish. At Sachsenhausen Jews were classified and given different uniform patches on a variety of grounds: Jewish political prisoner in protective custody; Orthodox Jew; Jewish prisoner in fixed-term preventive custody; Jewish anti-social; Jewish racial violator. All met the same end.

Impact and Future Hope

The camp at Sachsenhausen is a frightening reminder of events that occurred barely more than half a lifetime ago. It is surely right that all should be reminded of what happened. In Germany today there is evidence enough that a sharp political swing could again trigger the kind of authoritarian state which the National Socialists brought into being. One way to guard against such future madness is to lay bare the dreadfulness of the past and repeat, and repeat, the fundamental message: 'It must not happen again.'

In 1992 the Jewish Barracks were badly damaged by a mysterious fire. There seems little doubt that some extreme right-wing faction was responsible. Their foolish aim, presumably, was to obliterate the memorial, as if that would somehow prove there was no brutality to Jews, no Holocaust. Germany faces a grim future if it does not stand firm against this new wave of hysteria.

Walk 18

Grunewald

A taste of the great forest to the west of the city. See an art show at the Brücke Museum and walk through the pine and birch wood to Grunewaldsee. Beside the lake is Jagdschloss Grunewald, a former royal hunting lodge with a surprising collection of early Dutch and German masters. Essential for admirers of Cranach the Elder.

Allow   4-6 hours.

Best times   Not Monday-Tuesday. Brücke Museum also closes between special shows; check press, *Tip*, *Zitty*, etc., for details.

ROUTE

Begin at Pücklerstrasse bus stop on Clayallee (Bus 115 from Ⓤ Güntzelstrasse or Ⓤ Fehrbelliner Platz).

Walk along Pücklerstrasse (signs to Brücke Museum) and take next left down Fohlenweg. Turn right along Bussardsteig to **Brücke Museum** at end ☞; open 11.00 to 17.00, closed Tuesday. *Admission.*

Return to Pücklerstrasse and turn left towards woodland path leading to lake and **Jagdschloss** ☞; lodge open April to September 10.00 to 18.00, March *and* October 10.00 to 17.00, November to February 10.00 to 16.00, closed Monday and each lunchtime 13.00 to 13.30. *Admission.*

Also in courtyard see small **Hunting Museum** and **Woodland Centre for Children (Grunewaldschule)**, similar opening times to lodge.

Stroll into the woods or make a circuit of the lake. From the Jagdschloss, an alternative way back to Clayallee is to take right-hand footpath signposted to Dahlem. This passes eccentric Chalet Suisse restaurant. Walk ends at Clayallee. Nearest refreshment on left in woodland shack, the Waldbaude. Nearest buses: 115 back to U-Bahn stations, as above, or, opposite in Königin-Luise-Strasse, Bus 180 to Ⓤ Dahlem-Dorf.

Brücke Museum

Located at the fringe of the inhabited city, beside a huge and silent wood, the approach to the Brücke Museum stirs a strange excitement. The museum stands, ordinarily enough, in a low block typical of its vintage (1967) at the end of a cul-de-sac lined with expensive small villas. What is rare about this collection, certainly among Berlin's art museums, is that it specialises in the work of one movement.

The artists of the Brücke Group ('The Bridge') came together in Dresden in 1905. Theirs was the first avant-garde movement in German art, its programme formulated in 1906 by Ernst Ludwig Kirchner. In 1911 the group moved to Berlin to try and improve its position in the contemporary art market, and broke up in 1913. Chief founding members were, in addition to Kirchner, Karl Schmidt-Rottluff and Erich Heckel. They were later joined for varying periods by Emil Nolde, Max Pechstein and Otto Mueller.

In their different styles, the Brücke artists form a connecting link be-

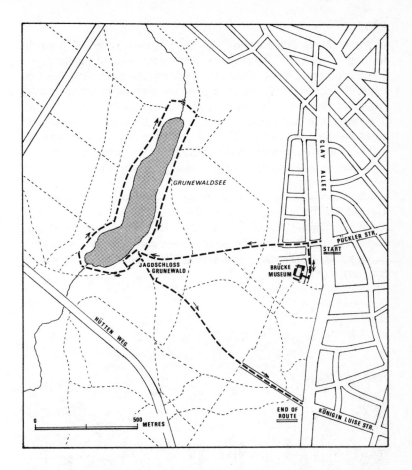

tween Post Impressionism and Expressionism. Heckel and Mueller, and on occasion Pechstein, were closest to the compositional methods and Oriental influences of Gauguin; Schmidt-Rottluff in those years took colour painting close to abstraction in both portraiture and land-scape. Kirchner moved towards the spiky evocations of disconnected urban life for which he is most famous.

The collection is weighted towards Schmidt-Rottluff and to a lesser extent Heckel, who themselves made the largest donations and helped to establish the museum. Individual shows may turn on a group theme or focus on one artist, for example the 'Water Colours of Schmidt-Rottluff (1904-1970)'. Quality varies accordingly (Schmidt-Rottluff is not, alas, in the same league as Matisse). For me Kirchner is the giant of the group, but the museum holds only ten of his paintings whereas its stocks of Heckel and Schmidt-Rottluff are virtually comprehensive. The visitor may be lucky, or not so lucky. In any event it is prudent to view this museum as the study centre of a broad artistic programme, and what its members accomplished later in their careers, rather than as some permanent stage for the 'Brücke's Greatest Hits'.

Grunewald

This 'green wood', originally part of Spandau Forest, might also be dedicated to the dog. Some of its component parts already are. There is a Dog's Throat Lake and a Dog's Throat Marsh, as well as a Dog's Bathing Station (visited later).

Hunting Lodge, Grunewald

The four hundred and fifty-year history of the royal hunting lodge beside the lake is loud with the clamour of dogs: initially they were the liver and white pack-hounds of mounted huntsmen and the other breeds and mixtures, usually large and long in the fang, which fared best against the wild boar, a fearsome adversary, very deft with its tusks. (They do say, though sometimes with a detectable smile, that wild boar lurk still in these woods. Then they usually spoil it by adding, 'No, no. They're very shy. You'll never see one.' Which still leaves the visitor not quite sure what to expect.)

Today the pack-hounds have gone – the last court hunt at Grunewald was in 1907. Now the forest is a wonderful leisure ground for the family dog. A walk there, particularly at the weekend, offers a free insight into the Berliner's choice of canine pet. The prospect would not be encouraging for potential housebreakers. At least half look far too large and powerful for the average family *Wohnung*, but must fit in somehow. The accent is on lithe hunters and huge-shouldered hulks which look as if they could push a tree down with one paw. It's not so surprising, really, in a country where the so-called 'shepherd's dog' (*Schäferhund*) is not some tail-wagging light-middleweight relative of the collie but a dog bred to see off wolves – the one our friendly British policemen employ to knock over criminals, more commonly known as the Alsatian.

Then there are the fighting dogs. Well, we must not call them that as dog fighting is illegal. There they are, though, and in numbers: bull mastiffs, American pit bulls, dobermanns, rottweilers and giant schnauzers, kitted out with bondage collars and harnesses by their fearless owners who themselves parade in spiky haircuts, leather jackets and, in summer, the most virulent purple-yellow-green shorts to which the C & A range will stretch itself.

Here, though, a word of praise is also due. Off the lead, the vast majority of Berlin house dogs are almost serenely well-behaved. Above temptation. Other dogs may sniff their bottoms but they don't care. They're above that. Sniffing the breeze all very aloof – ears pricked for some faint and far more interesting movement in the vegetation. That over there, under the silver birch, no it's gone now – could've been a blackbird, take a lot of chances, blackbirds – no, well mostly I come here Saturdays, with him in the mauve trainers and hairy legs – d'you like my new collar, it's from the dog shop in Halensee.

Leaving them to their private ways, keep on down the straight woodland path, beside neat stacks of felled and stripped pine trees, and arrive shortly at the whitewashed enclosure of the Royal Hunting Lodge.

Jagdschloss Grunewald

Through the rounded archway lies a broad cobbled courtyard, surrounded by handsome outbuildings like a model farm. In the long barn on the right is a small Hunting Museum; on the far side is the Grunewaldschule, a woodland study centre for young visitors.

Courtyard of Hunting Lodge

The Hunting Lodge overlooks the lake beside a screen of tall upstanding beech trees. It was built in 1542 for Elector Joachim II of Brandenburg and the two-storey entrance and hexagonal stair turret are from the original building which was surrounded by a moat. Around 1700 the lodge was altered and enlarged, and under Frederick the Great a hunting equipment magazine was built. Hunting parties from the court stayed overnight at the lodge and there were separate quarters for the chief huntsman (*Jägermeister*) and the head forester (*Hegemeister*). After a period of decline the lodge was repaired and refurnished in the early to mid-nineteenth century. Collections of various kinds were installed – hunt paintings and animal scenes, and stuffed birds and antlers. They proved to be heralds of a major change at the lodge. After the First World War, when the monarchy ceased, the building was turned into a museum.

Georg Poensgen assembled collections of furniture and paintings from other Hohenzollern castles now in the state's charge. A gallery was built and the museum took shape. The paintings are of mixed origin and quality. Best by far are the Dutch and German masters from the seventeenth century, and the group of Cranachs, father and son and their school, which were handed down through the monarchy from the time of Joachim I. Other fine works came from the Solly collection purchased by Friedrich Wilhelm III.

The lodge survived the Second World War and in 1947 was the first museum in Berlin to reopen. It was restored and enlarged in 1973, in part to receive the paintings of the *Passion Cycle* by the Cranach School which came from the Berliner Dom.

The tour of the lodge (self-guided) begins in the Great Hall. A useful, modestly priced guidebook (in German and English) is available at the ticket desk (*Kasse*). Some highlights are:

Great Hall, portraits of Brandenburg rulers and family by Lucas Cranach the Elder and Younger, and Heinrich Bollandt.

Room 1, nine *Scenes from the Passion* from the workshop of Cranach the Elder. The *Crucifixion* is missing.

Room 7, animal portraits, including a two-headed deer and a rather sweet white marten, head cocked and pink nose bristling.

Room 8 (former kitchen of chief huntsman). Extraordinary heraldic picture by unknown German artist *c*.1720: *The Tossing of Fox and Boar*. At the centre of a canvas enclosure twelve men in a circle hold a white sheet and toss a wild boar in the air. In surrounding friezes courtly figures stroll about, slender hounds leap, two large dogs in harlequin costume carry a man in a sedan chair, white-ruffed men ride galloping boars, and at top and bottom two rows of foxes are tossed by footmen holding narrow nets.

Room 6, view of lodge and courtyard on *The Arrival of Kaiser Wilhelm I for the 'Red Hunt' at Grunewald*. Also *Court Hunt near Letzlingen*, by Eduard Grawert, which shows Friedrich Wilhelm IV shooting boar at close range.

Up stairs of turret to first floor.

Room 16, relief portrait in wood of *Tiedemann Giese* by Hans Schenk, known as Scheusslich (*c*.1528). He was the chief sculptor employed on the original Jagdschloss building.

Room 18, the principal room for Cranach the Elder. Familiar subjects include an unusually serene *Lucretia* (1529); a lethargic *Adam and Eve* (1537); a fiery *Judith*, dressed as a sixteenth-century noblewoman; and a pensive *Fountain Nymph*, not wishing to be disturbed. Also two fine portraits in armour of *Johann, Prince of Anhalt* (1520) and his brother *Joachim* (*c*.1521).

Room 13, *Susannah and the Elders*, by Jacob Jordaens (1657). The nearby *Allegory of Smell* by Frans Muntsaert (1649) fails to live up to the promise of its title.

Room 12, *Julius Caesar*, by Peter Paul Rubens (1619) in a collection of portraits of the first twelve Roman emperors, acquired by the Great Elector Friedrich Wilhelm.

Room 11, a delicate but dark *Landscape with Nymphs* by Jan Brueghel the Younger (*c*. 1650); and *The Prodigal Son and the Harlots*, by Cornelis Cornelisz van Haarlem (1596).

Up the spiral stair to the second floor.

In the main this floor has routine German portraits, but in the hall (*Room 25*) see a finely executed plant and animal picture by Otto Marsens van Schriek, *Orache, Toadstools, Snakes and Butterflies* (*c*.1670). Decorations in the rooms include antlers reworked as candelabra, one such fronted by a stern-faced mermaid with two tails which curve in harmony with the antler branches. Finally:

Rooms 27 and 24, two tiny baroque picture cabinets crammed with small works, among them two smoking pictures – that by Jan Steen too dark to enjoy fully, alas. Also a charming fragment of a larger, cut-down original, Willem Kool's *Beach with Fishermen* (*c*.1650).

Hunting Museum

In the long barn facing the lodge is an interesting collection of hunting guns and swords overlooked by portraits of slaughtered boar, deer and elk, these last specially imported by the Hohenzollern rulers; in 1728 they had a stock of seven hundred and five. Amongst the other hunting ephemera: cartridge bandoliers, powder flasks, game bags, a huntsman's red coat, hunting horns and photographs from the good old days when Kaiser Wilhelm I attended the hunts of the *Rote Jagd*. Also here is an immensely detailed Meissen enactment of the *Vision of St Hubertus*, when the inveterate hunter met a stag bearing a crucifix between its antlers. Hubertus was overcome by the vision and renounced earthly things; in about the year 727 he became Bishop of Tongeren.

By the entrance are two large canvases of wild boar by C.G. Merck. The special distinction of these animals came at the very end of their lives, when they were personally shot by Friedrich Wilhelm I, in 1720 and 1724 respectively.

Around the lake

No refreshments are to be had inside the Jagdschloss compound, though here and there around the lake are mobile *Imbiss* stands selling sausages and drinks – in winter they do a very acceptable *Glühwein* spiked if desired with a shot of rum or amaretto.

Another option is to walk down a hundred metres or so, past the Grunewald Riding Club, to the luxurious Forsthaus Paulsborn which has a pleasant tree-shaded garden behind the high front hedge, and drinks at average terrace prices. From here the lakeside path turns uphill and joins the *Neue Rundwanderweg*, bending back above the foot of the lake to a vantage-point opposite the Jagdschloss. On a still day the reflection of the lodge is rendered perfectly in the water.

In time the footpath reaches a terraced beach (the *Nacktbadestelle*) shared by nudist sunbathers and pétanque players (at some risk to the former, I would have thought). Nude sunbathing is no great rarity in Berlin. Around the city, and within it, are various beaches and meadows where sunbathers may quite unselfconsciously remove all clothing and lie in the sun. On maps these places are designated by the initials FKK (*Freikörperkultur*); they are to be found, for example, at Halensee in the West and at Strandbad Müggelsee in the East (on the Rahnsdorf side of the lake). Elsewhere, as in the Tiergarten, people just follow their instincts and trust they will not be disturbed.

The rest of the walk is dominated by dog culture, by the huge abundance of breeds on view. The bright-eyed dobermann with pin-sharp ears; the long-haired dachshund which truffles past, its nose skimming the fallen leaves, oblivious of all else, and the black beast which canters up with a four-foot length of tree-branch in its jaws, its coat shiny from a recent dip at the Dogs' Bathing Beach.

The *Hundebadestelle* lies at the north-east end of the lake – a shady paradise where dogs may freely chase after each other, dig holes in the sand, dash through the shallow water or take a more studied swim out in the lake (more or less what we humans do on our beaches). On this stretch of sand, humans are entirely surplus to requirement, except as instruments for throwing bits of tree into the water.

In deep-frozen winter, the cold air is cut by the shouts of skaters and the *click-clack* of hockey sticks, as Berliners seize the moment to revive their old skills with stick and puck. 'The skaters were out on the lake,' I reported one evening to a friend. 'I know,' she said, 'it's been on the radio all day. They've been warning everybody the ice isn't thick enough.'

This walk visits but a tiny fragment of Grunewald. To see more, it's best to have a bicycle. Then it is a joy to pedal west from here, across the Avus and the S-Bahn, to see the Grunewaldturm and drop dramatically down to the Havel Lake on the far side. In summer, cycles may be hired at Schmetterlingsplatz, outside S-Bahnhof Grunewald, tel. 811 58 29.

Walk 19

Wannsee

West Berlin's lakeside resort with Europe's largest inland beach. Beautiful lakeside views and forest walks. This is not so much one walk as a series of excursions mostly radiating by boat and bus from the S-Bahn station at Wannsee.

Allow   All day and more.

Best times   Good dry weather from April to October. Not Monday for Schloss on Pfaueninsel (closed November to March). Not Saturday for Wannsee Conference House.

ROUTE
To the Beach (Strandbad Wannsee)
Begin at Ⓢ Nikolassee. Take Bus 513 to front entrance of **Strandbad** or walk there via Rosemeyerweg bridging motorway and along Wannseebadweg. Beach open May to September 07.00/08.00 to 18.00/20.00, last two weeks April and first two weeks October 10.00 to 17.00, closed rest of year. *Admission*.

After beach, return to Ⓢ Nikolassee or bear right at exit along woodland path to Youth Hostel (*Jugendherberge*). Turn right and catch Bus 118 to Ⓢ Wannsee.

Boat Trips
Begin at Ⓢ Wannsee. At exit, turn left and cross road, continuing past bus stops and right down steps to boat dock (there is also a foot tunnel across the road from the station).

Quickest and cheapest trip, using Berlin travel pass, is on the BVG ferry which crosses the lake to **Kladow**. Boats leave on the hour from *Brücke B*. From Kladow, onward trips go to Pfaueninsel and other destinations; or ride back to Wannsee.

Main boat-trip operators are Stern und Kreisschiff-fahrt and Reederverband. See large noticeboard for details. Best local trips tour Wannsee island or continue to Potsdam calling at **Kladow-Pfaueninsel-Glienicker Brücke-Potsdam**.

Nikolskoë and Peacock Island (Pfaueninsel)
Begin at Ⓢ Wannsee. At bus stop facing station take Bus 216 to **Nikolskoë** via Moorlake. Walk past Blockhaus restaurant for marvellous views over lake. Turn right down path to **Church of Sts Peter and Paul**.

Continue on upper level through woods or down beside lake in direction of **Pfaueninsel**, emerging beside timbered Wirtshaus – good for snacks or a lunch stop. There is no catering on Pfaueninsel – no cars either, nor dogs, nor smoking. Take ferry across and explore the peaceful nature reserve and the Schloss.

Island open as follows: March and October 09.00 to 17.00
April and September 08.00 to 18.00
1 May to 31 August 08.00 to 20.00
1 November to end February 10.00 to 16.00
Schloss open 1 April to 30 September 10.00 to 17.00, October 10.00

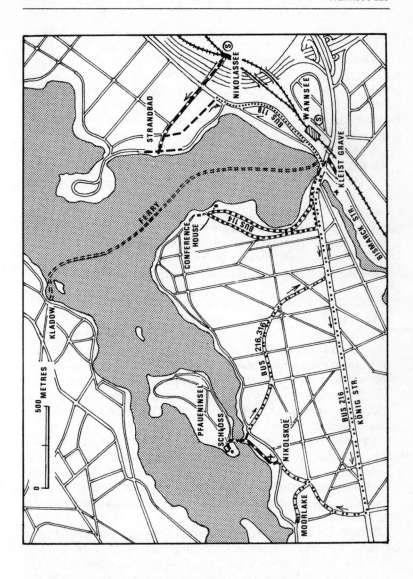

to 16.00, closed Monday and 1 November to 31 March.

Continue by boat round island or return by Bus 216, 316 to Ⓢ Wannsee.

Kleist Grave and Wannsee Conference House

Begin at Ⓢ Wannsee. At exit, turn left down to T-junction. Cross and turn left, then right before railway bridge into Bismarckstrasse. Opposite No.3, and just past large rowing club HQ, take footpath downhill to grave of writer **Heinrich von Kleist (1777-1811)** who committed suicide here after first killing his lover Henriette Vogel.

Return to main road and cross to bus stop in Königstrasse. Take Bus 114 which turns down Am Grossen Wannsee to **Conference House** at Nos.56-58; get off at Lion Monument (*Löwendenkmal*). House open 10.00 to 18.00, Sunday opens 14.00, closed Saturday. Ground-floor rooms give fully documented account of Nazis' persecution of Jews, and of conference here in January 1942 which set in motion the Final Solution to deport and murder the Jews of Europe.

Walk ends here. Refreshments nearby at Bolles Bootshaus (recommended) or Seehase. Return by bus to Ⓢ Wannsee.

Strandbad Wannsee

As beaches go, it is not that extraordinary: straight and undoubtedly long (said to be the largest inland bathing station in Europe) and furnished with orderly blockhouses for changing rooms, shops and eating-places. Out on the water stand sculptural chutes and diving boards. The flavour is late Twenties, for that was when the original beach resort of 1907 was enlarged and the pioneering fenced-off sections for men and women merged into one.

There is something antiseptic about the rigid symmetry of the buildings. Although the style is international, in the context of Berlin it is difficult not to think of all the 'people programming' that went on shortly afterwards under the guise of *Kraft durch Freude* (Strength through Joy) and other movements urging the virtues of healthy minds in healthy bodies.

Today's clientele are more relaxed. They use the beach as a kind of apparatus on which to perfect the *bronzage* of skin. Many of the more desirable tints on view are the fruit of pre-season training under the lamp at one of Berlins numerous *Bräunungstudios*. In the Cold War years West Berliners poured out here on the S-Bahn, twenty thousand at a time, to enjoy the only true beach on their island in the Sea of Communism. Numbers now are not so great, though the beach is still a useful place to prepare for the annual getaway to the Med (*das Mittelmeer*), sectors of which the Germans have colonised with uncanny socio-economic results. A Berlin teacher I know, asked about her spring break in Crete, said with some puzzlement, 'It was fine, except our village was full of teachers from Berlin.' It's much the same at Strandbad Wannsee, only more so. A West Berliner, especially from the Spandau area, would be surprised not to find at least half a dozen familiar faces snoozing on the sand.

Boat Trips

The once famous name of the Weisse Flotte (White Fleet) ship company, formerly an Eastern concern, has disappeared. The fleet was swallowed by its main Western rival, the Stern und Kreisschiffahrt (Star and Circle Voyages), who now run an enormous programme of waterway tours in and around Berlin.

The boat dock at Wannsee is a great departure point for trips reaching westwards around Wannsee island to Potsdam and beyond, and for exploring the upper waters of Lake Havel as far as Spandau and Tegel. The most flamboyant vessel based here is a kind of motorised 'Jaws' called *Moby Dick*, its bow windows framed by an awning of monstrous teeth. Much more modest – and free to holders of a Berlin travel pass – is the BVG ferry which runs across the lake to Kladow and back. The advantage of this service is that it operates all year round, whereas the pleasure boats only run in season, mostly from early April until the end of October.

Kladow itself is unremarkable, a quiet enclave of tidy villas. The road beside the piers is discreetly populated with cafés and restaurants, but otherwise there is little to do here but get on the next ferry back, or even turn round immediately, that is, as soon as the skipper has taken his *Pause* in the tumbledown shack across the way.

On the journey out, the ferry pushes briskly into the heart of the lake. To the right are the broad yellow sands of Strandbad Wannsee. On the other side, on Wannsee island, are yacht moorings and a clutch of boathouses. The last of these before the headland is Bolles Bootshaus, incorporating an attractive restaurant. Next to it lights sparkle in the Wannsee Conference House, a broad three-storey villa with three oval windows above the garden doors. The ferry rounds the Heckeshorn and heads across the lake to Kladow, first wheeling round Imchen island, a nature reserve. In season, pleasure boats call at Kladow and may be joined for an onward journey to Pfaueninsel and Potsdam.

A more ambitious boat trip tours the whole of Wannsee island. The Stern und Kreis vessel heads south into a chain of narrow lakes flanked by wooded hills and large desirable houses. Stops are made at Stölpchensee and Kohlhasenbrück, on the fringe of former East Germany. (A little way south of Kohlhasenbrück is the hamlet of Steinstücken, which from 1961 to 1989 was entirely walled in except for one narrow corridor linking it to the West.)

The old border followed the south shore of Griebnitzsee, crossed briefly onto Wannsee island and then continued to Glienicker Brücke. Here the boat makes a further stop by the East-West bridge which became renowned for the exchange of political prisoners. Most famous of these was the American pilot Gary Powers, swapped for a Soviet agent in 1962.

From here the boat turns round the north side of Wannsee island to Moorlake and Pfaueninsel, then heads back to Wannsee. The complete round trip takes about two hours.

Nikolskoë and Peacock Island (Pfaueninsel)

The small ferry linking Wannsee island to Pfaueninsel is also reachable by road. From Wannsee S-Bahn station, Bus 216 (the 316 is very infrequent) crosses the Wannseebrücke and runs along Königstrasse towards the far side of the island. Then it turns up a winding forest road, detours into Moorlake and out again, and stops at Nikolskoë.

This extraordinary settlement was the inspiration of King Friedrich Wilhelm III. The Blockhaus, now a pretty timbered restaurant, was copied from a Russian model and built in 1818 in honour of the King's daughter, Princess Charlotte, and her husband, the future Tsar Nicholas I. The name and strange spelling of 'Nikolskoë' imitates the Russian pronunciation of a word meaning 'Nicholas's own'. The first Blockhaus was burnt out in 1984 but was fully restored the following year.

From the Blockhaus a steep flight of wooden steps runs down to the lake. A wonderful view extends across the still water to a long horizon on the far side, dense with dark fir trees. When the church bells ring out through the silence, it is a magical place.

The Church of Sts Peter and Paul was founded in 1834. It was designed by Friedrich August Stüler in a style sympathetic to Russian church buildings, with a high square onion-domed tower rising above the simple portico. The interior is neatly symmetrical: twin galleries run down to the apse beneath a coffered ceiling. To the left of the apse is a tall wooden pulpit, supported on four eight-sided pillars with Corinthian capitals and decorated with mosaic medallions of the apostles Peter and Paul, and a *Christ Crowned with Thorns*.

Fountain on Peacock Island

It is just a short stroll through the woods to the Pfaueninsel ferry. A path drops gradually to the lakeside and there is soon the welcoming courtyard terrace of the Wirtshaus zur Pfaueninsel. In season the ferry crosses constantly to and from Peacock Island, but it is a good idea to eat and drink before setting off. The island is a nature reserve and has strict rules forbidding picnics, dogs, smoking and other worldly pastimes.

Pfaueninsel is something of a tourist trap, and the open-decked ferry is usually packed. Wander up to the Schloss Pfaueninsel and on the way look out for resident peacocks strutting freely round the paths. They too may not be fed but no one seems to take much notice of this regulation, it being somehow thought necessary to bribe the male birds with breadcrumbs before attempting to pose with them for the family album.

The so-called castle is a purpose-built ruin, a folly contrived in 1794 by Johann Gottlieb Brendel for King Friedrich Wilhelm II and his mistress Wilhelmine. I find it cold and ugly, unredeemed even by the quaint bridge which spans the void between two castellated towers. An altogether better building is Schinkel's Kavalierhaus (1825) at the far end of the island, which also involves a pleasant walk through the wild gardens landscaped by the prolific Peter Joseph Lenné; rich in wild flowers and satisfyingly peaceful despite the regular flow of visitors up and down the paths.

Kleist's Grave and Wannsee Conference House

On a wooden slope overlooking the Kleiner Wannsee, Heinrich von Kleist shot himself in a suicide pact with his lover Henriette Vogel. The Romantic author was thirty-four years old. Today he is chiefly remembered for his comedy *Der zerbrochene Krug* (The Broken Jug), the drama *Prinz Friedrich von Homburg* and a number of sporadically brilliant stories including *Die Marquise von O* — and *Michael Kohlhaas* which is based on the story of a horse-dealer from Kohlhasenbrück, less than two miles from this spot.

Kleist is buried at the place where he died. A simple pink granite stone marks his grave; the inscription reads:

NOW	HEINRICH VON KLEIST
O · IMMORTALITY	18 OCTOBER 1777
ARE · YOU · WHOLLY · MINE	21 NOVEMBER 1811

From the grave a path leads down to the lakeside, where there are benches to sit on but alas, no through road or towpath to follow. In the built-up parts of Wannsee, territorial rights are zealously guarded and only limited parts of the lakeside are available to walkers.

One remedy is to go back to Königstrasse and board Bus 114. This shortly turns down a winding lane, Am Grossen Wannsee. At the Lion Monument (*Löwendenkmal*) bus stop, several possibilities offer themselves.

The first is to visit the Wannsee Conference House at No.58, which in 1992 opened as a memorial site and museum of Jewish oppression under the Nazis.

The second is to walk to the monument and turn left down a sometimes muddy path to Bolles Bootshaus, a place I find remarkably well-adjusted to long and relaxed lunching at more or less any daylight hour. The fish is good, and the terrace runs out to the water where sailing dinghies clunk and tremble at their moorings.

The third possibility is to take a refreshing walk along the lakeside path, heading north past the Heckeshorn and rounding the tip of the island. The path continues all the way to Pfaueninsel and beyond. Alternatively, strike uphill into the woods and work out some kind of loop which returns to the starting point. The woods are liberally equipped with footpaths and occasional signs which note the walking time to various destinations.

The Wannsee Conference House, originally the lakeside villa of a Berlin industrialist, was acquired by the SS in 1940 and used mainly as a guest house for visiting police and SS officers. In 1941 Reinhard Heydrich, head of the Nazi Security Office, began planning the *Endlösung der europäischen Judenfrage* (final solution to the Jewish question in Europe). On 20 January 1942 he presided at a historic meeting in this house. Its subject was not *whether* to murder the Jews – that was already decided – but how to go about it. The meeting laid the ground rules for the 'Final Solution'. Jews would be rounded up in every occupied country, sent east to concentration camps and there be put to death.

The exhibition is well laid out in a series of fourteen rooms on the ground floor of the house. They trace the history of anti-semitism from the rise of the Nazi Party to the Liberation of Europe. Many of the illustrations are disturbing but the exhibition is not so large that it threatens to swamp the visitor. Room 6 is the Conference Room, overlooking the lake, where fifteen men set about organising the greatest act of racial oppression in history. The minutes of the meeting have survived, after coming to light at the German Foreign Office in 1947. The name of the man who wrote them will be familiar to many: Adolf Eichmann.

Walk 20

Köpenick and Grosser Müggelsee

A handsome township on the edge of former East Berlin. See the Old Town and Schloss, and its Museum of Applied Art, and take a bus out to the forest, the Devil's Lake and the waterside attractions of Grosser Müggelsee.

Allow   All day.

Best times   Not Monday-Tuesday.

ROUTE

Begin at Ⓢ Köpenick (on the eastbound line to Erkner). At exit, turn left into dingy Bahnhofstrasse and walk down to junction with Lindenstrasse (or take this stretch aboard Tram 86 or Bus 168, 169).

Turn left at park along Lindenstrasse and cross bridge over River Spree to **Old Town** (*Altstadt*). Bear right towards **Town Hall** (tower with clock), in cellar of which is useful restaurant (Ratskeller Köpenick).

At Schlossplatz, keep ahead to stone arch leading to Schloss Köpenick. On right in courtyard is **Museum of Applied Art (Kunstgewerbemuseum)** 👁 ; open 10.00 to 18.00, closed Monday-Tuesday. *Admission*. Refreshments in café-restaurant across courtyard.

Return to Schlossplatz and turn right. Take Bus 169 out of town to E on long straight road between pine and birch woods. Get off at stop signposted Teufels-see (facing sign to Rübezahl).

Turn right and walk through woods to **Teufels-see**. Bear right at terrace of *Gaststätte* and take stepped path up to **Müggelturm** (ugly buildings but good all-round view from top of tower).

From front of tower turn left to footpath along ridge and after about 400m turn left down rough path beside fenced-in toboggan run. Keep on past wooden bridge to foot of run near E end of Teufels-see. Turn right and keep on to concrete road, passing *Wanderlehrkabinett*. At main road, cross and continue to **Grosser Müggelsee**.

To right on lake, Müggelsee Perle is a big resort establishment with tennis courts, cafés and a boat jetty (lake trips in season). Turn left beside lake to Rübezahl, a brash and noisy watering hole which also has a boat jetty. From here, return up path to main road. Bus 169 goes all the way to Ⓢ Köpenick – or stop off in Old Town at the Ratskeller.

To return by another route, take the ferry from Rübezahl across to Friedrichshagen. From the jetty on the far side, perhaps explore the Spree Tunnel and the park beyond, then catch Tram 25 or 84 up Bölschestrasse to the S-Bahn station.

In the train

The S-Bahn line from Alexanderplatz meanders through a belt of factories, marshalling yards and worker flats. Look out for long-distance trains which share the track – the express to Vilnius and the khaki-

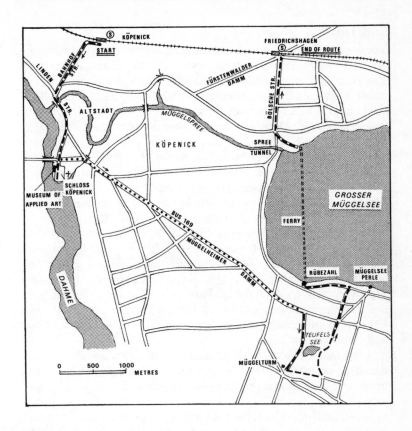

green sleeper from Moscow, the green wagons of the German Post Office (Deutsche Bundespost) and orange ones from Poland, and trains to all points in the reunited country – Heidelberg, Karlsruhe, Hamburg, Frankfurt Main and Frankfurt Oder.

Ostkreuz is a spaghetti junction of the rail network, with lines swerving off to join the overhead routes to north and south. The train to Köpenick, and eventually Erkner, prowls on to Karlshorst and the open heath of Wuhlheide – flat and scrubby, here and there a small wood of birch and pine – and shortly pulls in at Köpenick.

Old Town

The railway station is in the Dammvorstadt, a nineteenth-century sub-urb some way north of the Old Town. Linking the two is Bahnhof-strasse, a shopping street of dull façades in a uniform dirty cement colour, very East German, about as charming as Streatham High Road just after they took the barrage balloons away in 1945 (roughly the date when the houses of Köpenick had their last lick of paint). Little reason not to hop on a bus or tram and ride down to the T-junction with Linden-strasse, a meeting-point also known as the Platz des 23. April as a salute to the arrival of the Soviet Army in the last weeks of the war.

On the left here is a park, and in the surrounding space the archi-tecture is more stately – apartment blocks with semi-domed corner turrets, the pink and sand gabled front of the Post Office and, on the junction itself, the Gothic excrescences of the Realgymnasium (1910). Across the park swans cruise on the water and away on Baumgarten Island is a small colony of *Kleingarten* chalets. Orange trams well qualified by age for the transport museum clang along with impressive regularity. A sizeable congregation files out beneath the red-brick tower of the Catholic Church of St Josef, and next door the District Council offices occupy a neat neo-classical villa that has not worn too badly, considering.

At the Damm Bridge, the River Spree divides into the narrow arm of the Alte Spree which flows into Grosser Müggelsee, and the broad reaches of the Dahme where huge pleasure boats run down to Langer See.

Ahead the Gothic clocktower and ship weathervane of the Town Hall (*Rathaus*) rise above the roofs of the Old Town. The surrounding streets are cobbled and narrow, retaining the closed atmosphere of the medieval market community which grew up here from the thirteenth century. In modern times two notable events have occurred in Köpen-ick, and the more amusing of them took place in the Town Hall. This was the affair of the *Hauptmann von Köpenick* (Captain from Köpenick) which Carl Zuckmayer later converted into a successful comedy.

In 1906 Wilhelm Voigt, a disgruntled shoemaker, pulled off an anti-establishment stunt which crisply illuminated the false values of authority, particularly if it presented itself in the shape of a military uni-form. Voigt got himself up as a Prussian captain, went to the military bathing station at Plötzensee, placed a squad of twelve grenadiers in his charge and took them to Köpenick. Here he marched on the Town Hall, arrested the Mayor, took the contents of the town treasury from his hands, and vanished.

Although Voigt did not remain at large for long, his story captivated popular imagination and is re-enacted each year in the town's summer festival.

The brick-vaulted cellar of the *Rathaus* is a comfortable and attractive restaurant. It needs to be said that the food leans towards *nouvelle cuisine* and consequent stinginess with the portions. More to the point, however, the focus of decorative interest is a waxwork tableau in which the bogus *Hauptmann* poses before a period plate camera in his borrowed military cap and greatcoat.

The second event in the recent history of the town was not at all amusing. This was the Week of Blood (*Köpenicker Blutwoche*). The town, already known as something of a left-wing outpost, rumbled with dissent on the day Hitler came to power in 1933. A red flag flying from the brewery at nearby Friedrichshagen proved more than the new regime could tolerate. Reprisals were savage. SA storm-troopers arrested some five hundred people suspected of being Communist or Social Democrat supporters. During and after a week of vicious raids, ninety-one people were put to death.

Schloss Köpenick and the Museum of Applied Art

At Schlossplatz, cross the tram tracks to the footbridge and sandstone gateway leading to Castle Island. On the west side of the courtyard stands the Dutch Baroque Schloss, charming but crumbling somewhat. It was designed by Rutger van Langefelt for the Elector Friedrich and completed in 1681. Today it houses the Museum of Applied Art (Kunstgewerbemuseum) which since the *Wende* has been twinned with its much more opulent Western counterpart in the Kulturforum, to the consternation of many locals who fear cuts and closures. Meanwhile the museum jogs on in a state remarkably close to shabby gentility, though that can hardly be the phrase for a palace which was in Communist hands for forty years. 'Fraternal decay' might be more accurate.

Climb the creaky wooden staircase to begin at the top with the Art Nouveau collection. Alas, there is not much here, but some of the glass is by Emile Gallé and the Daum Brothers, and I liked an ornate *Schatulle* or money-box by the Russian artist Khlebnikov (1913). Also on this floor look for the virtuoso limewood carvings of Aubert Parent (c.1795), amazingly thin reliefs of flowers in vases and a portrait medallion of Friedrich Wilhelm II.

The most splendid room is the *Wappensaal* (Hall of Arms), the creation of Giovanni Carove who from 1683 held the splendid title of 'Electoral Stuccoist in Cöpenick'. Beneath a lavish acanthus-leaf ceiling stand the principal shields of the Mark Brandenburg and subject territories, each one supported by a pair of classical figures. Nearby is the Treasury, its star item the silver-gilt buffet made *c*.1698 for Friedrich I by Ludwig & Biller of Augsburg, flanked by three oversized silver tankards studded with medieval silver *Thaler*. On the middle and ground floor is a mixed collection of glass, porcelain and furniture and, under the *Wappensaal*, a grand reception room with an elaborate cherub-laden ceiling, unfortunately flaking in parts.

On the far side of the castle courtyard is the fine Baroque Chapel (1682-5), designed by Johann Arnold Nering who also built the original Palace at Charlottenburg. The chapel is rarely open. Next to it is a slightly stuffy museum café with views across the Dahme to the boatsheds of the Kietz, the medieval fisherman's quarter.

Grosser Müggelsee

Bus 169 (*27 on old maps*) heads east past the top of the Kietz and through a dull modern suburb which incorporates the Salvador Allende Quarter. Soon it reaches an arrow-straight road, the Müggelheimer Damm, cleaving through the birch and pine of the Berliner Stadtwald. When the road bends to the left, push the button above the exit door to alert the driver and get off at the next stop.

Signposts point left to Rübezahl, beside the lake, and right through the forest to the Devil's Lake (Teufels-see). Beside the broad path are timber picnic tables and things for children to swing on and crawl through. Traffic noise soon dies away and walkers amble peacefully towards the Teufels-see. The Devil is associated with a number of lakes around Berlin but this one – still and dark, surrounded by marsh and heavily shaded with trees – carries a stronger hint of supernatural occupancy than the average forest pool.

Beside the lake stands a terraced *Gaststätte* which never seems to be open when it should be. From here a nature trail (*Wanderlehrpfad*) sets off through the trees, its route accompanied by picture panels and details of rock types, names of trees, birds and so on, all innocent enough but carrying unmistakable echoes of 'constructive leisure' in the GDR mode.

Another path, broad and stepped with timber risers, bends upwards to the top of not exactly a mountain range but known for all that as the Müggelberge. On the ridge is a Brutal café-restaurant attached to the Müggelturm. From the top of this remarkably ugly tower – it looks like an emergency staircase somehow come adrift from its office block – excellent views may be had over the surrounding lakes and woods.

Follow the ridge eastwards to a toboggan run which snakes downhill through the forest, stoutly guarded on each side by a cross-mesh of timber poles. A rough footpath winds down beside the run to a marshy expanse on the edge of the Teufels-see. Close by, a concrete road leads off to the Müggelheimer Damm, passing the nature wardens' museum (*Wanderlehrkabinett*). From the main road it is a short walk down to the Grosser Müggelsee, arriving beside the Müggelsee Perle.

This concrete holiday fortress was once where deserving citizens of the GDR rested from their labours at the state machine; played tennis, sunned themselves on the terraces and feasted and drank in a chain of restaurants and bars along the lake front. 'Were the rooms bugged?' I asked a Western businessman. 'Almost certainly,' he replied. 'When my company took over a hotel in the East we found one room which was always kept locked and no one would admit to having a key. We broke in and there was the complete control room, tape-recorders and the whole works.'

In recent free market times the Müggelsee Perle went through a rough patch and is currently in the care of the Treuhand, the trust organisation which has been selling off still workable enterprises in East Germany and shutting down those deemed hopeless.

The boat from Friedrichshagen puts in at the jetty here, or may be caught at Rübezahl just along the lake. This is another old GDR pleasure garden, noisy at weekends with a vast open terrace seating 1,800 visitors where you can buy barbecued sausages and steaks, and eat them at a rustic table.

The ride across the water to Friedrichshagen takes about twenty minutes. Look back to the tree-covered tops of the Müggelberge and forward to the landing-place at the corner of the lake. Here the River

Spree joins the lake through a narrow passage. Overlooking the Spree is the Berliner Bürgerbrauerei, source of the demonstrations which provoked the dreadful Blood Week in Köpenick. Beneath the river a foot tunnel leads up to a quiet park on the far side, a good place to laze for a few minutes with a rich ice cream, then set off for the S-Bahn station. If you don't feel like walking, there are ancient orange trams to ease the way.

Walk 21

Potsdam Town

A charming baroque town in former East Germany. See the gabled Dutch Quarter, the old city gates and many streets of fine domestic architecture. From the Brandenburger Tor by Park Sanssouci, return to the station past the historic Film Museum.

Allow All day.

Best times Not Monday.

Note 1 Potsdam Town is worth a full day's exploration. Frederick the Great's Park Sanssouci, described in the next walk, is vast and most visitors will find it too much to attempt both in one day.

Note 2 Berlin travel passes are valid on Potsdam buses and trams.

ROUTE

Begin at ⑤Potsdam Stadt. From the station yard walk up to the main road and turn right over Lange Brücke. On right the **Nikolaikirche** and **Altes Rathaus (Old Town Hall)**. On left the long pavilion of the **Filmmuseum** (formerly the **Marstall** or **Royal Stables**).

Continue to first grim yellow block, housing the useful Tourist Information Centre which offers an Accommodation Service.

Keep on to **Platz der Einheit (Unity Square)**. Turn right to Post Office and walk up E side of square to corner of Bassinplatz, where two churches flank a large ugly bus station and occasional street market.

On left side of square, turn left along Brandenburger Strasse (*Klement-Gottwald-Strasse*), a pedestrian shopping street, and right up Friedrich-Ebert-Strasse. On right, look along picturesque streets of the **Dutch Quarter**. Keep on to the **Nauener Tor**. Turn left beside splendid villas of Hegelallee. At the **Jägertor**, turn left down Lindenstrasse (*Otto-Nuschke-Strasse*) to Brandenburger Strasse and turn right to **Brandenburger Tor**.

To visit **Park Sanssouci**, keep straight on to Luisenplatz (*Platz der Nationen*) and join *Walk 22*.

Walk down to Charlottenstrasse (*Wilhelm-Pieck-Strasse*) and turn left to the **Alte Wache** on the corner of Lindenstrasse. Turn down Lindenstrasse to **Breite Strasse** (*Wilhelm-Külz-Strasse*). Look right to see the extraordinary **Waterworks (Pumpwerk)** in the style of an Eastern mosque.

At the corner of Lindenstrasse is the **Potsdam Museum**; open 10.00 to 17.00, closed Monday. *Admission*.

For agreeable refreshment, cross to **Kiezstrasse** and Der Froschkasten. Look along the fine baroque houses and return to Breite Strasse. Keep on to the **Filmmuseum**; open 10.00 to 17.00, closed Monday. *Admission*. Continue past the **Portal** or **Havelkolonnade des Stadtschlosses**, and turn right to the S-Bahn station.

Perfumes of the East

An experienced Western nose can tell at a sniff when the old border has been passed. Somewhere between Griebnitzsee and Babelsberg the unmistakable odour drifts in through the carriage window. The quintessential pong of Herr Honecker's undemocratic republic lives on, pungent yet strangely difficult to define. There is certainly more to it than

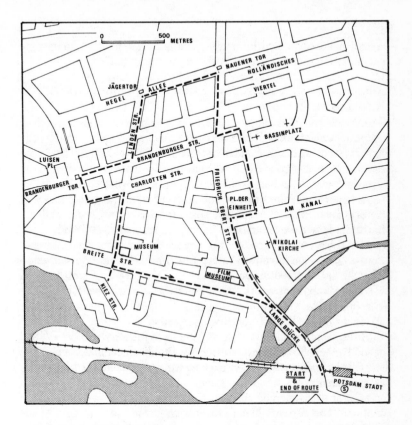

the expected after-fug of brown coal and woodsmoke which overhangs every built-up area in former East Germany. A friend offered this analysis:

'It's more of a mixture than just one smell. It's got old paper in it as well as the coal, and sometimes drains and cooking fat too. Around hotels you also get that engine oil stuff they put in the cabbages and salads.'

Welcome, then, to the aromatic, as well as historic and handsome, capital of the new *Bundesland* (regional state) of Brandenburg. Now through the window looms the huge dome of Karl Friedrich Schinkel's Nikolaikirche, modelled on Wren's St Paul's. Fortunately, the ugly square block on which the dome rests is hidden for the moment by neighbouring rooftops.

Into Town

The cobbled station yard is wholly East European, crisscrossed by tramtracks and bordered by a huddle of shacks and *Imbiss* stands, the footways a packed compound of brown earth and sand. At the top of the rise leading to the Long Bridge (*Lange Brücke*) a new vista unfolds, the aftermath of an RAF bomb raid which in April 1945 flattened more than eight hundred buildings in the Old Town (*Altstadt*). Among others of historic importance, the Stadtschloss, the Garrison Church and the Barberini Palace were damaged beyond repair and demolished.

The replacement architecture is universally cheap and slablike. Across the bridge the unwelcoming tower of the Hotel Potsdam rears over the site of the baroque Schloss. Ahead a parade of prefabricated yellow cells extends across one end of the Old Market, forming the Teacher Training Institute; at shop level on the near corner are the useful offices of the Tourist Information service.

Three restored survivors stand witness to the town that once stood here. To the left, across the main road, the Filmmuseum occupies the former Marstall or royal stables: a long elegant pavilion which began life as an orangery, designed by Johann Arnold Nering in 1685. Ahead stands the Nikolaikirche, built in three stages in the mid-nineteenth century. The fortress-like base was the work of Ludwig Persius (1830-7) and Schinkel's dome was added in 1843-9. To contain its massive outward thrust, four bell towers were attached to the corners of the building; the effect is unfortunate, creating the impression of a Turkish mausoleum rather than a neo-classical church. Next to it is the more orthodox Old Town Hall (Altes Rathaus) designed in 1753 by Johann Boumann in the style of the Italian classicist Andrea Palladio. Above the central dome a gilded Atlas supports a monstrous globe, representing the weight of municipal responsibility resting on the town council (which vacated the building in 1885). The premises now serve as a rather lame-looking arts centre.

History and Growth

Potsdam was a thousand years old in 1993. Its first official mention was in July 993 when King Otto III presented the Slav villages of Poztupimi (Potsdam) and Geliti (Geltow) to his aunt, the Abbess of Quedlinburg. For the next six hundred years Potsdam remained an unremarkable settlement of fishermen and farmers, then in 1660 the Great Elector ordered the building of a castle. In the eighteenth century Friedrich Wilhelm I, the 'Soldier King', decided Potsdam would be an ideal garrison town for his expanding army. In 1732 building began of the 'Second Baroque Extension', virtually a new town arranged on a grid and bordered by present-day Hegelallee, Schopenhauerstrasse, Charlottenstrasse (*Wilhelm-Pieck-Strasse*) and Hebbelstrasse. A customs wall pierced by gates surrounded the new district and palisades ran down to the banks of the Havel. It was this extension which gave the town its form and character. Much of it escaped the bombs of 1945 and we may still enjoy its elegant terraces and the richness of detail added to porches, windows and rooflines.

Between 1713 and 1740 the number of houses in Potsdam rose from 220 to 1,154. In the reign of Frederick the Great (1740-86) the great park of Sanssouci was laid out to the west of the town, and the simple city gates were replaced by altogether grander versions. The town acquired a further 700 buildings, of which almost a hundred provided living quarters for the military.

The Hohenzollerns remained permanently based at Potsdam until 1918, and up to the Second World War the city retained its character as a former *Residenzstadt* with a large garrison and several thriving factories producing a diversity of goods from textiles to crystalware and guns.

Unity Square (Platz der Einheit)

The quarter we now reach is a sorry substitute for the *Altstadt* destroyed in April 1945. The prefabricated Seventies blocks on Platz der Einheit (Unity) are shoddy and worn, and here as elsewhere the old Communist memorials have been derided by a scornful and bitter population. In the middle of the square the official mural celebrates:

OUR SACRIFICE OUR STRUGGLE AGAINST FASCISM
AND WAR
A REMINDER TO THE LIVING OF THEIR DUTY

Between the lines someone has sprayed a counter-assessment in thin black letters:

28 Years of GDR-Ghetto 40 Years of SED -
Lies ††† Stasi-Terror †††

Other messages, on nearby buildings, speak of more immediate hopes and fears:

WE DON'T NEED THE ARMY
RUSSIANS OUT
NO NEW GERMANY

Next to the Post Office a plaque on the yellow wall of a dismal block of flats records that the Synagogue of the Jewish Community of Potsdam stood here. On the night of 9-10 November 1938 (*Kristallnacht*) it was plundered and destroyed as part of the Nazis' anti-Jewish campaign.

Unity Square indeed. It was once less controversially known as Wilhelmplatz.

Second Baroque Extension

Walk ahead to the gabled wings of the Dutch Quarter (*Holländisches Viertel*) whose best aspects will be shortly revealed. First is Bassinplatz, a huge square sprinkled with market stalls and dominated by three edifices. In the middle are the painted masts and angular suspended roof of the bus station, a nasty piece of People's Progressive architecture made more offensive by its location between two historic churches.

To the right is the eighteenth-century French Church, built for the Huguenots who came to Brandenburg after suffering persecution in their own land. The church was designed by Johann Boumann in 1751 and features a saucer dome comparable to St Hedwig's Cathedral in Berlin (see *Walk 4*); both were modelled on the Pantheon in Rome.

Across the square is the gaunt Catholic Church of Sts Peter and Paul, a huge building in pale brick dating from 1867-8. Its design, by Wilhelm Salzenberg, borrows extensively from two different sources. The campanile follows the lines of San Zeno Maggiore in Verona and the body of the church draws elements from St Sofia in Constantinople. The church closes the view at the eastern end of Brandenburger Strasse. Turn along here to find houses typical of the standard models used for the Second Baroque Extension. Attractive in a style reminiscent of English Georgian, each house is carefully varied from the rest, the front elevations rendered in bright pink, lime green, beige or a custard shade of yellow.

At the first intersection, where the trams run, turn into Friedrich-Ebert-Strasse towards the yellow gateway at the end (the Nauener Tor). On the right is the elegant Town School building. The school was founded in 1739 and the writer Heinrich von Kleist was a pupil there before going on to university at Frankfurt-an-der-Oder. Look right along Gutenbergstrasse and Mittelstrasse to see the shuttered red-brick houses of the Dutch Quarter.

The quarter consists of four handsome blocks designed by Johann Boumann, who came from Amsterdam and built these streets in his native style between 1732 and 1742. Originally the quarter was intended for Dutch craftsmen coming to Potsdam to work for Friedrich Wilhelm I. Recent restoration work has been piecemeal and slow, but now the terraces are almost back to how they looked two hundred and fifty years ago.

The Nauener Gate is a strange piece of work, the result of Frederick the Great's plan to aggrandise the entrances to the Second Baroque Extension with a new set of gateways. Each was designed in a different style, chosen at the king's whim. Fancying a chunk of English Gothic, in 1754 he briefed the architect Johann Gottfried Büring to produce a round-towered gate with side wings. Today, with its newly spruced-up yellow sandstone walls and contrasting castellations it looks remarkably as if it is on loan from Disneyworld. Elsewhere in this quirky bout of pastiche building, new gates appeared with Egyptian obelisks and Roman triumphal arches. The only one to escape renewal was the Jägertor, which stands halfway along Hegelallee.

This fine broad avenue is richly endowed with eighteenth-century villas. There are columned porches, wrought-iron balconies, turrets and rows of urns parading at roof level. Incongruously, some houses on the north side are guarded by bored Russian soldiers whose active part in the phased withdrawal of former Soviet troops has yet to begin. Then comes the Jägertor (Huntsman's Gate), now isolated at the centre of a broad crossroads. Above the arch a sculpted stag is trapped by hunting dogs, the group flanked on each side by trophies.

The houses of Lindenstrasse are more modest, and some have fallen into sad decay. But there is considerable beauty here, behind the grey and dusty façades which seem to be frozen from another age. At the junction with Brandenburger Strasse turn towards the massive gateway which spans the western end of the street – and which for almost a year has been shrouded in scaffolding and builders' sheets. Beneath the wraps is a monumental sandstone arch with two side passages, modelled on the triumphal arches of Ancient Rome and built in 1769.

There is no shortage of café-stops along here – for example Babette and Am Stadttor in the piazza by the Brandenburg Gate – though if returning to the station my choice would be the Froschkasten in the old fishermen's district, the Kiez, about ten minutes away. Walkers seeking at least a taste of the huge Park Sanssouci should now cross the tramtracks behind the Brandenburger Tor and join the route of *Walk 22*. Best plan for a relatively quick visit would be to take in the Friedenskirche, Schloss Sanssouci and Bildergalerie, then return to the centre.

To continue this walk, turn down to Charlottenstrasse to find one of Potsdam's best buildings, the colonnaded Guard House or Alte Wache. Designed by Andreas Ludwig Krüger in 1795, its paired columns and accented keystones, coupled with the patterned stonework of the upper walls, forge an immediately satisfying blend of classical and Moorish styles. (It is less pleasing, somehow, to find that the building has now been captured by the omnivorous Commerzbank.)

Along Breite Strasse

Continue to the Potsdam Museum, and on the corner look west to see Moorishness run riot – and at a pumping station of all places! Ludwig Persius designed the Potsdam Pumpwerk in 1841 to resolve a problem which had defeated mechanical engineers in Frederick the Great's day:

how to pump water from the Havel up to the reservoir on the Ruinenberg and so activate the fountains in Park Sanssouci. Not only did the Pumpwerk work, its glorious banded façades, mosque-like dome and elegant slender minaret are a visual triumph which even the boring backdrop of GDR worker flats cannot diminish.

Potsdam Museum has yet to haul itself into the post-Wall world, but there may be an interesting special exhibition with a local flavour. Across the road the pink and yellow blocks of the Hiller-Brandtsche Häuser (1769) now serve as an annexe to the museum. Along the roof-line is an eye-catching row of figures from Roman mythology.

Kiezstrasse is a cobbled backwater, its low varied house-fronts dating from 1777, by which time the medieval fishermen's village had been absorbed into the town. For hungry and thirsty walkers the panelled and pleasantly atmospheric rooms of the 'Frog Box' (*Froschkasten*) offer a calm setting for a late lunch and reflective thoughts on the day, perhaps before setting off for a final round of twentieth-century culture at the Filmmuseum.

The final stretch of Breite Strasse is decorated with a sandstone colonnade which formerly linked the demolished Stadtschloss with the royal stables, present home of the Filmmuseum. The columns are by Knobelsdorff, probably best known for his work at Charlottenburg Palace (see *Walk 14*) and there are other sculptural fragments retrieved from the wartime wreckage of the Castle.

The Potsdam Filmmuseum opened here in 1982, its chief function to record and pay tribute to the work of the famous film studios in nearby Babelsberg. Under the original name of UFA, which was changed to DEFA when the GDR state took them over, the studios were the birthplace of many legendary movies. Here in the Twenties they made, among a great list of fine films and box-office hits, *Das Kabinett des Doktor Caligari* (1919), *Nosferatu* (1922), Murnau's *Faust* (1926), Lang's *Metropolis* (1926) and Pabst's *Die Büchse von Pandora* (1928). The museum has plentiful scope for viewing clips, from 1895 to 1980, an excellent cinema and a café that is one of the best in town.

Walk 22

Park Sanssouci

The palaces and landscaped grounds which Frederick the Great built as his 'Park Without Cares'. Though the buildings are damp and faded from long neglect, the dreamland of the warrior-intellectual is still a place of wonder.

Allow All day.

Best times Mid-May to mid-October (some buildings closed in winter). See opening times in Route section for current details. Restoration programmes make it difficult to say precisely what will be open at any given time. Early start recommended.

Note Berlin travel passes are valid on Potsdam buses and trams.

ROUTE

Begin at Ⓢ Potsdam Stadt. From the station yard walk up to the main road and catch Tram 91, 96 to Luisenplatz (*Platz der Nationen*).

Walk ahead up Allee nach Sanssouci. Turn right to the **Friedenskirche** 👁; open mid-May to mid-October 10.00 to 18.00.

From the cloisters walk up to Hauptweg. Look right to see the ceremonial **Obelisk Portal**. Turn left to the **Great Fountain** and here turn right up the six terraces to the **Palace (Schloss Sanssouci)** 👁; entrance at rear, open 09.00 to 17.00, closes earlier in winter and all day on 1st and 3rd Monday of month. **Ladies' Wing (Damenflügel)** on W side open mid-May to mid-October 09.00 to 17.00. *Separate admission to each part.*

From E end of terrace to rear of palace a path leads to the **Picture Gallery (Grosse Bildergalerie)** 👁; open mid-May to mid-October 09.00 to 17.00, closed 4th Monday of month. *Admission.*

Return to rear of palace. Walk to W end of terrace and turn along a narrow path which arrives at roof level of **New Chambers (Neue Kammern)**. Go down steps to front; open 09.00 to 17.00, closes earlier in winter and all day on Friday. *Admission.*

Walk down to park and turn right through **Sicilian Garden**. At end turn right up to main road (Maulbeerallee) and take a narrow path uphill to E side of **Orangery** 👁; occasional exhibitions in Viewing Tower (*Aussichtsturm*), open mid-May to mid-October 09.00 to 17.00, closed 4th Thursday of month. *Admission.*

From end of Orangery terrace, bear left down sloping path, cross Maulbeerallee and keep straight on to Karl von Gontard's sadly dilapidated **Antikentempel**. Walk round and continue to Hauptweg. Turn right towards **Neues Palais** 👁; tickets at S side, entrance at rear, open 09.00 to 17.00, closes earlier in winter and all day on 2nd and 4th Monday of month. *Admission.*

At exit, facing grand staircases and colonnade of the **Communs**, turn right and leave park. At bus stop ahead (*Abzweig der Eiche*), Bus 695 returns to Bassinplatz in town centre. For best refreshment possibilities in area, try along Brandenburger Strasse (see *Walk 21*).

From centre, walk down Friedrich-Ebert-Strasse to S-Bahn station, or continue on Bus 695 to **Schloss Cecilienhof** 👁; open 09.00 to 17.00, closes earlier in winter and all day on 2nd and 4th Monday in month. *Admission.* Return by bus to town centre and S-Bahn station.

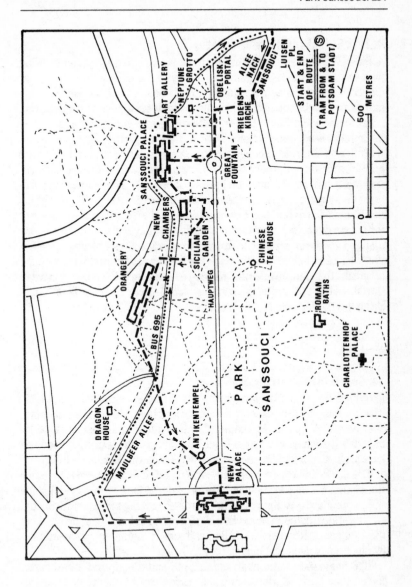

A few words before we set off

A Slow Walk in an eighteenth-century park ringed by palaces. What bliss in the prospect, though what agony in the execution – if, that is, one tries to consume the whole place in one visit. Park Sanssouci is simply too large, too filled with palaces, galleries, rococo conceits and other attractions. Far better to taste its pleasures a few at a time, and return for more some other day.

This walk therefore concentrates on the older, northern half of the park, for the development of which Frederick the Great was chiefly responsible. There was a second phase of building, under Friedrich Wilhelm IV, which brought into being Charlottenhof Palace, the Orangery, the Roman Baths and the Friedenskirche, as well as Lenné's series of formal gardens. We visit some of these too, but in the interests of our feet and good temper do not attempt to stand on every blade of grass in the park's 290 hectares (720 acres) or tread every footpath the longest of which, the Hauptweg, runs for more than 2 km (1.2 miles) between the Obelisk Portal at the main entrance and the bombastic hulk of Neues Palais on the far side of the grounds.

To the Church of Peace

From the tram junction at Luisenplatz, a modest side street helpfully labelled Allee nach Sanssouci delivers the visitor without formality into the heart of the park. Soon one arrives beside an administrative building, next to which is a gate. It looks as if it might lead to someone's garage, but is in fact the easiest way to reach the Friedenskirche.

The Church of Peace was conceived by Friedrich Wilhelm IV to mark the centenary of Sanssouci and to provide himself with a burial place which breathed nostalgia for other days. (A brochure written during the GDR's stewardship explains that the king 'had not grasped the sense of the Bourgeois Revolution of 1848 and sought refuge in a romantic reproduction of medieval kingship.')

The foundation stone was laid in 1845 and the church arose in the form of an Early Christian basilica flanked by a freestanding seven-storey bell tower. The architect was Ludwig Persius, a pupil of Karl Friedrich Schinkel. A later addition was the mausoleum of Frederick III, completed in 1890.

Great Fountain

From the cloisters, follow the path northward which crosses the Sheep Ditch (Schafgraben) stream and meanders up to the east-west axis path of Hauptweg. To the right is the Obelisk Portal, the principal gateway to the centre of Potsdam. Beyond the columns of Knobelsdorff's portal, and centred between them, is an ornamental obelisk decorated with hieroglyphs in the Egyptian style and dating from 1748; the portal was built the previous year. To the north of Hauptweg is the Neptune Grotto (Knobelsdorff, 1753), a monumental garden ornament with two cascades flanking an arched recess lined with shells.

To the left, facing into the park, is the Great Fountain, shooting a single jet of water high in the air which then, caught by the breeze, falls back into a marble basin in a triangular fan, like the plume on the helmet of a Prussian dragoon. Surrounding the fountain are a huddle of Roman gods and groups symbolising the four elements.

The Great Fountain was the focal point of the eastern pleasure garden which Frederick the Great laid out from 1744. Its chief eminence lies directly to the north: the terraced vineyard crowned by the low rococo pavilion of Schloss Sanssouci.

Schloss Sanssouci

The German word *Schloss* is applied to castles and palaces with little apparent distinction, though nothing could be further from the image of a castellated fortress than this saucer-domed single-storey palace which crouches on top of the hill. Thirty-six sandstone bacchantes support the eaves, set between long arched windows; adorning the balustrade is a row of portly urns. The design is by Georg von Knobelsdorff, to a recipe provided by Frederick the Great and conforming to his ideal – a palace where he could withdraw from the pomp of court life and follow his enthusiasm for French culture 'without cares'.

The siting of the palace is also true to its function: it stands away from the main axial path and has no grand entrance from the park, only the staircase passing up through the six terraces of the vineyard. The palace was built in only two years from 1745.

The principal entrance is at the rear, through the Cour d'Honneur. Here a splendid view reaches out between the colonnade, across the valley to the Ruinenberg: a collection of fake ruins put there to mask a reservoir installed to provide water for the Great Fountain.

In the west wing, added in 1840, are the rooms of the *Damenflügel*, once occupied by courtiers: a two-storey set of tiny panelled rooms now decorated on the upper level with topographical paintings by Eduard Gärtner and others. In the main part of the palace the principal rooms are the Marble Hall (*Marmorsaal*) and the Concert Room (*Konzertzimmer*). It was in this ornate setting that the French writer, wit and philosopher Voltaire lived for three mainly uncomfortable years from 1750 in the role of cultural mentor to the king.

Picture Gallery

Unmistakably Friderician in appearance, the Art Gallery (Grosse Bildergalerie) was built in 1755-63 by Johann Gottfried Büring. It is the oldest surviving museum building in Germany and supplied much of the original stock of paintings to Schinkel's Altes Museum when it opened in 1830. Many were later returned, but wartime losses were severe and the present collection is a patchwork of acquisitions and transfers from other sources in former East Germany. Greatest of the masters represented are Van Dyck, Rubens and Caravaggio. The garden front overlooks the Dutch Garden, laid out in 1764-6, and is itself decorated with eighteen marble statues symbolising the Arts and Sciences.

Refreshment Break

From the west end of Schloss Sanssouci go down to the road and cross to a choice of watering holes. The largest is the Gaststätte Historische Mühle (Historic Mill). It has a self-service cafeteria, a terrace and a restaurant with faintly creaky service on the East German model.

New Chambers and Orangery

The mustard façade of the Neue Kammern conceals a former orangery which in 1771-4 was converted into a guesthouse. The ensemble was restored in the 1980s by Polish craftsmen, and the principal rooms are the oval Buffet Room (*Büfettraum*), Ovid Gallery (*Ovid-Galerie*) – with reliefs illustrating the poet's *Elegies* – and the central Jaspis Room (*Jaspisraum*).

From here it is a short stroll to P.J. Lenné's restful Sicilian Garden, laid out in 1857 in a geometrical style and richly furnished with palm trees in ochre-painted barrels. Then it is time to scale the northern hill once more to visit the Orangery. This enormous structure – 300m (1083ft) long – looks considerably more like an Italian Renaissance palace than an indoor garden. It was built in 1851-60 in the Park's second phase of development, the first edifice of a triumphal way that Friedrich Wilhelm IV wanted to erect here, and thankfully never did. It was here that the king's sister Charlotte stayed when she visited Berlin with her husband Tsar Nicholas I. (They were the couple who inspired the Russian church and Blockhaus at Nikolskoë, Wannsee – see *Walk 19*.)

No longer an orangery, the building is dark and damp with peeling plaster and rotted walls. Visitors may nonetheless climb to a Viewing Tower (*Aussichtsturm*) where art exhibitions are sometimes held.

Neues Palais

Around now visitors may feel the onset of 'palace fatigue', so huge is the Sanssouci complex. Keep on though for just one more, the largest of them all.

The way to the New Palace is downhill across Maulbeerallee (Mulberry Avenue) and through a delightful expanse of wild garden, formerly the Deer Park. Nestling not far from the straight path of Hauptweg is a sadly dilapidated Antique Temple, built in 1768 by Karl von Gontard to house Frederick the Great's sculpture collection. This was later transferred to the Altes Museum in Berlin. The temple is one of a pair; the other, on the far side of Hauptweg, is the Friendship Temple, also designed by Gontard and dedicated to Frederick the Great's sister, the Countess Wilhelmine von Bayreuth.

Turn past the temple to face the mighty bulk of Neues Palais, erected as a bragging monument, or fanfaronade, to Prussian military success in the Seven Years' War. The front is 213m (699ft) broad and the decorations include 428 statues. The architects were Johann Gottfried Büring and Karl von Gontard.

Years of neglect have rendered the palace rooms tawdry, dusty and altogether *triste*. Minor Italian paintings hang or sag from the walls beside those of the ubiquitous Antoine Pesne. Most spectacular of the rooms are the renovated Theatre (*Schlosstheater*), the Marble Gallery

(*Marmorgalerie*) and the central Grotto Hall (*Grottensaal*), its walls and ceilings covered with architectural rock-forms and shells, a kind of Jugendstil fantasy more than a century ahead of its time.

To the rear of the palace is a grand ensemble of domestic buildings, the Communs, distinguished by a pair of curving stone staircases and a central colonnade.

Schloss Cecilienhof

It so happens that Bus 695 stops near the park exit to the north of Neues Palais, and from there grumbles uphill over the cobbles of Maulbeerallee, returns to the middle of Potsdam and then heads north to the Cecilienhof. If time allows at the end of the day, those with an interest in the Second World War may wish to visit the site of the Potsdam Conference, where in July-August 1945 Stalin, Truman and the British tandem of Churchill-Attlee confirmed the post-war divisions of Europe.

The building is a picturesque imitation of the English Tudor country house style and was designed by Paul Schultze-Naumberg in 1913-16. Focus of interest is the *Konferenzsaal* and the massive round table at which Stalin effectively secured the right to subject Eastern Europe to a form of despotic Communism which cast a blight on the lives of two generations.

BRIEFING

HISTORY NOTES

Albert the Bear

In the early Middle Ages, Germanic peoples moved eastwards across the North European Plain. Albert (Albrecht) I the Bear (1100-70) was the founder of the important Ascanian dynasty. He subdued the local Slavs and encouraged Frisians and Saxons to settle in the border region, or march, which became known as the Mark Brandenburg.

Within the present boundaries of Greater Berlin, four village settlements grew up in the marshlands of the Spree river valley. Those to west and east were the fortified Slav villages of, respectively, Spandau and Köpenick. Midway between them, in about 1160-70, fishermen built huts on an island they named Cölln (the present Museuminsel-Fischerinsel) and another group settled on the neighbouring bank to the north-east, calling their village Berlin. Cölln and Berlin became a major stopping-place on the route of merchants working the east-west trade route between Posen (Poznań) and Magdeburg.

Albert the Bear assumed the title of first Margrave of Brandenburg (margrave = governor of a border region). The Ascanians ruled this eastern wing of the German Empire until 1319. Meanwhile Berlin and Cölln grew as rival centres, though sharing some institutions in common. In 1307 they formed a federal union with a joint council housed in a new town hall next to the Lange Brücke (present Rathausbrücke).

See Early artefacts and history of the two towns at the Nikolaikirche (*Walk 6*), Märkisches Museum (*Walk 7*) and Berlin Museum (*Walk 10*).

Anarchy and Iron Tooth

Control under the Ascanians was followed by bloody turmoil as local robber barons fought for supremacy. Berlin and Cölln built up alliances with neighbouring communities and in 1359 joined the Hanseatic League, a powerful trading association of north German towns.

In 1411, Burgrave Friedrich VI of Nuremberg became Governor of the Mark Brandenburg and in 1415 took the title of Elector (*Kurfürst*) Friedrich I. He was a member of the Hohenzollerns, the dynasty which ruled Berlin for the next five hundred years.

Berlin and Cölln continued to press for municipal freedoms and virtual autonomy but the Elector's son Friedrich II 'Iron Tooth' imposed ruthless direct rule on the two towns, separating their joint powers and building a palace in Cölln. He quelled a revolt in 1447-8 (known as the *Berliner Unwille*) and established his own seal which showed the Hohenzollern eagle clamping its talons on the back of Berlin's black bear.

See Medieval buildings, usually dating from after 1376-80 when fires destroyed earlier versions. Examples: fragments of city wall and ruined Franciscan church (*Walk 7*), Marienkirche (*Walk 5*) and Nikolaikirche (*Walk 6*).

Court Life under the First Electors

In 1486 Berlin-Cölln became the Elector's official *Residenz*. A new class of courtiers and officials took control. This civilising influence stimulated the craft guilds and launched a building programme symbolised by the Renaissance palace (Stadtschloss) begun in 1538. The following year the two towns accepted the Reformation.

Periodic outbreaks of plague and other epidemics took a heavy toll, grievously felt during the Thirty Years' War (1618-48) when Imperial troops occupied Berlin-Cölln and subjected the citizens to butchery and extortion.

See Site of Stadtschloss, now and for the time being partly occupied by the Palast der Republik (*Walk 4*). Medieval events – fairs and jousting – are sometimes staged nearby on the former ground of the palace tilt-yard.

Friedrich Wilhelm the Great Elector

In 1640 the young Elector Friedrich Wilhelm took over a city shorn of nearly half its population (7,500 from 12,000). He fortified it with bastions and outworks and encouraged new waves of immigrants to settle, in particular Huguenots fleeing from Louis XIV's France.

His son crowned himself Friedrich I, King of Prussia and set in train the dynamic growth of Brandenburg-Prussia, soon to be the dominant German state. In Berlin-Cölln new outer districts appeared – Dorotheenstadt, Friedrichstadt, Friedrichswerder. In 1709 these were united with the original centre to form one city, which took the name Berlin. **See** Statue of Great Elector at Charlottenburg, and Queen Sophie Charlotte's Palace (*Walk 14*); Huguenot Museum in French Church and the Zeughaus (*Walk 4*).

Frederick the Great

Friedrich II '*der Grosse*' reigned from 1740 to 1786. He developed the rigorous system of Prussian militarism begun by his father but also encouraged the flowering of the Enlightenment, raising Berlin to the status of a major European city. Leading intellectual figures were the dramatist Lessing, the philosopher Mendelssohn and the publisher Nicolai.

See Buildings in Unter den Linden – Opera House, St Hedwig's Cathedral, Old Library – and statue of Frederick the Great (*Walk 4*); Ephraimpalais in Nikolai Quarter (*Walk 6*); Park Sanssouci at Potsdam (*Walk 22*).

Nineteenth Century and German Unification

Berlin recovered from the blight of Napoleon's occupation (1806-8), symbolised by the removal to Paris of the Quadriga above the Brandenburg Gate, and grew to become an industrial power. New suburbs were built and the population soared, reaching 826,000 by 1871.

Under the expansionist rule of Bismarck, the 'Iron Chancellor', a string of military victories hardened the general wish for national unity, and this was proclaimed in 1871. Berlin was now the capital of a country spanning all German territories apart from Austria and German-speaking Switzerland.

In the 1880s Berlin acquired electric trams, the S-Bahn, a power station and a telephone service. By 1900 the population was 1.9 million, many living in cramped conditions in *Mietkaserne* (tenements or 'rental barracks').

See Early 19C buildings by Schinkel – Neue Wache, Schauspielhaus, and home of Schinkel Museum (*Walk 4*), and Altes Museum (*Walk 12*); Victory Column (Siegessäule) and Reichstag (Walks 2-3); Kurfürstendamm and the New West, with KaDeWe department store and Wittenberg U-Bahn station (*Walk 1*).

First World War and the Twenties

Failure on the battlefield, followed by the harsh conditions of the Versailles Treaty, brought severe hardship and led to mass strikes and political agitation. In 1920, at the stroke of a pen, the city expanded massively to become Greater Berlin, swallowing neighbouring towns and rural communities from Wannsee to Köpenick. The uncertainties of high unemployment and economic crisis coexisted uneasily with a cosmopolitan café and night life. Expressionist artists showed up the confusions of the city, its hypocrisies, excesses and corruption.

See Twenties buildings in Alexanderplatz (*Walk 5*); Bauhaus Archiv and works by Grosz, Dix, Kirchner and others in Neue Nationalgalerie (*Walk 13*).

Nazi Period and Second World War

Hitler and his National Socialists (Nazis) seized power in 1933 and in Berlin established totalitarian rule under Josef Goebbels, the party's area commander. The city staged the Olympics of 1936 and in 1938 suffered the shameful *Kristallnacht* ('Crystal Night') when synagogues were destroyed and Jewish premises attacked and burnt.

In the Second World War, Berlin was intensively bombed from 1943. On 30 April 1945 Hitler committed suicide in his bunker beneath the Chancellery garden. The city fell to Russian troops on 2 May.

See Reichstag and Topography of Terror Museum (*Walk 3*); Synagogue and other memorials in Old Jewish Quarter (*Walk 8*); Plötzensee Memorial (*Walk 16*); Sachsenhausen Concentration Camp (*Walk 17*).

Recovery and Partition

The city was left a flattened wreck, bereft of food and public services, as the survivors began clearing away the debris. Much of the wreckage was stacked in gigantic Rubble Mountains which were grassed over and now form part of the cityscape.

Berlin was divided into four occupied sectors, controlled by British, US, French and Soviet forces. The city had become an island in the larger Soviet Zone of Germany which extended westward to the Elbe. Relations between East and West deteriorated and in July 1948 the USSR withdrew from the Allied Kommandatura, having already blockaded supply lines from Berlin to the West. The Western Allies responded with the Berlin Airlift, flying in 1.7 million tons of food until

May 1949, when the USSR backed down and the blockade was lifted.

That month the Western Allies founded the Federal Republic of Germany and the Soviets replied in October by proclaiming the German Democratic Republic in the eastern part of the country. Berlin remained a divided island but suffered creeping partition as crossing-points between East and West were blocked; in 1952 tram and bus routes were severed.

Economic recovery in the West far outpaced that in the East, where the Communists' attempt to raise the work norms provoked the uprising of 17 June 1953, brutally suppressed by the Soviet army. Numbers of East Germans fleeing to the West continued to increase, and in August 1961 Ulbricht's GDR regime sealed all Berlin's borders and began building the 'Anti-Fascist' Wall (*Mauer*).

See Soviet War Memorial in Tiergarten (*Walk 2*); route of the Wall (*Walk 3*); Luftbrücke (Airlift) Memorial at Tempelhof (*Walk 9*).

Era of The Wall 1961-89

Hundreds risked their lives to escape to freedom in the West by climbing over, driving through or tunnelling under the Wall, which circled West Berlin and cut the city in half. In the late 1960s the West began a policy of *détente* and secured the Quadripartite Agreement of 1971. This achieved international recognition for the GDR, eased travel and transit arrangements between the two parts of Berlin and restored telephone communications.

In the Gorbachev period, from 1985, the GDR remained resistant to the spread of democracy growing in other Warsaw Pact countries. In 1989 Hungary removed part of its fortified border with Austria and GDR residents poured out through this and other avenues of asylum. Massive protest demonstrations in Leipzig and East Berlin weakened the authorities' grip until, recognising that the Wall had outlived its purpose, they opened the crossing-points on 9 November and the Wall crumbled.

See Remains of the Wall and Museum at Checkpoint Charlie (*Walk 3*); urban decay and renewal in Prenzlauer Berg (*Walk 11*).

After the Turn

Germany was officially reunited on 3 October 1990, and Berlin became its capital. The decision to re-establish the German Government in

Berlin has been taken and the move is scheduled for the late 1990s.

The Wall has largely disappeared and what survives *in situ* has to be protected from the chisels of souvenir hunters. Development schemes proceed apace to cover the unsightly swathe left by the Wall. A bigger task is to solve the underlying cultural problems and successfully reunite the inhabitants of East and West, whose values and expectations have differed radically for forty years.

See Site of new Government centre around Lustgarten (*Walk 4*); housing in East, e.g. Old Jewish Quarter (*Walk 8*) and Prenzlauer Berg (*Walk 11*) and compare with its equivalents in the West, e.g. Schöneberg (*Walk 9*), also quality of shops and restaurants in, say, Alexanderplatz (*Walk 5*) and Kurfürstendamm (*Walk 1*).

THE GERMAN LANGUAGE – Words and Phrases

Speaking good German is demanding and calls for rapid thinking and facial flexibility. It is rather like turning out tiny pieces of high-precision engineering, one after the other and all different. Each clause or sentence is a perfect, ingeniously hinged unit composed of nouns, pronouns and other indispensable parts, all locked up tight with a verb which must be positioned in particular locations according to laws which are in theory immutable but in practice have been complicated by the march of usage. The completed unit is then delivered for public inspection, and *thereby itself with others fusing which gone before have may*.

Readers who learned German at some stage, and can remember enough of its structures and vocabulary, will be streets ahead of those who are just beginning. No one should be put off from trying to cross the great divide; in fact, the sooner you start the better. What then happens, as many advanced learners will I hope agree, is that you find this particular linguistic bridge is built on rollers and you are unlikely to get the whole way across in a lifetime of trying. Berliners, with their gobble-gobble accent, machine-gun delivery, elisions and rich vein of local slang, do little to smooth the way.

A consoling aspect is that many people in Berlin speak some English and some speak very good English, though less so in the East where Russian was until recently the second language most taught in schools. In general, too, Berliners *want* to communicate, and so everybody usually gets there in the end.

Some guide-books attempt to teach simple German in about a page and a half, which I think is nonsense. Learning any language is bound to take time and application. In the following pages are some words and phrases which I nonetheless hope will be useful. Some general points to note are:

- In German, the nouns begin with a capital letter.
- Double *s* may be written as β – the sharp *s* or *scharfes S*.
- For general vocabulary you will need an up-to-date dictionary. Go for the largest one you can comfortably carry.

Pronunciation Guide

This is my own fabrication and I take responsibility for its shortcomings. Some sounds are alien to English: these I point out below and offer the best near-miss alternative I have been able to find.

A helpful feature of German is that every letter or combination of letters is pronounced. This should help both listening and speaking. When you speak, go for *cla-ri-ty*. English speakers do not, as a whole, move their mouths around as much as Germans.

Problem sounds

consonants	The trickier consonants are j (like English *y*); s (before vowels is like *z*, before *p* and *t* is like *sh*); v (like *f*); w (like *v*) and z (like *ts*).
ch	This is a distinctive throat-clearing sound. Pronounce like the *ch* in Scottish *loch*.
u	There are two *u* sounds. Long *u* is like *oo* in English *noon*. Short *u* is like *u* in English *put*. In the words below, short *u* is shown as *u*, long *u* as *oo*.
umlaut	Appears as two dots on some uses of *a*, *o* and *u*.
ä	This changes the *ar* sound of long *a* to something like the *ae* in English *encyclopaedia*. Example: pronounce *spät* as *shpaet*.
ö	This changes the short *o* of English *bottom* to something like the *ea* in *earl*. Example: pronounce *Öl* as *earl* but with the lips more rounded.
ü	This changes the short *u* of *put* to something like the *ue* in *true*. Example: pronounce *fünf* as *fuenf*.

In the pronunciation column below, hyphens denote significant sound breaks, usually in longer words; in general, run syllable clusters together without pausing.

English	German	pronunciation
good morning	guten Morgen	*gooten morgen*
good day	guten Tag	*gooten targ*
good evening	guten Abend	*gooten arbent*
good night	gute Nacht	*goote narcht*
hello	hallo	*halloo*
goodbye	auf Wiedersehen/tschüss	*owf veederzayn/ tchuess*
do you speak English?	sprechen Sie englisch?	*sphrechen zee ennglish?*
I don't speak German	ich spreche kein deutsch	*ich shprecher kine doytsh*
yes/no	ja/nein	*yar/nine*
I don't know	ich weiss nicht	*ich vice nicht*
I don't understand	ich verstehe nicht	*ich fair-shtayer nicht*
all right (understood)	alles klar	*alice klar*
please/thank you/ not at all	bitte/danke/bitteschön	*bitter/danker/bitter- shern*
excuse me, please	entschuldigen Sie mich, bitte	*ent-shooldigen zee mich, bitter*
how do I get to . . .	wie komme ich nach . . .	*vee kommer ich narch . . .*
where is . . .?/ where are . . .?	wo ist . . .?/wo sind . . .?	*voe ist . . .?/voe zint . . .?*
When?	wann?	*vann?*
I'm looking for . . .	ich suche . . .	*ich zoocher*
is it far?/is it near?	ist das weit?/ist das nah?	*ist das vyte?/ist das nar?*
to the right/to the left	nach rechts/nach links	*narch rechts/narch links*
straight on/round the corner	gerade aus/um die Ecke	*ge-rarder owce/um dee ecker*

here/there/over there	hier/da/da drüben	*heer/dar/dar-drueben*
upstairs/downstairs	oben/unten	*oh-benn/un-tenn*
my name is . . .	mein Name ist . . .	*mine narmer ist . . .*
do you have a room free?	haben Sie noch ein Zimmer frei?	*harben zee noch ine tsimmer fry?*
a single room	ein Einzelzimmer	*ine ine-tsel-tsimmer*
a double room	ein Doppelzimmer	*ine dopple-tsimmer*
I'd like . . .	ich hätte gern . . ./ich möchte . . .	*ich hetter gairn . . ./ ich merchter . . .*
how much?	wieviel?	*veefeel?*
that's expensive/ cheap	das ist teuer/billig	*das ist toyer/billich*
the menu, please	die Speisekarte, bitte	*dee shpyzer-karter, bitter*
did it taste good? (waiter-speak)	hat es geschmeckt?	*hat es ge-schmeckt?*
the bill, please	bezahlen, bitte/die Rechnung, bitte	*be-tsarlen, bitter/dee rechnung, bitter*
(do you want to pay) together or separately?	zusammen oder getrennt?	*tsoo-zammen oh-der ge-trennt?*
open/closed	offen, geöffnet, auf/ geschlossen, zu	*offen, ge-erfnet, owf/ ge-shlossen, tsoo*

Streets, buildings and useful signs

underground/urban train	U-Bahn, S-Bahn	*oo-barn/ess-barn*
bus	Bus	*bus*
taxi	Taxi	*taxi*
street	Strasse	*shtrarsser*
square	Platz	*platz*
church	Kirche	*keercher*
museum	Museum	*moo-zayum*
palace/castle	Palast/Schloss	*pa-last/schloss*
exhibition	Ausstellung	*owce-shtellung*
police	Polizei	*pollits-eye*
hospital	Krankenhaus	*kranken-house*

memorial	Gedenkstätte	*ge-denk-shtetter*
push/pull	drücken/ziehen	*drueken/tsee-en*
free/occupied	frei/besetzt	*fry/be-zetst*
toilets	Toiletten	*toy-letten*
Gents/Ladies	Herren/Damen	*herren/darmen*
Men/Women	Männer/Frauen	*maenner/frow-en*
entrance/exit	Eingang/Ausgang	*ine-gang/owce-gang*
no entry	kein Eingang	*kine ine-gang*
emergency exit	Notausgang	*note-owce-gang*
arrival	Ankunft	*an-kunft*
departure	Abfahrt	*ap-fart*
no smoking	nicht rauchen	*nicht row-chen*
attention/take care	Achtung/Vorsicht	*ach-tung/for-zicht*

Time and date words

day and night	Tag und Nacht	*targ und narcht*
today	heute	*hoyter*
yesterday	gestern	*gestern*
tomorrow	morgen	*morgen*
in the morning	vormittags	*formittags*
in the afternoon	nachmittags	*narch-mittargs*
in the evening	abends	*arbents*
what's the time?	wie spät ist es?/wieviel Uhr ist es?	*vee spät ist es?/ veefeel oohr ist es?*
midday	Mittag	*mittarg*
midnight	Mitternacht	*mitternarcht*
one o'clock/two o'clock	ein Uhr/zwei Uhr	*ine oohr/tsvy oohr*
ten past seven	zehn nach sieben	*tseyn narch zeeben*
quarter past seven	viertel nach sieben	*feertel narch zeeben*
half past seven	halb acht	*halp-archt*
quarter to eight	viertel vor acht	*feertel for archt*
five to eight	fünf vor acht	*fuenf for archt*
When does the next bus/train leave?	wann fährt der nächste Bus/Zug ab?	*vann fairt dair nexte bus/tsoog ap?*
could you write that down, please	könnten Sie das bitte aufschreiben	*kern-ten zee das bitter owf-shryben*
Monday	Montag	*montarg*

Tuesday	Dienstag	*deanstarg*
Wednesday	Mittwoch	*mittvoch*
Thursday	Donnerstag	*donnerstarg*
Friday	Freitag	*frytarg*
Saturday	Sonnabend, Samstag	*zonnarbent, zamstarg*
Sunday	Sonntag	*zonntarg*
week	Woche	*vocher*
this week/last week/ next week	diese Woche/letzte Woche/nächste Woche	*deezer vocher/letzter vocher/nexter vocher*
January	Januar	*yanyooar*
February	Februar	*febrooar*
March	März	*maertz*
April	April	*apreel*
May	Mai	*my*
June	Juni	*yoonie*
July	Juli	*yoolie*
August	August	*ow-goost*
September	September	*zeptember*
October	Oktober	*oktober*
November	November	*november*
December	Dezember	*detsember*
month	Monat	*moan-art*
year	Jahr	*yar*
spring	Frühling	*fruehling*
summer	Sommer	*zommer*
autumn	Herbst	*hairbst*
winter	Winter	*vinter*

Numbers

one	eins	*einz (Heinz without the h)*
two	zwei/zwo	*tsvy/tsvo*
three	drei	*dry*
four	vier	*feer*
five	fünf	*fuenf*
six	sechs	*zex*

seven	sieben	*zeeben*
eight	acht	*archt*
nine	neun	*noyn*
ten	zehn	*tseyn*
eleven	elf	*elf*
twelve	zwölf	*tzvoelf*
thirteen	dreizehn	*dry-tseyn*
fourteen	vierzehn	*feer-tseyn*
fifteen	fünfzehn	*fuenf-tseyn*
sixteen	sechzehn	*zech-tseyn*
seventeen	siebzehn	*zeeb-tseyn*
eighteen	achtzehn	*archt-tseyn*
nineteen	neunzehn	*noyn-tseyn*
twenty	zwanzig	*tsvan-tsik*
twenty-one	einundzwanzig	*ine-und-tsvantsik*
twenty-two (etc.)	zweiundzwanzig	*tsvy-und-tsvantsik*
thirty	dreissig	*dry-sik*
forty	vierzig	*feer-tsik*
fifty	fünfzig	*fuenf-tsik*
sixty	sechzig	*zek-tsik*
seventy	siebzig	*zeeb-tsik*
eighty	achtzig	*archt-tsik*
ninety	neunzig	*noyn-tsik*
a hundred	hundert	*hundert*
a hundred and ten	hundertzehn	*hundert-tseyn*
a thousand	tausend	*tow-sent*
two thousand	zweitausend	*tsvy-towsent*

WHERE TO STAY

In previous books in this series I have avoided attempting a critical guide to hotels. Done properly, this would be a book by itself. Berlin, however, has special problems. In the Western part of the city there are not enough hotels, and in general they are expensive or very expensive. In the Eastern centre the provision of hotels is tiny – a residue of GDR days – and almost all are very expensive (which may have been fine in the old days for visiting czars from Bulgaria, etc., but perhaps not at all suited to the resources of thee and me).

In this book, therefore, I should like to offer an enjoyable and economic alternative to hotels. To avoid being flunkeyed and dined at premium rates, contact one of Berlin's thriving Rental or Accommodation Agencies, known as *Mitwohnzentrale*. They can arrange a room (*Gastzimmer*) in a private apartment for any length of stay. Expect the apartment to be clean and attractive, and your host or hostess considerate and helpful. Breakfast is usually provided, and an evening meal if desired. I can personally recommend the following agencies:

Agentur Wohnwitz Holsteinische Strasse 55, 1000 Berlin 31; tel 861 82 22, 861 91 92, 861 63 38; fax 861 82 72.

Erste Mitwohnzentrale Sybelstrasse 53, 1000 Berlin 12; tel 324 30 31.

Other agencies which have been in business for some while are:

Mitwohnzentrale Ku'damm-Eck Kurfürstendamm 227-8 (2nd floor), 1000 Berlin 15; tel 882 30 51; fax 882 66 94.

Freiraum Wohnagentur (West) Wiener Strasse 14, 1000 Berlin 36; tel 618 20 08; fax 618 20 06. (East) Marienburger Strasse 47, 1055 Berlin; tel 426 54 47; fax 427 46 31.

Wohnagentur Last Minute Yorckstrasse 72, 1000 Berlin 61; tel 786 52 84, 786 48 36; fax 786 95 58.

When writing or faxing in advance, tell them roughly where you would like to stay in Berlin. In the West, the most agreeable central districts are Wilmersdorf, Charlottenburg, and Schöneberg around Winterfeldplatz; in the East, opt for Mitte and Prenzlauer Berg. The agencies also need to know, in addition to the obvious requirements of dates and how many people, which sex you are and whether you smoke. If a booking is made, a deposit will be asked for and usually you pay the whole of the balance to the agency.

TRANSPORT

S-Bahn and U-Bahn

The urban rail network, including the mainly underground U-Bahn, covers the whole city and extends to outlying *Slow Walk* destinations such as Potsdam, Wannsee, Oranienburg (Sachsenhausen) and Köpenick. East-West lines severed in the Cold War are being restored, and new links are being built to further bind the two halves of the city together.

Trains are frequent and reasonably quick, though the distances involved are great. To travel from somewhere in West Berlin to a destination in the Eastern centre, or vice-versa, usually takes at least forty-five minutes door-to-door.

Stadt-Bahn train at Charlottenburg

Trains run from approximately 04.00 to 00.30. Intervals between trains are longer at the weekend.

Buses and Trams

These are slower than the trains and bring swift acquaintance with the word *Stau* (traffic jam). If you are not in a hurry, the views from the double-decker buses more than make up for odd stagnant episodes, and the Eastern trams have an antiquated charm that many will find delightful – a pleasure increased if you manage to find a seat.

Buses run from approximately 05.00 to 00.30 when a good night service takes over on many routes, mainly in West Berlin.

For recommended sightseeing routes, see 'The Geography of Berlin'.

Tickets

Tickets are valid for urban trains and buses alike. Make sure you have a valid ticket before beginning a journey. There are no barrier checks at train stations but roving bands of ticket inspectors do sometimes pounce and the penalty for being caught travelling *schwarz* (black) is a fine of DM 60.

You can buy single journey tickets from the orange machines in station halls and on platforms, and at some bus stops. Short-stretch (*Kurzstrecke*) tickets are cheapest and may be used for up to three train stops and six bus stops. Otherwise, the single (*Einzelfahrschein*) ticket allows travel anywhere within the network for up to two hours; any number of changes may be made.

Better value, just, is the *Sammelkarte*, a card covering four journeys. At the beginning of any journey using this or a single trip ticket, cancel the ticket in the special machines provided (usually in a red post on station platforms or a smaller machine near the front stairs on buses).

For better value still, buy a Day Ticket (*Tageskarte*) or a Weekly Ticket (*Wochenkarte*) which runs from Monday to Sunday. The Monthly Ticket (*Umweltkarte*) works out cheaper still for longer-stay visitors and runs from the first of each month. First-time buyers need the basic card and the monthly stamp which is fixed to the back of it. Always show this side to ticket inspectors and bus drivers who are unimpressed at being offered the pretty picture on the front.

In theory these tickets may be bought at all S-Bahn and U-Bahn stations. In practice, they are not available in the East where document-holding residents of the *Neue Bundesländer* (the old GDR) still receive subsidised fares in line with their lower wages (currently around seventy per cent of the Western rate). At the start of a visit to Berlin it is best to go to a big rail station in the West, of which Bahnhof Zoologischer Garten (Zoo) is the biggest and best equipped (see also explanation in *Walk 1*).

For bus journeys up and down Kurfürstendamm there is a special one trip *Ku'damm Ticket*, currently costing DM 1.50 and valid anywhere between Wittenbergplatz and Rathenauplatz at the top (Halensee) end.

Taxis

Berlin's taxi drivers are the first to complain that they have too many rivals shrinking their weekly take. This is of course beneficial to customers and taxis can be hailed on main streets in the West at most hours of the day or night. In the East the city goes dead at night – or it does on the surface – and it is best to telephone in advance. Taxi numbers to call are: (W) 6902 or 691001; (E) 9644.

TELEPHONES

Public call boxes are widely available in the street (most are yellow) and in post offices, cafés, bars and restaurants. They are thinner on the ground in East Berlin, and suffer more from vandalism. Roughly a third to half take *Telefonkarten* which may be bought at a post office (*Postamt*) in denominations of DM 12 and 50. Follow the dialling instructions in the box (translated into several languages). A bell symbol on the box means you can be called back on that number.

There is still a huge shortage of lines and telephones in East Berlin and it requires a reservoir of patience to call one half of the city from the other in business hours. International calls are now much easier to make from the East than they used to be.

Formerly there were two code systems for West and East Berlin. These are being rapidly merged, but at the time of writing there are still differences.

- To call Berlin from abroad, the code is 49 30.
- To call Berlin from former West Germany, dial 030. To call West Berlin from former East Germany you may also need to dial the prefix code 0092, followed by 30.

International calls
- To make an international call from Berlin, dial 00 and the country code, e.g. 44 for Great Britain.
- Then dial the area code and number, deleting the initial 0 if there is one. Thus the code for Inner London from West Berlin is 00 44 71; for Amsterdam it is 00 31 20; for New York it is 00 1 212; for Stockholm it is 00 46 8.

Emergency numbers
Police 110
Fire, Doctor 112

MONEY

Until there is monetary union in the European Community, the DM (*Deutsche Mark*) is Germany's national currency. DM 1 = 100 pfennig or pf. Coins are Pf 1, 2, 5, 10, 50; DM 1, 2, 5. Banknotes in everyday circulation are DM 10, 20, 50, 100, 200, 500.

Banking hours vary. Most banks are open Monday to Friday from 09.00 to 13.30 or 14.00, and two afternoons a week until 15.30 or later on days that vary from bank to bank.

The best exchange office for out-of-hours transactions is outside Zoo Station on Hardenbergplatz.

Eurocheques and Travellers' Cheques are easy to change. Take a passport for identification, and with Eurocheques the encashment card as well. The usual cash limit is DM 400.

Some banks accept Visa and Access (Mastercard) cards for cash withdrawals. American Express cardholders should go to the company office at Kurfürstendamm 11.

Shops and restaurants prefer to see the colour of your cash and are not generally keen on credit cards or Eurocheques drawn on a foreign bank. If you need to pay by card or Eurocheque, make sure in advance that the shop or restaurant will accept yours.

Tipping

In cafés and restaurants, assume service is included. If you wish to add a tip, round up a small bill to the next whole DM or one higher, and for a larger bill add DM 2-3, perhaps more at an expensive restaurant.

Rather than leave money on the table, give the waiter or waitress the correct amount with tip and say 'Das stimmt' ('That's right'). If you do not have the correct amount, tell them in advance how much change you want. Example: the bill is DM 14.50. You want to leave a tip of DM 1.50. Hand over a larger note and say 'Sechzehn Mark' ('Sixteen marks').

Tip taxi drivers up to ten per cent of the fare. Cloakroom attendants put out signs listing their tariffs; offer less at your peril.

OPENING TIMES

Shopping hours are governed by frankly loony regulations devised in part to protect staff from exploitation by their employers. Shops usually open from Monday to Friday between 09.00 and 18.00 or 18.30 (city centre). On Thursday some stay open until 19.30 or later (but not food shops). On Saturday – barking mad but there you go – shops close at 13.00 (14.00 in centre) except on the first Saturday of each month ('Long Saturday' or *langer Samstag*) when they are open until 18.00 or so.

Many bakers open on Sunday for a few hours from 12.00 or 14.00. For out-of-hours food shopping, go to the shops at U-Bahn Stations Fehrbelliner Platz, Kurfürstendamm and Schloss-strasse – which are open evenings and weekends at not entirely reliable hours, and they charge a good bit more. In Kreuzberg, some Turkish food shops carry on regardless of the rules. Best place for newspapers, through the week from 07.00 to midnight, is Internationale Presse, Joachimthaler Strasse 1 (opposite Zoo Station).

Cafés, bars and restaurants open according to their view of themselves. If they serve breakfast, they may open early but most cafés and bars open at 11.00. Some are night bars and do not open until early evening. In West Berlin most cafés and bars stay open until late or very late; in East Berlin they tend to shut earlier if the regulars push off home.

Museum hours vary. State museums are usually open from 09.00 to 17.00; on Saturday-Sunday they open at 10.00, on Monday they are closed all day.

Opening hours for all main places of interest on Slow Walk routes appear in the appropriate chapter. Hours may be shorter in winter, particularly where gardens are involved.

Banking hours are described in 'Money', above.

List of Public Holidays

1 January: New Year's Day – *Neujahrstag*
Good Friday – *Karfreitag*
Easter Monday – *Ostermontag*
1 May: May Day – *Der erste Mai*
Ascension Day – *Christihimmelfahrtstag*
Whit Monday – *Pfingstmontag*
3 October: Reunification Day – *Wiedervereinigungstag*

1 November: All Saints' Day – *Allerheiligentag*
3rd Wednesday in November: Day of Prayer and Repentance – *Buss und Bettag*
25 December: Christmas Day – *Erster Weihnachstag*
26 December: Boxing Day – *Zweiter Weihnachstag*

CLOTHING SIZES

Sample conversation in shop:
Assistant: 'Welche Grösse haben Sie?' ('What size are you?')
Customer: 'Ich habe Grösse achtunddreissig' ('I am size 38')

For Women

Dresses, knitwear, blouses, coats (*Kostüme, Strickwaren, Blusen, Mäntel*)

German	36	38	40	42	44	46	48	50
GB	10	12	14	16	18	20	22	24
USA	8	10	12	14	16	18	20	22

Tights (*Strumpfhosen*)

German	0	1	2	3	4	5	6
GB (dress size)	10-12	12-14	14-16	16-18	18-20	20-22	22-24
USA (dress size)	8-10	10-12	12-14	14-16	16-18	18-20	20-22

Stockings (*Strümpfe*)

German	1	2	3
GB	8½-9	9½-10	10½-11
USA	8½-9	9½-10	10½-11

Shoes (*Schuhe*)

German	35½	36	36½	37	37½	38	39	40	41
GB	3	3½	4	4½	5	5½	6	7	8
USA	4	4½	5	5½	6	6½	7½	8½	9½

For Men

Shirts (*Hemden*)

German	36	37	38	39	40	41	42
GB	14	14½	15	15½	16	16½	17
USA	14	14½	15	15½	16	16½	17

Sweaters (*Pullover*)

German	46	48	50	52	54	56	58
GB	36	38	40	42	44	46	48
USA	36	38	40	42	44	46	48

Suits (*Anzüge*)

German	36	38	40	42	44	46	48
GB	35	36	37	38	39	40	42
USA	35	36	37	38	39	40	42

Shoes (*Schuhe*)

German	39	40	41	42	43	44	45
GB	5½	6½	7	8	8½	9½	10½
USA	6	7	7½	8½	9	10	11

WATERING HOLES

The marvellous abundance of cafés and bars in West Berlin is highly soothing for the foot-propelled visitor (even if some of the bars are slightly ropey *Eck-Kneipen*, see also 'Berlin from A to Z').

At the pinnacle of the city's coffee-house tradition are establishments like Cafe Möhring (the one in Kurfürstendamm on the corner of Uhlandstrasse is my favourite). Then there are the breakfast menus, offering anything from simple rolls and coffee up to a small feast and available until four o'clock in the afternoon. Nor is it a struggle to make yourself known at one of those countless agreeable bars where the waitress thoughtfully pops over every now and then to see whether she should not start the ritual of pouring you another.

Eating out is a natural part of life. Comparisons with London start me moaning with grief for my native city. Why, in Berlin, can I buy three dinners for the price of one in London – and eat them outdoors on a terrace or some glassed-in conservatory overlooking the local street-life? The answer, regrettably, has only a little to do with climate and much more with national economic policies over the last forty years, combined with the Germans' dogged insistence on living well and reasonably. Even though prices are beginning to climb in Berlin, the gulf between the two cultures, the British and the German, does not shrink.

One small but important recommendation. Just like anywhere else, Berlin has its high and high-middle price restaurants but, unless you have money to burn, you do not need them. Look around the local cafés instead. Their sheer good value, the quality of the food and the long serving hours are quite outstanding.

Attentive readers will have noticed that these remarks apply only to West Berlin. In the East, the prices are no higher but the choice is much more limited. Here it is wise to mark down likely restaurants as you go round during the day. Away from the Eastern centre, there are still a lot of dead streets at night.

TOILETS

Public facilities are few and far between, and some in the centre share their ground with drunks and dropouts. Use the loos in cafés and restaurants. Nearly all are clean with up-to-date plumbing – even if that does incorporate the inspection platform in the toilet bowl which some observers find hilariously Germanic.

WHAT'S ON/FURTHER INFORMATION

The best listings guides are *Tip* and *Zitty* which appear every two weeks and overlap with each other. Buy them from newsstands and station bookstalls. For local news buy a Berlin paper such as the *Berliner Morgenpost*.

The best central source for background information is the Verkehr-samt Berlin in the Europa-Center.

BERLIN BY NIGHT

The city is very good for opera and musical concerts. The problem at the major venues is getting in, thanks to the large take-up of seats by season-ticket holders. It is best to book as soon as dates are known. Advance bookings may be made at several ticket agencies in central West Berlin. These include:

Theaterkasse Centrum Meinekestrasse 25, 1000 Berlin 15; tel 882 76 11.

Berliner Theater und Konzertkasse Kurfürstendamm 16, 1000 Berlin 15; tel 882 65 63; fax 882 65 67.

Theaterkasse im Europa-Center Tauentzienstrasse 9, 1000 Berlin 30; tel 261 70 51, 261 70 52; fax 261 92 86.

KaDeWe department store Tauentzienstrasse 21, 1000 Berlin 30, tel 21 21 0.

Kantkasse Kantstrasse 54, 1000 Berlin 12, tel 313 45 54; fax 312 64 40.

Failing these, try the Yellow Pages (*Gelbe Seiten*) under *Theaterkassen*.

In East Berlin there is a *Theaterkasse* at the **Palast Hotel** in Spandauer Strasse; tel 212 52 58, 212 59 02.

For daily listings of what's on, refer to *Tip* or *Zitty*. The latter has separate categories for TV (*Fernsehen*), Radio, Cinema (*Kino*), This & That (*Dies & Das*), Stage (*Bühne*) and Music (*Musik*), this last including Folk, Jazz/Rock and Classical (*Klassik*).

Best late-night bars: try the streets around Savignyplatz, a pleasant area for wandering and pavement eating too. Many stay open until 02.00 or 04.00. They say you can drink round the clock in Berlin; I have not tried to verify this but am quite sure it is true.

There are a number of sleazy streets in West Berlin, if you like that sort of thing. If you hate it, or feel threatened by it, at night keep away from the streets south of Zoo Station, Lietzenburger Strasse near the corner of Uhlandstrasse, Potsdamer Strasse around Kurfürstenstrasse, and the area north of S-Bahnhof Charlottenburg. This is not an exhaustive list; in general, these shady parts are confined to just a block or two, so are not a great menace to the innocent passer-by.

QUICK BERLIN

If you are in the city for only a few days, the Slow Walks below will give a good introduction to Berlin. Before setting off on any of these walks, make sure the various opening times fit in with your plans.

Day 1   Take Bus 100 from Zoo Station to the Brandenburg Gate and join *Walk 4: Unter den Linden*. Go up the Television Tower (*Walk 5*) and eat out in the Nikolai Quarter (*Walk 6*).

Day 2   Ride west up Ku'damm on Bus 119 or 129. Turn round at Rathenauplatz (next to the white Italian garden statues) and ride back as far as Uhlandstrasse (Cafe Möhring on corner). Follow *Walk 1* from here to the Käthe Kollwitz Museum, etc.

Day 3   *Walk 12: Museum Island*. Visit the Pergamon Museum and perhaps a special exhibition at the Altes Museum.

Best museum for art-lovers is the Picture Gallery at Dahlem (*Walk 15*). For a view of East Berlin behind the scenes, take *Walk 8: Old Jewish Quarter* or *Walk 11: Prenzlauer Berg*.